WILLS AND THE ADMINISTRATION OF ESTATES

Second edition

Sheila Hamilton Macdonald

Series editors: Amy Sixsmith and David Sixsmith

First published in 2023 by Fink Publishing Ltd
Second edition published in 2023

British Library Cataloguing in Publication Data
A catalogue record for this book is available from the British Library
ISBN: 9781914213892

This book is also available in various ebook formats.
Ebook ISBN: 9781914213908

Multiple-choice questions advisor: Mark Thomas
Cover and text design by BMLD (bmld.uk)
Production and typesetting by Westchester Publishing Services (UK)
Commissioning by R Taylor Publishing Services
Development editing by Sonya Barker
Editorial management by Llinos Edwards
Indexing by Terence Halliday

Revise SQE
Fink Publishing Ltd
E-mail: hello@revise4law.co.uk
www.revise4law.co.uk

Contents

This book incorporates the updates to the SQE Assessment Specification published in April 2023 which came into force from 1 September 2023. Please note that, unless otherwise expressly stated, the law covered in this book applies in both England and Wales.

Contributors

THE AUTHOR

Sheila Hamilton Macdonald is a senior lecturer at Nottingham Law School, Nottingham Trent University, where she teaches on the Postgraduate Diploma in Law and SQE courses, including SQE Wills and Administration and SQE Property. She is a module leader for the LPC Private Client elective, teaching all aspects of probate practice, and she is also the module leader for the SQE2 courses in Property and Wills and Administration. She practised as a Chancery barrister for 25 years and has extensive experience in contentious and non-contentious probate cases.

SERIES EDITORS

Amy Sixsmith is a senior lecturer in law and programme leader for LLB at the University of Sunderland, and a senior fellow of the Higher Education Academy.

David Sixsmith is assistant professor at Northumbria Law School, and a senior fellow of the Higher Education Academy.

Introduction to Revise SQE

Welcome to *Revise SQE*, a new series of revision guides designed to help you in your preparation for, and achievement in, the Solicitors Qualifying Examination 1 (SQE1) assessment. SQE1 is designed to assess what the Solicitors Regulation Authority (SRA) refers to as 'functioning legal knowledge' (FLK); this is the legal knowledge and competencies required of a newly qualified solicitor in England and Wales. The SRA has chosen single best answer multiple-choice questions (MCQs) to test this knowledge, and *Revise SQE* is here to help.

PREPARING YOURSELF FOR SQE

The SQE is the new route to qualification for aspiring solicitors, introduced in September 2021 as one of the final stages towards qualification as a solicitor. The SQE consists of two parts:

SQE1	• **Functioning legal knowledge (FLK)** • two x 180 MCQs • closed book; assessed by two sittings, over 10 hours in total.

SQE2	• **Practical legal skills** • 16 written and oral assessments • assesses six practical legal skills, over 14 hours in total.

In addition to the above, any candidate will have to undertake two years' qualifying work experience. More information on the SQE assessments can be found on the SRA website; this revision guide series will focus on FLK and preparation for SQE1.

It is important to note that the SQE can be perceived to be a 'harder' set of assessments than the Legal Practice Course (LPC). The reason for this, explained by the SRA, is that the LPC is designed to prepare candidates for 'day one' of their training contract; the SQE, on the other hand, is designed to prepare candidates for 'day one' of being a newly qualified solicitor. Indeed, the SRA has chosen the SQE1 assessment to be 'closed book' (ie without permitting use of any materials) on the basis that a newly qualified solicitor would know all of the information tested, without having to refer to books or other sources.

With that in mind, and a different style of assessments in place, it is understandable that many readers may feel nervous or wary of the SQE. This is especially so given that this style of assessment is likely to be different from what readers will have experienced before. In this *Introduction* and revision guide series, we hope to alleviate some of those concerns with guidance on preparing for the SQE assessment, tips on how to approach single best answer MCQs and expertly written guides to aid in your revision.

What does SQE1 entail?

SQE1 consists of two assessments, containing 180 single best answer MCQs each (360 MCQs in total). The table below breaks down what is featured in each of these assessments.

Assessment	Contents of assessment ('functioning legal knowledge')
FLK assessment 1	• Business law and practice • Dispute resolution • Contract • Tort • The legal system (the legal system of England and Wales and sources of law, constitutional and administrative law and European Union law and legal services)
FLK assessment 2	• Property practice • Wills and the administration of estates • Solicitors' accounts • Land law • Trusts • Criminal law and practice

Please be aware that in addition to the above, ethics and professional conduct will be examined pervasively across the two assessments (ie it could crop up anywhere).

Each substantive topic is allocated a percentage of the assessment paper (eg 'legal services' will form 12–16% of the FLK1 assessment) and is broken down further into 'core principles'. Candidates are advised to read the SQE1 Assessment Specification in full (available on the SRA website). We have also provided a *Revise SQE checklist* to help you in your preparation and revision for SQE1 (see below).

HOW DO I PREPARE FOR SQE1?

Given the vastly different nature of SQE1 compared to anything you may have done previously, it can be quite daunting to consider how you could possibly prepare for 360 single best answer MCQs, spanning 11 different substantive topics (especially given that it is 'closed book'). The *Revise SQE FAQ* below, however, will set you off on the right path to success.

Revise SQE FAQ

Question	Answer
1. Where do I start?	We would advise that you begin by reviewing the assessment specification for SQE1. You need to identify what subject matter can be assessed under each substantive topic. For each topic, you should honestly ask yourself whether you would be prepared to answer an MCQ on that topic in SQE1.
	We have helped you in this process by providing a *Revise SQE checklist* on our website (revise4law.co.uk) that allows you to read the subject matter of each topic and identify where you consider your knowledge to be at any given time. We have also helpfully cross-referenced each topic to a chapter and page of our *Revise SQE* revision guides.
2. Do I need to know legal authorities, such as case law?	In the majority of circumstances, candidates are not required to know or use legal authorities. This includes statutory provisions, case law or procedural rules. Of course, candidates will need to be aware of legal principles deriving from common law and statute.
	There may be occasions, however, where the assessment specification does identify a legal authority (such as *Rylands v Fletcher* in tort law). In this case, candidates will be required to know the name of that case, the principles of that case and how to apply that case to the facts of an MCQ. These circumstances are clearly highlighted in the assessment specification and candidates are advised to ensure they engage with those legal authorities in full.

Revise SQE FAQ (continued)

Question	Answer
3. Do I need to know the history behind a certain area of law?	While understanding the history and development of a certain area of law is beneficial, there is no requirement for you to know or prepare for any questions relating to the development of the law (eg in criminal law, candidates will not need to be aware of the development from objective to subjective recklessness). SQE1 will be testing a candidate's knowledge of the law as it stands four calendar months prior to the date of the first assessment in an assessment window.
4. Do I need to be aware of academic opinion or proposed reforms to the law?	Candidates preparing for SQE1 do not need to focus on critical evaluation of the law, or proposed reforms to the law either.
5. How do I prepare for single best answer MCQs?	See our separate *Revise SQE* guide on preparing for single best answer MCQs below.

Where does *Revise SQE* come into it?

The *Revise SQE* series of revision guides is designed to aid your revision and consolidate your understanding; the series is not designed to replace your substantive learning of the SQE1 topics. We hope that this series will provide clarity as to assessment focus, useful tips for sitting SQE1 and act as a general revision aid.

There are also materials on our website to help you prepare and revise for the SQE1, such as a *Revise SQE checklist*. This *checklist* is designed to help you identify which substantive topics you feel confident about heading into the exam - see below for an example.

Revise SQE checklist

Wills and the Administration of Estates

SQE content	Corresponding chapter	*Revise SQE checklist*		
Validity of wills and codicils • Testamentary capacity	Chapter 1, pages 7–10	I don't know this subject and I am not ready for SQE1 ☐	I partially know this subject, but I am not ready for SQE1 ☐	I know this subject and I am ready for SQE1 ☐

Wills and the Administration of Estates (continued)

SQE content	Corresponding chapter	Revise SQE checklist		
Validity of wills and codicils • Duress and undue influence	Chapter 1, pages 10–12	I don't know this subject and I am not ready for SQE1 ☐	I partially know this subject, but I am not ready for SQE1 ☐	I know this subject and I am ready for SQE1 ☐
Validity of wills and codicils • Formal requirements	Chapter 1, pages 4–7	I don't know this subject and I am not ready for SQE1 ☐	I partially know this subject, but I am not ready for SQE1 ☐	I know this subject and I am ready for SQE1 ☐

PREPARING FOR SINGLE BEST ANSWER MCQS

As discussed above, SQE1 will be a challenging assessment for all candidates. This is partly due to the quantity of information a candidate must be aware of in two separate sittings. In addition, however, an extra complexity is added due to the nature of the assessment itself: MCQs.

The SRA has identified that MCQs are the most appropriate way to test a candidate's knowledge and understanding of fundamental legal principles. While this may be the case, it is likely that many candidates have little, if any, experience of MCQs as part of their previous study. Even if a candidate does have experience of MCQs, SQE1 will feature a special form of MCQs known as 'single best answer' questions.

What are single best answer MCQs and what do they look like?

Single best answer MCQs are a specialised form of question, used extensively in other fields such as in training medical professionals. The idea behind single best answer MCQs is that the multitude of options available to a candidate may each bear merit, sharing commonalities and correct statements of law or principle, but only one option is absolutely correct (in the sense that it is the 'best' answer). In this regard, single best answer MCQs are different from traditional MCQs. A traditional MCQ will feature answers that are implausible in the sense that the distractors are 'obviously wrong'. Indeed, distractors in a traditional MCQ are often very dissimilar, resulting in a candidate being able to spot answers that are clearly wrong with greater ease.

In a well-constructed single best answer MCQ, on the other hand, each option should look equally attractive given their similarities and subtle differences. The skill of the candidate will be identifying which, out of the options provided, is the single best answer. This requires a much greater level of engagement with the question than a traditional MCQ would require; candidates must take the time to read the questions carefully in the exam.

For SQE1, single best answer MCQs will be structured as follows:

A woman is charged with battery, having thrown a rock towards another person intending to scare them. The rock hits the person in the head, causing no injury. The woman claims she never intended that the rock hit the person, but the prosecution allege that the woman was reckless as to whether the rock would hit the other person.

The factual scenario. First, the candidate will be provided with a factual scenario that sets the scene for the question to be asked.

Which of the following is the most accurate statement regarding the test for recklessness in relation to a battery?

The question. Next, the candidate will be provided with the question (known as the 'stem') that they must find the single best answer to.

A. There must have been a risk that force would be applied by the rock, and that the reasonable person would have foreseen that risk and unjustifiably taken it.

B. There must have been a risk that force would be applied by the rock, and that the woman should have foreseen that risk and unjustifiably taken it.

The possible answers. Finally, the candidate will be provided with **five** possible answers. There is only one single best answer that must be chosen. The other answers, known as 'distractors', are not the 'best' answer available.

C. There must have been a risk that force would be applied by the rock, and that the woman must have foreseen that risk and unjustifiably taken it.

D. There must have been a risk that force would be applied by the rock, and that both the woman and the reasonable person should have foreseen that risk and unjustifiably taken it.

E. There must have been a risk that force would be applied by the rock, but there is no requirement that the risk be foreseen.

Now that you know what the MCQs will look like on SQE1, let us talk about how you may go about tackling an MCQ.

How do I tackle single best answer MCQs?

No exact art exists in terms of answering single best answer MCQs; your success depends on your subject knowledge and understanding of how that subject knowledge can be applied. Despite this, there are tips and tricks that may be helpful for you to consider when confronted with a single best answer MCQ.

1. Read the question twice	2. Understand the question being asked	3. If you know the answer outright	4. If not, employ a process of elimination	5. Take an educated and reasoned guess	6. Skip and come back to it later

1. Read the entire question at least twice

This sounds obvious but is so often overlooked. You are advised to read the entire question once, taking in all relevant pieces of information, understanding what the question is asking you and being aware of the options available. Once you have done that, read the entire question again and this time pay careful attention to the wording that is used.

- **In the factual scenario:** Does it use any words that stand out? Do any words used have legal bearing? What are you told and what are you not told?
- **In the stem:** What are you being asked? Are there certain words to look out for (eg 'should', 'must', 'will', 'shall')?
- **In the answers:** What are the differences between each option? Are they substantial differences or subtle differences? Do any differences turn on a word or a phrase?

You should be prepared to give each question at least two viewings to mitigate any misunderstandings or oversights.

2. Understand the question being asked

It is important first that you understand what the question is asking of you. The SRA has identified that the FLK assessments may consist of single best answer MCQs that, for example,

- require the candidate to simply identify a correct legal principle or rule
- require the candidate to not only identify the correct legal principle or rule, but also apply that principle or rule to the factual scenario
- provide the candidate with the correct legal principle or rule, but require the candidate to identify how it should be properly applied and/or the outcome of that proper application.

By first identifying what the question is seeking you to do, you can then understand what the creators of that question are seeking to test and how to approach the answers available.

3. If you know the answer outright

You may feel as though a particular answer 'jumps out' at you, and that you are certain it is correct. It is very likely that the answer is correct. While you should be confident in your answers, do not allow your confidence (and perhaps overconfidence) to rush you into making a decision. Review all of your options one final time before you move on to the next question.

4. If you do not know the answer outright, employ a process of elimination

There may be situations in which the answer is not obvious from the outset. This may be due to the close similarities between different answers. Remember, it is the 'single best answer' that you are looking for. If you keep this in your mind, it will thereafter be easier to employ a process of elimination. Identify which answers you are sure are not correct (or not the 'best') and whittle down your options. Once you have only two options remaining, carefully scrutinise the wording used in both answers and look back to the question being asked. Identify what you consider to be the best answer, in light of that question. Review your answer and move on to the next question.

5. Take an educated and reasoned guess

There may be circumstances, quite commonly, in which you do not know the answer to the question. In this circumstance, you should try as hard as possible to eliminate any distractors that you are positive are incorrect and then take an educated and reasoned guess based on the options available.

6. Skip and come back to it later

If time permits, you may think it appropriate to skip a question that you are unsure of and return to it before the end of the assessment. If you do so, we would advise

- that you make a note of what question you have skipped (for ease of navigation later on), and
- ensure you leave sufficient time for you to go back to that question before the end of the assessment.

The same advice is applicable to any question that you have answered but for which you remain unsure.

We hope that this brief guide will assist you in your preparation towards, and engagement with, single best answer MCQs.

GUIDED TOUR

Each chapter contains a number of features to help you revise, apply and test your knowledge.

Make sure you know   Each chapter begins with an overview of the main topics covered and why you need to understand them for the purpose of the SQE1 assessments.

SQE assessment advice   This identifies what you need to pay particular attention to in your revision as you work through the chapter.

What do you know already?   These questions help you to assess which topics you feel confident with and which topics you may need to spend more time on (and where to find them in the chapter).

Key term   Key terms are highlighted in bold where they first appear and defined in a separate box.

Exam warning   This feature offers advice on where it is possible to go wrong in the assessments.

Revision tip   Throughout the chapters are ideas to help you revise effectively and be best prepared for the assessment.

Summary   This handy box brings together key information in an easy to revise and remember form.

Practice example   These examples take a similar format to SQE-type questions and provide an opportunity to see how content might be applied to a scenario.

Procedural link   Where relevant, this element shows how a concept might apply to another procedural topic in the series.

Key point checklist   At the end of each chapter there is a bullet-point summary of its most important content.

Key terms and concepts   These are listed at the end of each chapter to help ensure you know, or can revise, terms and concepts you will need to be familiar with for the assessments.

SQE-style questions   Five SQE-style questions on the chapter topic give you an opportunity to test your knowledge.

Answers to questions   Check how you did with answers to both the quick knowledge test from the start of the chapter and the SQE questions at the end of the chapter.

Key cases, rules, statutes and instruments   These list the key sources candidates need to be familiar with for the SQE assessment.

SQE1 TABLE OF LEGAL AUTHORITIES

The SQE1 Assessment Specification states the following in respect of legal authorities and their relevance to SQE1:

> On occasion in legal practice a case name or statutory provision, for example, is the term normally used to describe a legal principle or an area of law, or a rule or procedural step (eg *Rylands v Fletcher*, CPR Part 36, Section 25 notice). In such circumstances, candidates are required to know and be able to use such case names, statutory provisions etc. In all other circumstances candidates are not required to recall specific case names, or cite statutory or regulatory authorities.

This *SQE1 table of legal authorities* identifies the legal authorities you are required to know for the purpose of the SQE1 Functioning Legal Knowledge assessments for *Wills and the Administration of Estates*.

Legal authority	Corresponding *Revise SQE* chapter/pages
Administration of Estates Act 1925 s 46	**Chapter 5: The Intestacy Rules pages 72–4**
Non-Contentious Probate Rules	**Chapter 7: Getting the grant of representation pages 114–17**
Inheritance (Provision for Family and Dependants) Act 1975	**Chapter 9: Claims under the Inheritance (Provision for Family and Dependants) Act 1975 pages 142–61**

TABLE OF CASES

Banks v Goodfellow [1870] LR 5 QB 549... 1, 2, 8–10, 12, 16
Parker v Felgate [1883] 8 PD 171... 8, 10, 12
Re Benjamin [1902] 1 Ch 723... 134, 140, 141
Re Coventry [1980] Ch 461... 146
Re Duranceau [1952] 3 DLR 714... 150
Ross v Caunters [1980] Ch. 297... 43
Saunders v Vautier (1841) Cr & Ph 240; 41 ER 482... 186
White v White [2000] UKHL 54... 150

TABLE OF STATUTES

Administration of Estates Act 1925 (AEA 1925) 21, 34, 41, 53, 70, 71–4, 76–80, 85, 87, 104, 131, 135, 141, 160
    First Schedule part II... 41, 53
    s 1(1)... 90–1, 104, 131
    s 2(1)... 141

s 18C... 29
s 20... 56, 58–63, 69
s 21... 35, 45–7, 53
s 33... 42
Wills Act 1837 (Electronic Communications) (Amendment) Order 2022/18
art 2(2) 6

REVISING WILLS AND THE ADMINISTRATION OF ESTATES

We have already noted earlier in the Introduction that this guide is designed to aid your revision and consolidate your understanding, and not to replace your substantive learning of the SQE1 topics. When you are revising Wills and the Administration of Estates, it is particularly important to remember:

- that this book does not deal with the professional conduct issues that can arise in this topic, which are dealt with in *Revise SQE: Ethics and Professional Conduct*
- that a good working understanding of trusts law is essential to understanding wills and the administration of estates, which is in a very real sense a topic of 'applied trusts'; you may need to refer frequently to *Revise SQE: Trusts Law* when revising this topic, and this book indicates where that may be necessary, but does not go through the trusts basics again
- that you are required to have a thorough knowledge not just of inheritance tax but also of capital gains tax and income tax in the context of estate administration; these topics are not dealt with in this book but will be available to you in *Revise SQE: Business Law and Practice.*

Essential requirements for a valid will

■ MAKE SURE YOU KNOW

For SQE, you need a good working knowledge of the three elements that must all be present in a valid will: formalities, testamentary capacity and intention (also called 'knowledge and approval'). You must be able to distinguish whether or not a given will or part of a will is valid, and the reasons why or why not. It is not enough simply to memorise the various elements: in order to pass this part of the examination, you must be able to understand and apply them.

■ SQE ASSESSMENT ADVICE

As you work through this chapter, remember to pay particular attention in your revision to:
- the technical requirements for due execution under s 9 of the Wills Act 1837
- in particular, the rules surrounding the witnessing and attestation of signatures
- what the *Banks v Goodfellow* test for testamentary capacity is, and how to use it
- what 'knowledge and approval' means in practice.

■ WHAT DO YOU KNOW ALREADY?

Have a go at these questions before reading this chapter. If you find some difficult or cannot remember the answers, make a note to look more closely at that area during your revision.

1) Who or what is a 'testatrix'?
   [Why make a will at all?, page 2]
2) True or false? A soldier on active service does not have to have any witnesses for their will.
   [Formalities, page 4]
3) If a will is not admitted to probate, can the beneficiaries organise distribution of the estate themselves?
   [Validity of wills, page 3]

4) True or false? A person cannot make a will if they have been diagnosed with dementia.
[The common law/*Banks v Goodfellow* test, page 8]

WHY MAKE A WILL AT ALL?

No one in England and Wales is obliged to make a will, and many people do not. If a person does not make a will, then they will die intestate and their estate will be distributed after their death according to the intestacy rules (see **Chapter 5**). If a potential **testator** decides that they are happy with the way their property will pass on intestacy, they do not need to make a will and they may well decide not to do so.

> **Key term: testator**
>
> The person who makes a will is traditionally called a 'testator', although in more old-fashioned books and cases you may also see a woman will-maker described as a 'testatrix'. For convenience, we are going to call the will-maker a 'testator' throughout this book.

There are many situations, however, in which making a will is undoubtedly the best thing for a testator to do. If the testator wants to leave their property to someone who would not benefit under the intestacy rules, the only way to do this is to make a will in that person's favour. Making a will also allows the testator to choose who will manage and distribute their **estate**, by appointing executors of the will (see **Chapter 2**). If the testator does not do this, then the people who manage and distribute the estate (the personal representatives; see **Chapter 2**) will be the persons specified in the Non-Contentious Probate Rules 1987 (SI 1987/2024) (NCPR; see **Chapter 5**). The testator may have good reasons for not wanting these people to have control of their property after they have died, and the only way to avoid this is to make a will.

> **Key term: estate**
>
> This is the property that passes to the heirs under the will. It is sometimes called the 'death estate'. However, not all of the property owned by the testator may pass under the will (see **Chapter 6**).

If the testator owns a lot of money and land – that is, they have a large estate – it is more likely that they will want to make a will. There are usually two reasons for this: first, in order to make sure that it is distributed exactly as the testator wishes; second, to make sure it is done in a way that is tax-efficient, ie by not paying any tax (particularly inheritance tax) which could legitimately be saved. We look at taxation in **Chapter 10**.

Further, testators with large estates often want to leave their property in complex ways, including under trusts (see **Chapter 11**), which require extra powers for the personal representatives that can only be given by will.

Finally, there are some private and personal matters – appointing guardians for the testator's children if the testator dies while they are still minors, for example; or dealing with funeral arrangements and whether they wish to be buried or cremated – that can only be dealt with in a will and not in intestacy.

After the testator has died, there is obviously no way to check with them what they 'actually' or 'really' meant by what is in the will, or indeed to check that the testator really made the will, ie whether it is genuine. The rules on validity of wills are there to make sure that the will is genuine and that only the testator's clearly expressed and attested wishes are implemented.

VALIDITY OF WILLS: FORMALITIES, CAPACITY AND INTENTION

If the contents of a will do not comply with the relevant rules, it is highly likely that part or all of it will be ineffective. If a will fails any of the rules on validity, it will not be **admitted to probate**. The probate registry will reject it, and the estate will either pass to the personal representatives under an earlier valid will, if there is one, or if not, under the intestacy rules.

Key term: admitted to probate
In order for a will to take effect, probate of the will must be granted by the relevant probate registry. When we say a will has been 'admitted to probate' we mean that it has been approved by the probate registry and a grant of probate issued. Until that has happened, the executors cannot carry out the instructions of the will (see **Chapter 7**).

There are three main sets of rules with which all wills must comply if they are to be valid: these are the rules on formalities, set out in s 9 of the Wills Act 1837; the rules on the testator's capacity; and the rules on intention.

Revision tip
In order for a will to be valid, it must comply with all the rules on formalities, *and* it must be clear that the testator had the mental capacity to make the will, *and* it must be clear that the testator knew what was in the will and intended to make those arrangements (not just, for example, to jot down some ideas about how they might want to leave their property). *You must always bear in mind that if any one of these elements is missing, the will is not valid.* Imagine the will as sitting on top of a tripod, where all three legs (elements) have to be present. Just like a tripod, if one of the legs fails, the whole thing will collapse!

Let's now look at these three elements one by one.

Formalities

These are the rules set out in s 9 of the Wills Act 1837. Broadly speaking, we can say that they are the rules specifying how the will must be **executed** and how correct execution of the will (which is normally called 'due execution') can be proved. As you will see, these rules are applied extremely strictly and failure to comply with any one of them is likely to render the whole will invalid.

Key term: executed

To 'execute' the will is to comply with all of the formalities under the law, but particularly the formalities under s 9 of the Wills Act 1837. It includes the testator signing the will but, as we will see, it includes a lot more than that.

Let's look at what s 9 says and then break it down. Remember that you need to understand what these terms mean in practice. Some words have been put into italics for emphasis.

Wills Act 1837, s 9

No will shall be valid unless:

(a) it is in writing, and signed by the testator or by some other person in his presence and by his direction; *and*

(b) it appears that the testator by his signature intended to give effect to the will; *and*

(c) the signature is made or acknowledged by the testator in the presence of two or more witnesses present at the same time; *and*

(d) each witness either –

   (i) attests and signs the will; or

   (ii) acknowledges his signature in the presence of the testator (but not necessarily in the presence of any other witness), but no form of attestation shall be necessary.

You will see that we have emphasised the word 'and' at the end of each subclause. *All* of these elements must be present in every valid will: if one of them is missing, *the entire will is invalid*. If a will is invalid, it will not be admitted to probate, and it will never take effect. You must therefore be sure that you fully understand what is meant by *every word* of s 9 so that you can, if need be, identify an invalid will in a multiple-choice question (MCQ). These rules govern all wills except for what are called 'privileged wills', which are wills made by members of the armed forces on active service, or sailors at sea. In battle conditions, it would be extremely difficult for armed personnel to comply with these requirements, so they are made an exception to the main rule.

Before moving on, let's pause to consider the requirement that the witness should '**attest**' the will at s 9(d).

Key term: attest/attestation

To 'attest' to something is to bear witness to it as a fact. When attesting a will, the witness is confirming that they saw the testator sign or heard the testator acknowledge their signature.

Table 1.1 looks at the wording of s 9 in more detail.

Table 1.1: Requirements under s 9 of the Wills Act 1837

9(a) 'it is in writing'	Any kind of writing will do, including handwriting, typewriting or printing off on a printer linked to a PC. However, note that handwritten wills in pencil, as opposed to ink, are only valid if there is further evidence that the testator intended the pencil writing to be final (see **Chapter 3**).
9(a) 'signed by the testator'	If the testator has signed with their usual signature, that will meet this requirement, but testators can also make a mark (such as an 'X' or a monogram) or a thumbprint, or even a rubber stamp. An incomplete signature will also suffice, as will initials. The key point is that the testator intended this to be read as their signature, and that is confirmed by the other elements of s 9.
9(a) 'by some other person in his presence and at his direction'	There are two elements here which are essential. The first (direction) is that the testator must be asking the other person, 'please sign this will on my behalf'; these words or their equivalent must be said. The second (presence) is that the other person must sign *with the testator present* when they do so.
9(b) 'the testator by his signature intended to give effect to the will'	The classic way of doing this is to sign at the end of the will, though if the signature is elsewhere, it may still pass s 9(b) if the signature and all of the provisions were written at the same time.
9(c) Signature made or acknowledged 'in the presence of two witnesses present at the same time'	*Both* witnesses must be present* to see the testator sign or acknowledge their signature.
9(d) 'each witness either attests and signs the will' ... 'no form of attestation shall be necessary'	By signing, the witness is confirming that they witnessed the testator's signature. The will does not have to contain the statement, 'I saw T sign the will' ('no form of attestation shall be necessary'), but it is standard practice to have an 'attestation clause' to confirm this: see below.

(*Please note that s 9(2) states that 'For the purposes of paragraphs (c) and (d) of subsection (1), in relation to wills made on or after 31 January 2020 and on or before 31 January 2024, *"presence"* includes presence by means of videoconference or other visual transmission'. This provision was inserted by virtue of the Wills Act 1837 (Electronic Communications) (Amendment) Order 2022/18 art.2(2) (1 February 2022) to deal with the challenges associated with requiring physical attendance during the Covid-19 pandemic.)

Remember that *all* of these rules must be complied with (except that the witnesses can either comply with 9(d)(i) or (ii)) or the *whole will is invalid.*

Practice example 1.1 illustrates how the topic might be assessed in an MCQ.

Practice example 1.1

Perry has asked his brother Franchot and his friend Sylvestra to witness his will. They have a cup of tea and a chat in Perry's sitting room before they attend to the will. Perry has a fountain pen ready, but when he tries to sign the will with it, it does not work. He asks Sylvestra to fetch another fountain pen from his study upstairs, and she leaves the room to do so. While she is away, the original fountain pen begins working and Perry signs the will. Sylvestra comes back into the room as Franchot is signing as a witness, and she then signs straight after him without any further discussion.

Has the will been properly executed?

No. The will has not complied with the rule at s 9(c). It was not signed before two witnesses present at the same time. Only Franchot saw Perry sign the will; Sylvestra did not. Any attestation that she made would be untrue. It does not matter that Perry really did sign the will, and that Franchot saw him. The requirement is that *both* witnesses must see the testator sign *at the same time.* Remember that this means that the will would not be admitted to probate!

Attestation and attestation clauses

Attestation is the process of confirming that the signature on the will has been witnessed according to the provisions of s 9. There is no legal or formal requirement to put plain words in the will that the witnessing formalities have been complied with, but in practice all well-drafted wills contain an **attestation clause** which states that the witnessing of the will complies with the statutory requirements.

Key term: attestation clause

This is a clause in a will that sets out the requirements of s 9(d) of the Wills Act 1837. An example would be: 'Signed by [the testator] in our joint presence and attested by us in his presence [witness' signatures]'.

An attestation clause in a will is important because, if the clause is there, there is a legal presumption that the will has been executed in accordance with s 9. This is called a 'presumption of due execution'. If the attestation clause is not there, the will may still be valid, but evidence would have to be produced to show that the s 9 requirements had been complied with. We deal further with this point in **Chapter 7**.

Bear in mind that a presumption of due execution is exactly that: a *presumption*. It can be challenged. We can see how the presumption works in **Practice example 1.2**.

Practice example 1.2

Frieda's will was witnessed by Greig and Hannah but contained no attestation clause, only their signatures below Frieda's signature. It left all of her property to a local charity. Frieda's nephew, Rolo, has now challenged the will on the basis that it was not properly witnessed in accordance with the provisions of s 9. He relies on the fact that there is no presumption that the will has been duly executed.

What, if anything, can Frieda's executors do to meet Rolo's challenge?

Frieda's executors can gather evidence that proves that Greig and Hannah saw Frieda sign the will in their presence and the presence of each other. The usual way to do this would be to obtain a statement from both Greig and Hannah setting out the circumstances in which they witnessed the will. If these circumstances comply with s 9, and the evidence is accepted and reliable, the will has been duly executed and will be admitted to probate.

Blind or illiterate testators

There are special rules about attestation if the testator was blind, illiterate or could not read over the will themselves for some other reason. There is an obvious danger in these circumstances that the testator may sign the will not knowing its contents. This would mean that the testator may not have had *knowledge and approval* of the will (see **Intention** below). For this reason, a special attestation clause should be added where this danger is present. The clause will set out that the will was read over (aloud) to the testator in the presence of the witnesses, and that the testator confirmed that they understood its contents; then that the testator signed the will (or had someone sign at their direction) and the witnesses then attested the will in the usual way. If this clause is included, this will give rise to a presumption of due execution.

Testamentary capacity

You will remember that compliance with the formalities is only one of the three things that must be proved if a will is to be valid. We are now going to look at the second of the three things, which is testamentary capacity. This element must also be proved, as well as intention, which we will look at in the next section.

Finally, it may surprise you to learn that it is not essential for a will to be dated (although all well-drafted wills do have a date). However, if the will does not bear a date, it will not be granted probate unless some external evidence is submitted confirming the date of execution (see **Chapter 7**).

What exactly is 'testamentary capacity'?

Testamentary capacity is the mental ability to make a will. A testator must be at least 18 years old (s 7 Wills Act) to have capacity. As we have now seen, a will is a very important document, which can radically change the lives of those who are affected by it. It is therefore vital to prove that the testator understood what they were doing when they signed the document, and what the implications were. If these points cannot be proved to the required standard, then the will is not valid and, again, will not be admitted to probate. There is a legal presumption that a testator has testamentary capacity, but again it is only a presumption, and can be displaced by any evidence that this was not the case. If that happens, as we will now see, there is a legal test for whether or not the testator had testamentary capacity.

When should a testator have testamentary capacity?

The strict answer to this question is that testamentary capacity must always be present when the will is executed. However, as a matter of logic, capacity must also be present when the testator gives instructions for drafting their will. Problems can arise if the testator did have capacity when they gave instructions, but had lost it by the time of execution. This can happen where the testator has either a deteriorating or a variable condition: Parkinson's disease and dementia are typical examples. What happens in this situation?

The exception to the strict rule that capacity must be present at the time of execution is known as the rule in *Parker v Felgate* [1883] 8 PD 171. That rule states that if there was capacity when instructions were given; if the will was prepared in accordance with those instructions; and if, now, the testator understands that they are signing a will prepared in accordance with those instructions (even if they cannot remember what those instructions were), then there is sufficient capacity on execution for the will to be valid.

The common law/Banks v Goodfellow test

The standard test for whether a testator has testamentary capacity comes from the Victorian case of *Banks v Goodfellow* [1870] LR 5 QB 549. Even though there have been major advances in understanding mental health and mental capacity since that case was decided, the basic rules are still very sound and are applied to this day. The *Banks v Goodfellow* test can be broken down into three questions which must be answered if the will is to be valid (see **Table 1.2**).

Table 1.2: Components of the Banks v Goodfellow *test*

Question 1: did the testator understand the *nature* of the will and its *effects*?	The testator would not understand the *nature* of the will if, for example, they thought that they were simply jotting down notes about what they might eventually put in a will.
	They would not understand the *effects* of the will if, for example, they believed that it made provision for a favourite grandchild who in fact received nothing.
Question 2: did the testator understand the *extent of the property* they were disposing of by the will?	The testator does not need to know exactly how much is in their estate down to the last penny or even pound, but they do need to understand, for example, that there are different types of property in their estate (eg land and shares), and approximately how much their estate is worth, particularly if it is of high value.
Question 3: did the testator understand *the claims to which they ought to give effect*?	This element is problematic, and you need to be careful. What it means in basic terms is 'did the testator consider everyone that they ought to have considered?': children, brothers and sisters, parents and so on. It does *not* mean that they should have given any property to any particular person. However, if when making the will they forget that they have a son or daughter (as can happen when a testator has dementia, for example), that would be an example of not understanding the claims to which they ought to give effect.

Exam warning

'Testamentary capacity' versus mental capacity under the Mental Capacity Act: you may already have come across the definition of 'mental capacity' under the Mental Capacity Act 2005 (MCA 2005) in your studies and wondered how it relates to the question of testamentary capacity. In two recent cases, the courts have decided that the relevant test for capacity when making a will is the *Banks v Goodfellow* test and not the MCA 2005 test. Be careful, therefore, not to mix up the two tests in an MCQ.

Delusions and the Banks v Goodfellow *test*

It may surprise you to know that the *Banks v Goodfellow* test allows for testators who suffer from delusions to have testamentary capacity. The key element is not whether the testator suffers from delusions but whether those delusions affect any of the three tests set out above (see **Practice example 1.3**).

Practice example 1.3

Jorge suffers from visual and auditory hallucinations. He has an imaginary friend called Fernando, a giant pink and purple rabbit who he can see and who talks to him, although Fernando never discusses anything but football. However, Jorge also knows exactly what property he owns, and who his close relatives are. He has come to you wanting to make a will in which he leaves all his property to his sister, with whom he lives, but nothing to his brother. He is not intending to leave anything to Fernando.

Do you consider that Jorge has testamentary capacity?

There is nothing in Jorge's delusions that affects his understanding that he is making a will, or the property of which he is disposing, or the claims of his relatives. Jorge has the mental capacity to make a valid will.

All of the elements in the *Banks v Goodfellow* test must be met or the testator does not have testamentary capacity; and remember that if there is no testamentary capacity, then the entire will is invalid.

Intention (aka 'knowledge and approval')

The final part of the trio that makes up a valid will is the requirement of intention. Two things are needed here: the testator must have intended to make a will (as opposed to, say, making a gift in their lifetime); and more specifically, they must have intended to make the actual will that they signed. So first they must *know* all of the contents of the will and then, second, they must think that they are a good idea; in other words, they must *approve* them. This is why you will sometimes find the requirement of intention described as 'knowledge and approval'.

Exam warning

Candidates often get confused between the key concepts of testamentary *capacity* and testamentary *intention*, or they consider (wrongly) that the two concepts are very much the same. They are quite distinct concepts and you must not mix them up. Remember that the *Banks v Goodfellow* test applies to testamentary capacity but *not* to testamentary intention. You should ensure that you can define both concepts in a way that means you can easily tell one from the other in an MCQ.

Intention, like testamentary capacity, has to be present at the time that the will is executed (though if the testator had intention at the time of giving instructions but lost it prior to execution, the will can be saved using the rule in *Parker v Felgate*).

It is possible for a testator to have knowledge and approval only of parts of the will and not of others, and if this is the case, only the parts known and approved will be admitted to probate. There is a general presumption of law that a testator with testamentary capacity did have knowledge and approval of the will, but once again, it is only a presumption: if there is evidence that outweighs it, then the presumption will fall. This presumption does not apply if the testator was blind or illiterate, or where the circumstances in which the will was made are suspicious, for example where the will benefits the person who drafted it for the testator. In these cases, the probate registry will require positive evidence that the testator intended to make the specific will under question (see **Chapter 7**).

However, the most common factor that brings intention into doubt is where there is reason to believe that the testator has been induced, or sometimes forced, to make a will that they did not really wish or intend to make.

Force, fear, fraud and undue influence

There is always a danger that a vulnerable testator, particularly an elderly person or someone suffering from a serious illness, can be frightened or threatened into making a will in favour of someone who is in a position of power over them: a carer, for example. Let's call this person Carey. If Carey hopes to gain an inheritance, they may make fraudulent representations to the testator (about other family members, say), or even act fraudulently; or they may even gain such a strong manipulative influence over the testator that the testator no longer knows their own mind. If any of these elements are proved, then the will made as a result is not valid; but the force, fear, fraud or undue influence must be proved by the person asserting them on the balance of probabilities (see **Chapter 7**).

This can be very problematic if the s 9 formalities have all been complied with, and there is no doubt that the testator had testamentary *capacity*. The validity of the will cannot be challenged on those grounds. The only possible challenge can be on the basis of 'knowledge and approval'. Was the testator so frightened, or duped, or manipulated by Carey that in reality, they either did not really know what was in the will or did know what was in the will and did not 'approve' it, but felt too frightened or browbeaten to say so? (For more information on duress, undue influence and fraud, see *Revise SQE: Contract Law*.)

For this reason, a solicitor taking instructions for a will usually asks to see the testator on their own without any other persons present, to be sure that the instructions really do come from the testator and from their own free will. Sometimes this is not possible for practical reasons – for example, if the testator's spoken English is poor and an interpreter is needed – but it is one reason why solicitors, when taking instructions for wills, should as a matter of professional conduct always take a very careful note of those instructions, including any questions and answers about whether the testator understands the instructions that they are giving and what they will mean after their death.

■ KEY POINT CHECKLIST

This chapter has covered the following key knowledge points. You can structure your revision around these, making sure to recall the key details for each point, as covered in this chapter.

- Only valid wills can be admitted to probate.
- To be valid, a will must satisfy *all* of the requirements on formality, testamentary capacity and testamentary intention.
- The rules on formalities are set out in s 9 of the Wills Act 1837 and are strictly interpreted.
- Testamentary capacity is established by using the test set out in *Banks v Goodfellow*.
- Unless the rules in *Parker v Felgate* apply, testamentary capacity is evaluated at the time that the will is executed.
- There is a presumption of law that a testator has knowledge and approval of a will unless they are blind or illiterate.
- This presumption can be overturned if there is evidence that the testator did not know what was in the will and/or did not approve its contents.
- Particular care must be taken by legal advisors to ensure that testators are making a will freely and are not being duped, forced or manipulated into making it.

■ KEY TERMS AND CONCEPTS

- testator (**page 2**)
- estate (**page 2**)
- admitted to probate (**page 3**)
- executed (**page 4**)
- attest/attestation (**page 5**)
- attestation clause (**page 6**)

■ SQE1-STYLE QUESTIONS

QUESTION 1

An eccentric billionaire writes out his will in pencil on two sides of a blank page that he has torn out of a paperback book. The billionaire asks his personal assistant, his chauffeur and his bodyguard to witness the will. When the three witnesses are present, the billionaire signs only the front page of the will at the top with a runic symbol and not with his name, explaining to the witnesses that he is doing so because there are so many forgeries of his normal signature. The witnesses sign the will at the bottom of the back page.

Which of the following statements is the most accurate description of the validity of the will?

A. Provided that no legal presumption can be displaced, this will is valid.

B. This will is invalid because a will can have a maximum of two witnesses only.

C. This will is invalid because it is written on a page torn out of a book.

D. This will is invalid because it is not signed by the testator at the bottom.

E. This will is invalid because a runic symbol cannot be a signature and therefore it is not signed by the testator.

QUESTION 2

A UK-based man spends most of his time travelling internationally for business purposes. For personal reasons, the man now needs to execute a new will urgently on a stopover between flights at the airport. The man drives his car to a car park next to the airport where one of the two witnesses has already parked. The first witness is disabled and cannot easily get out of his car. The man, who is in a hurry, puts the will on the bonnet of the first witness' car and signs it with the first witness watching him through the windscreen. The second witness then arrives. The man says to the second witness, 'Where have you been? I've already signed this. See?' He points to the signature on the will. The first and second witness then sign the will as witnesses.

Which one of the following options best describes whether the will is valid?

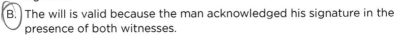

A. The will is not valid because only one witness was present when the man signed it.

B. The will is valid because the man acknowledged his signature in the presence of both witnesses.

C. The will is not valid because the man signed in the presence of the first witness but only acknowledged his signature to the second witness.

D. The will is not valid because the man did not acknowledge his signature.

E. The will is not valid because it cannot be executed in an exterior space such as a car park.

QUESTION 3

A woman, aged 55, has been diagnosed with early onset dementia and is living in a care home. The woman's solicitor visited her and took instructions from her for her will. The woman instructed that all her property, which consists now of a small balance in her savings account, should pass to her brother, who is her only living relative. The solicitor then drew up the will and has returned to the care home today to have it executed. The woman does not remember giving instructions for the will, can no longer remember that she has a brother, and does not remember the solicitor's previous visit. The solicitor has explained the purpose of today's visit to the woman. The woman seems to understand no more than that she is being asked to sign an important legal document.

Which of the following most accurately reflects the legal position *today*?

A. This will can never be executed because the woman had dementia when she gave her instructions.

B. This will cannot be executed today because the woman cannot remember the instructions that she previously gave.

C. This will can be executed today because although the woman no longer has testamentary capacity, she did have such capacity when she gave her instructions.

D. This will cannot be executed today because the woman does not understand that she is being asked to execute a will.

E. This will can be executed today because the woman understands that she is being asked to execute an important legal document.

QUESTION 4

A man is a professor of mathematics at a university. He has the full mental capability to organise and control his day-to-day life, and also to perform complex mathematical calculations beyond the scope of most people. However, the man also believes that famous scientists appear to him in 'visions' and give him help and advice, which he always follows. The man has told you that a vision has told him to exclude his daughter from his will. The daughter is 14 years old, without any disabilities and currently at a school for gifted children.

Which of the following most accurately describes whether the man has mental capacity to make a will?

A. The man does not have the capacity to make a will because he is suffering from delusions.

B. The man does not have the capacity to make a will because his delusions mean that he does not understand the nature and effects of the will he is proposing to make.

C. The man does not have the capacity to make a will because his delusions mean that he does not understand the claims of his relatives.

D. The man does have the capacity to make a will because his delusions do not affect his understanding of the claims of his relatives.

E. The man does not have the capacity to make a will because he does not understand the nature of the property in his estate.

QUESTION 5

A woman, a Japanese national living in the UK, died recently. The woman had a will which was written entirely in English. The will is signed by the woman in Japanese, and witnessed by two of her British work colleagues, but contains no attestation clause. The woman's family have told a solicitor that although the woman was able to speak English well, she was unable to read or write it.

Which one of the following statements most accurately describes the validity of the will?

A. The woman's will may be valid if sworn evidence is produced that the two witnesses saw her sign the will.

B. The woman's will may be valid if it can be proved that it was translated into Japanese before she died.

C. The woman's will cannot be valid under any circumstances because she did not have knowledge and approval of its contents.

 D. The woman's will may be valid if evidence is produced that it was read over to her and that she understood it before she signed.

E. The woman's will cannot be valid under any circumstances because she did not have any testamentary intention at the time that she signed.

■ ANSWERS TO QUESTIONS

Answers to 'What do you know already?' questions at the start of the chapter

1) A testatrix is a female testator. It is a slightly old-fashioned term these days, and 'testator' is often used interchangeably for will-makers of both sexes (as we use it in this book), but you should be aware of the word's meaning.

2) True. The reason, as you will see if you think about it, is that if a soldier is on active service and in battle conditions, it may be extremely difficult to comply with all of the conditions under s 9 of the Wills Act 1837, including the witness requirements. In this very exceptional case, the s 9 requirements therefore do not apply.

3) No. If the will is not admitted to probate, it cannot have any legal effect, and in particular it cannot pass legal ownership of the estate on to the

named executors (or anyone else). The beneficiaries named under that will have no legal rights to deal with the estate in any way and they must not do so.

4) False. There is no rule that says that a person diagnosed with dementia, or any other condition that affects their mental functioning, cannot make a will. On the contrary, the rule in *Banks v Goodfellow* must be applied and followed.

Answers to end-of-chapter SQE1-style questions

Question 1:

The correct answer was A. The legal presumptions of due execution and testamentary capacity would apply, and, as long as there is no evidence to displace them, there are no other factors which would invalidate this will. There is no rule that a will can have no more than two witnesses, so B is incorrect. The will can be written on any material at all, so C is incorrect. The billionaire indicated clearly to his witnesses that he intended the runic symbol to be his signature, and in these circumstances where he placed the signature is not relevant, so D is incorrect. There is no requirement that a signature must contain the testator's name, so E is incorrect.

Question 2:

The correct answer was B. This is because although only one witness was present when the man actually signed, both witnesses were present when he pointed to the signature and confirmed that it was his. It is not necessary for both witnesses to be present when the testator signs, provided that they are both present together, and in his presence, when he acknowledges his signature, so A is incorrect. C is a little more difficult. It is incorrect because it is not an accurate statement of what happened. If the first witness had left before the second witness arrived, then it would be correct, and the will would not be valid; but we know that all three were present when the man acknowledged his signature. The key thing is that all three people must be in each other's presence either at the time of signing or the time of acknowledgement of the signature. D is incorrect because the man did enough to tell both witnesses that the signature was his: he pointed to it and identified it as his signature. He does not have to use formal words such as 'I acknowledge this as my signature' as long as the witnesses are clear about the substance of what he is saying. Finally, E is incorrect because there are no rules about where a will should be executed. The only provision is that the three people, the testator and the witnesses, should be present together.

Question 3:

The correct answer was D. A person who has lost testamentary capacity between giving instructions and executing the will may still be able to execute it (so B is wrong), but one of the minimum requirements is that they must understand that it is a will that they are executing, and not some other document. The solicitor has tried and failed to explain this to the woman and therefore the woman does not have testamentary capacity. A is wrong because the fact that someone has been diagnosed with a mental impairment such as dementia does not automatically mean that they do not have testamentary capacity. Testamentary capacity is a question of fact on the relevant day. C is incorrect because the testator must understand at the very least that they are being asked to execute a will and that it has been drafted according to their previous instructions. E is incorrect because the testator must understand that they are being invited to execute a will and not some other legal document, no matter how important.

Question 4:
The correct answer was C. This is because the delusions directly affect the man's understanding of the claims that his young daughter has on his estate. Therefore all other options are incorrect.

Question 5:
The correct answer was D. This is because the woman is functionally illiterate; therefore, a straightforward confirmation of attestation will not suffice (so A is wrong). This question is not just specifically testing your knowledge of the rules relating to illiterate testators (the woman cannot read or write English so she is functionally illiterate), but your wider knowledge of other key concepts. Note that although C is also wrong, evidence would have to be brought forward that the woman had understood the contents of the will, or there would be no knowledge and approval. There is no evidence at all in the question that the woman did not know that she was making a will and so there is no basis for E. B is wrong as it does not matter that there may have been a translation of the will at some point before the testator died; what matters is whether the woman knew what she was signing at the time she signed it.

■ KEY CASES, RULES, STATUTES AND INSTRUMENTS

The SQE1 Assessment Specification does not require you to know any specific case names for this topic. There are a lot of case law examples in this chapter, but do not worry about the names; concentrate on the principles.

2

The personal representatives

■ MAKE SURE YOU KNOW

This chapter provides an overview of the role of personal representatives (PRs). For the SQE1 assessments, the required legal knowledge includes how executors and administrators are appointed, how executors can reserve their powers under the will and how PRs generally can renounce (in other words, refuse to act as PRs).

■ SQE ASSESSMENT ADVICE

As you work through this chapter, remember to pay particular attention in your revision to:
- who can and cannot be appointed as a PR
- the difference between the two types of PR, and the practical effects of that difference
- the procedural rules for appointing executors and administrators
- the rules to be applied when executors refuse or are unable to act
- the rules to be applied when no one is able or willing to act as a PR.

■ WHAT DO YOU KNOW ALREADY?

Have a go at these questions before reading this chapter. If you find some difficult or cannot remember the answers, make a note to look more closely at that area during your revision.

1) How does an executor know that they have been appointed?
   [Executors of the estate, page 19]

2) What is the difference between a PR, an executor and an administrator?
   [Who are the personal representatives and why are they appointed?, page 19]

3) Does a PR have to have professional qualifications, for example, as a solicitor or accountant?
   [Who can be an executor?, page 22]

4) Can anyone other than the PRs deal with the property in the estate?
   [Unwilling executors and renunciation, page 23]

WHO ARE THE PERSONAL REPRESENTATIVES AND WHY ARE THEY APPOINTED?

The **personal representatives (PRs)** are the persons who are in charge of the administration of the estate (see **Chapter 1**).

> ## Key term: personal representatives (PRs)
>
> PRs are the *only* people who are allowed to deal with the assets of the estate while it is being wound up and distributed. Nobody else has any right to deal with the estate, not even someone who is named as a substantial beneficiary. Anyone who attempts to deal with assets of the estate and is not a PR runs the risk of being held personally liable for any losses incurred by the estate. There are two types of PRs: executors, who are always appointed under a will, and administrators, who are appointed by the court.

Both executors and administrators are appointed to administer the estate, which means in basic terms to wind up the estate and distribute the assets either according to the terms of the will (if they are executors) or according to the rules on intestacy (if they are administrators; see **Chapter 5** for the intestacy rules). There is also a special category of administrators 'with the will annexed' (see **Administrator with a will** below) who distribute the estate according to the will.

The primary task of all PRs is not to hold on to the estate assets indefinitely but to distribute the assets to the right people at the earliest practicable moment. It should be a task for a limited period only. Bear this in mind as we proceed.

EXECUTORS OF THE ESTATE

As we have said, executors are appointed under the will of the testator (see **Chapter 1**). That means that they are selected to perform the role of executor by the deceased, and this distinguishes them from administrators, who are appointed by the court because they fall within a certain class of relations of the deceased. Executors are actively chosen in a way that administrators are not.

Two things follow from the fact that executors are appointed under the will: the first is that if the will is completely invalid for any reason, then the appointment of the executor will also be invalid. The second is that it is not possible for a person not named as an executor in the will to 'volunteer' to act as an executor.

The testator has an almost completely free choice in naming their executor(s) and there are, surprisingly, very few bars to acting as an executor.

Wording of the will

The wording of the will has to make clear two things about the executor(s): firstly, who the executor is to be. Generally, this is unproblematic as the testator describes the person so that there is no room for doubt: for example, 'my brother Safiz', 'my daughter Lupita', 'my dear friend Leon'. However, if there is room for doubt, for example naming 'one of my cousins' as an executor – even if only one of the testator's cousins outlives them – the appointment will be void for uncertainty (except in limited circumstances which do not concern us here).

Secondly, the will has to make it clear that this named person is being asked to perform all of the duties of an executor. This can cause problems in poorly drafted (particularly homemade) wills, where there is sometimes no express wording to say that Person A is intended to be the executor. In general, if the will directs that some of the essential tasks of an executor – eg paying funeral expenses or selling property within the estate – shall be carried out by some named person, then the court can conclude that the testator intended that person to be the executor, even if there is no express appointment.

There is one significant exception to the rule that executors have to be specifically named. This is where the testator wishes a solicitor from a particular firm to act as their executor. The testator can nominate one of the partners from the firm, or a successor firm, to act as their executor. In these circumstances, the wording of the will can make it clear that any person who is, for example, a partner in the firm at the relevant time can act (see **Practice example 2.1**).

Practice example 2.1

Rishi has been a client of Maxton & Co., a firm of solicitors, for many years and he has always instructed Jill Maxton, one of the partners of the firm, to act for him. He knows Jill well and trusts her, and wishes her to be one of his executors if she is able. However, Jill may have retired by the time Rishi dies, or may not be able to act for other reasons. If that happens, Rishi would still want one of the partners of Maxton & Co. to be his executor, but he does not know who the partners will be when he dies.

How should this be covered in Rishi's will?

Rishi's will could contain a clause which appoints Jill Maxton, but also the other partners of Maxton & Co. at the time of Rishi's death, to be his executors. The clause could restrict the number of such partners acting as his executor to one.

This means that when Rishi dies, Jill Maxton would be the first choice to act as his executor, but if she has retired by that time, then another partner from Maxton & Co. can act as executor in her place.

The will has to appoint at least one executor. There is no upper limit to the number that can be appointed, but probate (see **Chapters 1** and **7**) will only be granted to a maximum of four.

What if there is only one executor and that executor cannot act for any reason?

If the will only appoints one executor and that person for some reason cannot act, meaning that there would be no executor for the estate, there are two options.

The first is that if there is a single executor but that executor is *refusing* to act, then the person who would be first entitled to act as an administrator of the estate can make an application to the court for a **citation** under s 112 of the Senior Courts Act 1981.

Key term: citation

The citation procedure (NCPR r 46) is a means of forcing reluctant or hesitant executors to decide whether or not to accept executorship. A person interested in the estate (usually but not always a beneficiary) issues a court application which requires the reluctant PR to 'enter an appearance': that is, to choose whether or not to act as executor. If the PR does not enter an appearance, then they lose the right to administer the estate, which will then be taken over by the next eligible person: a co-executor, if named in the will, or an administrator if not.

How would this work in practice? Let's look at **Practice example 2.2**.

Practice example 2.2

Susie was named as the sole executor of Desmond's estate in Desmond's will. However, Susie has lived in New Zealand for the past 10 years and is also currently unwell. She has not taken any action in winding up Desmond's estate since Desmond died two years ago. Desmond left most of his property to his mother, Wilma, who is also the first person who would be entitled to act as administrator of his estate under the Non-Contentious Probate Rules (NCPR), but Wilma cannot receive her legacies until Susie starts acting as executor.

What action can Wilma take to receive her legacy?

Wilma can apply to the court for a citation under s 112 of the Senior Courts Act 1981 requiring Susie to 'appear'; in other words, to state whether she is willing to act as executor. If Susie does not respond ('fails to appear') to the citation at all, her rights in respect of the executorship will completely cease (s 5 of the Administration of Estates Act 1925). Wilma can then apply to be appointed as an administrator of Desmond's estate and move matters along.

The second possibility is that by the time the testator dies, every person named by the testator in the will as an executor has predeceased the testator, so there is no living person who can act as executor. If this happens, then the court will appoint an administrator, using the rules set out in **Administrators of the estate** below.

Extent of executors' powers

In most wills, the executors are granted full power over all of the assets in the estate. You should note, though, that it is possible to limit an executor's power over estate assets. For example, a 'literary executor' may be appointed in their will by a professional writer to deal with their literary work only and not with the rest of their estate.

Who can be an executor?

There are very few limits to acting as an executor. A minor under the age of 18 can be an executor (though a minor cannot apply for a grant of representation (see **Chapter 7**) or probate, until they reach the age of 18, so there is a significant problem there), as can an insolvent (bankrupt) person, a person with mental capacity issues and someone with a criminal record.

Exam warning

Be careful with issues around mental capacity. It is not impossible for a person suffering with a mental illness, for example, to be an executor, but the key question for the court is going to be whether or not that person is able to make a decision about the management of the estate, using the guidelines in ss 2 and 3 of the Mental Capacity Act (MCA) 2005. If the estate is relatively small or simple, for example, it may well be that a person suffering from a mild mental illness could make most if not all of the important decisions. You must always bear in mind that under the MCA principles, suffering from, say, schizophrenia or dementia *does not by itself mean* that the person concerned cannot act as an executor.

In fact, will the role of executor need not be taken by a human being at all, but by a legal 'personality': for example, a department of government known as the Public Trustee can act as an executor, as can a 'trust corporation' (broadly, a company appointed by the court to act as an executor or trustee; see **Chapter 11** for more on trusts)?

Professional and 'lay' executors

In broad terms, the choice for the testator tends to be between the professional and the non-professional executor. We have already seen that the testator may ask their solicitor to be an executor. They could also ask their accountant or their stockbroker/fund manager. All three have considerable expertise in dealing with the issues that will arise when distributing an estate, so they are good choices. However, they will usually be paid a fee for acting as professional executors, so they can be expensive choices. Where solicitors are concerned, an appointment as executor can frequently give rise to professional conduct issues. Professional executors will also be covered by indemnity insurance (that is, insurance which protects their clients from losses if they are negligent in any way), which is clearly of assistance to the beneficiaries of the estate if things go wrong during administration.

A non-professional (sometimes called a 'lay') executor will generally be a family member or friend who has known the testator well but is not professionally qualified as a lawyer or financial expert. It is very common, for example, for those in a marriage or civil partnership to name their spouse or civil partner as their executor. As this suggests, executors can also be beneficiaries of the estate, and this is extremely common. These lay executors will not be paid for the work they do, which of course means that the estate spends less on them. However, the main reason that the testator chooses them is not usually because they are the cheaper option but because the testator believes that they know the testator well enough to carry out the testator's wishes properly and to the full. Non-professional executors will almost always require professional advice anyway, and as this will probably be paid for out of the estate, the cost difference between the two types of executors may be relatively slight.

Unwilling executors and renunciation
There is no legal obligation for a testator to forewarn the executors that they are named in the will. As a result, someone may not find out that they have been nominated as an executor until the testator dies and the will is revealed. When they find out that they have been named, they may not want to act. In other cases, executors may know in advance that they have been nominated, but decide when the time comes that they do not want to act. What do they do? Are they forced to apply for a grant of probate even though they do not want to?

It is possible for executors to refuse to act: this act is called renouncing probate. To renounce, they must file a written form with the probate registry. They must, however, generally do so as quickly as they can, because the right to renounce is lost if the executor has taken any steps, however slight, in starting to administer the estate. Acts stopping the executor from renouncing include calling in any debts due to the estate, or advertising for beneficiaries, or even arranging for insurance for property in the estate: in summary, acting as an executor in any way. These actions are called 'intermeddling' with the estate, and if an executor is found to have intermeddled in any way, they are considered to have agreed to act and will not afterwards be able to renounce.

There is another way in which a named executor can avoid involvement with the administration of the estate. This procedure is called 'reserving a power to the executor involved'. It can only be used where there is more than one executor. The effect of reserving a power is that the executor to whom power is reserved is, so to speak, on the substitutes' bench unless and until they are needed (see **Practice example 2.3**).

Practice example 2.3

Manju and Ishmael were both named as executors in the will of their good friend Morton. Manju is happy to proceed as an executor, but Ishmael is reluctant to do so for personal reasons. However, Manju has been unwell recently, and both she and Ishmael are worried about what will happen if she falls ill again. If Ishmael renounces probate now and Manju later falls ill, the estate will be left without an executor and this will be complicated and expensive to remedy. It would also be contrary to Morton's wishes, which Manju and Ishmael want to respect.

What can Manju and Ishmael do in this situation?

Manju and Ishmael can agree that power will be reserved to Ishmael, but that only Manju will currently take out the grant of probate. If Manju later falls ill and cannot continue as an executor, Ishmael can step in as her replacement because he has a reserved power to do so.

Revision tip

The key difference to remember is that if an executor renounces, they are no longer an executor once the renunciation has taken effect. If an executor reserves a power, they continue to *be* executors although they do not *act* as executors unless they are called upon to do so.

Acting as an executor without authority: the executor *de son tort*

We have already seen that an executor's authority comes from the will. If you reverse that principle and look at it the other way around, you will see that if someone is not named in the will, they have no authority to act as an executor. Obviously they should not do so, but it does sometimes happen that a person starts acting as if they are an executor – calling in the testator's debts, dealing with the testator's bank and so on. This is another kind of intermeddling with the estate, and the person who does this is called an executor *de son tort* (or, in a loose translation, an executor 'by their own wrong'). You should bear in mind that executors *de son tort* will be held *personally* liable for the assets with which they have intermeddled, including paying losses, or any chargeable inheritance tax.

Revision tip

Always keep in mind that a person cannot appoint themselves an executor. An executor must be named in the will. Make sure that you can tell the difference between an executor *de son tort* and a duly appointed executor. Remember too that an executor *de son tort* is *personally* liable to pay any loss caused from their acts out of their own pocket.

ADMINISTRATORS OF THE ESTATE

Administrators are appointed by the court to administer the estate because no, or no appropriate, executor has been named to deal with the deceased's estate. The obvious example is where the testator has left no will, or in other words has died fully intestate (see **Chapter 5**).

There are two types of administrators: administrators without a will and administrators with a will. The difference between the two types is the validity of the will that the deceased has left behind. If there is no existing will (full intestacy), then there will be an appointment of an administrator without a will. If the will is valid but there is a problem or issue with the executorship (a type of partial intestacy; see **Chapter 5**), then an administrator will be appointed with a will.

Administrator without a will

The classic example is a full intestacy, where the deceased has left no will at all. If there is no will, then it follows that there is no executor.

A further example is where a will document exists but for some reason it is formally invalid. We have already seen that if all of the formalities for execution are not present, then there is no valid will (**Chapter 1**). If there is no valid will, then there is no valid executor. In that case, one or more administrators have to be appointed using Rule 22(1) of the NCPR (see **Chapter 5**). Note that wills where the testator was found to have no testamentary capacity, or where there was want of knowledge and approval, would also fall under this heading.

Where there is no will at all, it is not the case that any relative of the deceased, or indeed anyone else, can apply to be an administrator. Rule 22(1) of the NCPR sets out a list of candidates who must be considered in the order set out in the rule, generally relatives of the deceased who are entitled to apply (see **Table 2.1**).

NB You are looking for the first person who is alive and over the age of 18 years as you work through the table. In each case, if there is nobody alive in that category, then you move on to the next category. When you find that first person, then they are the person with the best right to be appointed administrator of the estate. Although there can be a maximum of four administrators, generally only one administrator will be appointed, unless there is either a minority interest (that is, a child beneficiary of the estate) or a life interest, in which case there must be at least two administrators (s 114(2) Senior Courts Act 1981).

Table 2.1: The order in which relatives of the deceased must be considered to be administrators

	Definition in NCPR Rule 22(1)	Explanation
1	Surviving spouse or civil partner	This must be someone who entered into a marriage or civil partnership with the deceased; cohabitees have no rights to administration, nor do previous spouses after divorce
2	Children of the deceased and the issue of any deceased child who died before the deceased	Any living children of the deceased, or if the deceased left no living children, any living grandchildren of the deceased
3	Father and mother of the deceased	Either surviving parent of the deceased
4	Brothers and sisters of the whole blood and the issue of any brother or sister of the whole blood who died before the deceased	Any sibling of the deceased who has the same parents as the deceased, or if the deceased's full brother and sisters have all died, then any living child of theirs (the deceased's nieces and nephews)
5	Brothers and sisters of the half blood and the issue of any brother or sister of the half blood who died before the deceased	Any sibling of the deceased who shares one parent with the deceased, or if the deceased's half-brother and sisters have all died, then any living child of theirs (the deceased's nieces and nephews)
6	Grandparents	Any living grandparents of the deceased
7	Uncles and aunts of the whole blood and the issue of any uncle or aunt of the whole blood who died before the deceased	Any uncle or aunt who was a full brother or sister of either of the deceased's parents, or if no such uncle or aunt is living, then any one of their children (the deceased's cousins)
8	Uncles and aunts of the half blood and the issue of any uncle or aunt of the half blood who died before the deceased	Any uncle or aunt who was a half-brother or sister of either of the deceased's parents, or if no such uncle or aunt is living, then any one of their children (the deceased's cousins)
9	The Treasury Solicitor if the Crown claims **bona vacantia**	NCPR r 22(2)

Key term: *bona vacantia*

Bona vacantia (literally, 'vacant goods') is a legal principle by which, if no person can be found to inherit the deceased's estate (either under a will or intestacy), the Crown can claim the estate for itself.

Let's work through **Table 2.1** using **Practice example 2.4**.

Practice example 2.4

Alkmund died recently without leaving a will. He was over 90 when he died and most of his relatives had predeceased him. He had only two *living* relatives: his daughter-in-law Monica, who was the widow of Alkmund's son Tristan; and Sabena, who was the daughter of Alkmund's half-brother Chad. Monica and Alkmund were close and Alkmund saw Monica at least once a week. He saw Sabena only about once a year.

Which of them has the best right to be appointed administrator?

If you use Table 2.1, you will see that the person with the best right is Sabena. Monica is not a surviving spouse; she is not Alkmund's child; she is not his father or mother; and so on. In fact, if you go all the way down the table, you will see that a daughter-in-law has no right to be appointed administrator at all. However, if you go down the table looking for Sabena, you will find her in category (5).

Note that the question of who is appointed administrator has nothing to do with how personally close to the deceased the 'candidate' may be. Alkmund knew Monica very well and Sabena hardly at all, and he might be both surprised and shocked if he were told that it would be Sabena who would have control over his estate when he died. Remember what we said when considering wills: if you want someone specific to look after your property when you die, it is generally better to make a will and appoint them as an executor!

However, what if the first person on the list does not want to be the administrator? As with executorship, it is possible to refuse administratorship. A potential administrator can renounce, for example. Some administrators will not be suitable because they are minors (see **Practice example 2.5**) or do not have sufficient mental capacity. If there are people who have a prior right to be appointed administrators, and they do not want to be appointed but someone else further down the table does, then the person with prior right must be 'cleared off'. This means that either they must have renounced their right to be appointed, or have been passed over by the court for some other reason.

> **Practice example 2.5**
>
> Petrus, who died recently without making a will, has an only daughter, Wynona, who is 11 years old. Petrus was not married to Wynona's mother, Clarice, and therefore there is no surviving spouse. Petrus also has a sister, Magda. Wynona cannot be appointed as an administrator as she is a minor.
>
> What should happen in this situation?
>
> **Where the person entitled to administration is a minor, it is possible to appoint the parent or guardian of that minor as administrator 'for the use and benefit of the minor' (NCPR r 32(1)) until the minor comes of age. However, if Wynona's mother Clarice says that she is not willing to act, then the next suitable person in the table is Petrus' sister Magda, provided she is willing to act.**
>
> **Note that before appointing Magda as administrator, the court will want proof that any person with a prior right to administration – in this case, Wynona – has been 'cleared off'; that is, that evidence has been given that the person with the prior right is unable or unwilling to act.**

Once appointed, the administrator without a will is bound to distribute the estate strictly according to the intestacy rules (see **Chapter 5**): this is very different to the position of an administrator with a will, which we will look at now.

Administrator with a will

The situation here is that the will is valid, but there is an issue with appointing an executor. This could be because the will did not name an executor at all, or because somebody is named but the testator does not make it clear whether this person was to be an executor. It can also be because the named executor will not or cannot act (they predeceased the testator, for example, or they do not have mental capacity, or they were cited and failed to appear). Finally, if the named executor is a former spouse or civil partner of the deceased, then the appointment will automatically fail.

In each of these cases, an administrator will be appointed ('with the will annexed') using NCPR Rule 20. This provides that the grant should go first to any named executor (if they are not otherwise disqualified from acting as such); or if none, then to a residuary legatee who is holding the estate or part of it in trust for another person (see **Chapter 11** for more on trusts); or if none, to any other residuary legatee under a complex set of rules which are outside the scope of this book.

The will did not name an executor

We looked in the previous section at the problems there can be under this heading, either because it is impossible to identify who the executor was to be or it was not clear that the testator wanted the person to act as executor.

If the rules cannot help, then an administrator will have to be appointed by the court instead.

The named executor will not or cannot act

The executor may already be dead, having predeceased this testator; or they may have lost mental capacity since the will was made; or they may be too young. We saw previously that minority is no bar to being appointed as an executor, but because a minor cannot apply for a grant of probate, the person entitled to the residuary estate will be granted administration of the estate until the minor attains majority: NCPR r 32.

The named executor is a former spouse or civil partner of the deceased

There is a special rule in these circumstances, set out in ss 18A and 18C of the Wills Act 1837. If the named testator is a former spouse or civil partner from whom the deceased is now divorced, then the appointment of that person as an executor will fail.

Exam warning

The NCPR Rule governing the order of administrators *with* a will is Rule *20* and not Rule *22*. The provisions are significantly different. Be sure that you are referring to, and applying, the correct rule!

Revision tip

Because there is a valid will in existence, the administrator's duties here are to distribute the estate in accordance with the will and *not*, you must note, in accordance with the intestacy rules.

DUTIES OF PERSONAL REPRESENTATIVES

We will look at the duties of PRs in more detail in **Chapters 7** and **8**.

■ KEY POINT CHECKLIST

This chapter has covered the following key knowledge points. You can structure your revision around these, making sure to recall the key details for each point, as covered in this chapter.

* Who can and cannot be appointed as a PR.
* The difference between the two types of PR, and the practical effects of that difference.
* The procedural rules for appointing executors and administrators.
* The rules to be applied when executors refuse or are unable to act.
* The rules to be applied when no one is able or willing to act as a PR.

■ KEY TERMS AND CONCEPTS

- personal representatives (PRs) **(page 19)**
- citation **(page 21)**
- *bona vacantia* **(page 27)**

■ SQE1-STYLE QUESTIONS

QUESTION 1

A woman wrote out a homemade will on a will form. The woman expressed a wish that one of her aunts should be her executor. At the time that the will was made, the woman had five aunts living; at the time of the woman's death, three of the aunts are still alive. The will also expressed a wish that the woman's civil partner should arrange and pay for a humanistic funeral for her.

Which of the following statements most accurately reflects the legal position?

A. The executor of this will is the woman's civil partner.

B. This will is formally invalid because it does not name an executor.

C. The executors of this will are all three of the woman's surviving aunts.

D. The executor of this will is the aunt that all three aunts agree should act.

E. There is no valid executor of the will, and an administrator must be appointed by the court.

QUESTION 2

A will appoints three people as executors. Person 1 has been convicted of a fraud-related offence and is currently imprisoned. Person 2 is 17 years of age and a mathematical prodigy currently in the second year of a degree at a prestigious university. Person 3 was declared bankrupt two months ago.

Which of the people appointed under the will can be an executor?

A. All persons are unable to be executors.

B. Persons 1 and 3 can be executors. Person 3 cannot be an executor because they are insolvent.

C. Persons 1 and 3 can be executors. Person 2 cannot be an executor because they are too young.

D. Persons 2 and 3 can be executors. Person 1 cannot be an executor because they have been convicted of a criminal offence.

E. All persons are able to be executors.

QUESTION 3

A businessman told his brother that he had made a will which appointed his brother as his sole executor. When the businessman died, the brother immediately contacted the customers of his business and asked them to pay to him the amounts due on any current invoices. As a result of this, the brother received the cash sum of £50,000. The brother kept the money in a safe in his house where it was subsequently destroyed in a fire. The house was not insured at the time of the fire. The businessman's will has now been found and it does not name his brother as his executor.

Which of the following most accurately reflects the legal position of the brother?

A. The brother can claim the loss of the £50,000 from the businessman's estate.

B. The brother is liable to pay the sum of £50,000 to the businessman's estate out of his own pocket.

C. The brother is not liable to pay the sum of £50,000 to the businessman's estate because he was not insured.

D. Because the brother genuinely believed that he was the executor of the estate, the businessman's estate cannot claim the sum of £50,000 from the brother.

E. The businessman's estate cannot claim the sum of £50,000 from the brother because the brother was entitled to act as executor until the will was found.

QUESTION 4

A divorced woman died childless, leaving no will and an estate worth £2 million. The woman's surviving relatives were her ex-husband, the daughter of her half-sister (her niece), the son of her half-brother (her nephew) and her grandmother. The woman and her ex-husband had been on distant terms for over 10 years prior to her death. The woman lived with her grandmother, to whom she was very close, and saw her every day. The woman was not aware that her half-brother had had any children and she had never met her nephew.

The niece and the nephew are on very bad terms after a family argument five years ago and have refused to speak to each other since.

Who is/are the person(s) most likely to be appointed to be an administrator of the woman's estate?

A. The grandmother.

B. The ex-husband.

C. Either the niece or the nephew.

D. Both the niece and the nephew.

E. None of them are eligible to be an administrator of the estate.

QUESTION 5

An artist died while 10 of her paintings were being exhibited in a gallery. At the time of her death, four of the paintings had been sold for the sum of £25,000 and six remained unsold. The artist's will left her paintings to her brother and any cash in her estate to her son. The artist appointed her sister as the executor of her will. The sister is still collecting the assets of the estate and is not yet in a position to distribute them.

Which of the following best describes to whom the gallery should send the £25,000 and the six paintings?

A. The gallery should send the £25,000 and the six paintings to the artist's brother.

B. The gallery should send the £25,000 and the six paintings to the artist's sister.

C. The gallery should send the £25,000 and the six paintings to the artist's son.

D. The gallery should send the £25,000 to the artist's son and the six paintings to the artist's brother.

E. The gallery should send the £25,000 to the artist's sister and the six paintings to the artist's brother.

■ ANSWERS TO QUESTIONS

Answers to 'What do you know already?' questions at the start of the chapter

1) The executor will be named by the testator in the will.

2) This is a slightly tricky question. In fact, executors and administrators are two different types of PR: so one person can be both an executor and a PR at the same time, and another person can be both an administrator and a PR at the same time.

3) No. Although it can be helpful for a PR to be a professional, there is no obligation to appoint professional executors or administrators.

4) No. This is the most important thing to grasp at the outset about PRs. Nobody else is allowed to deal with any property in the estate. Anyone else who does so will be liable to the beneficiaries of the estate for any loss that they have caused.

Answers to end-of-chapter SQE1-style questions

Question 1:

The correct answer was A. In order for one of the aunts to act, that aunt must be specifically named. As that did not happen in this case, an attempted appointment of the aunts is void for uncertainty (so C is incorrect) and the aunts cannot remedy the situation amongst themselves (so D is incorrect). Although the civil partner was not appointed as an executor, the will directed that he was to pay for the funeral. This is an essential task of an executor and the court may therefore conclude that the intention was that the civil partner was intended to carry out some of the functions of an executor, which means that A is the best answer. The omission of a named executor can never affect the formal validity of a will, so B is incorrect. As it is likely that the court will find sufficient evident that the civil partner was intended to be the executor, an administrator will not be needed and E is incorrect.

Question 2:

The correct answer was E. A criminal conviction is not a bar to being an executor, so D is incorrect. Neither is an insolvency, so B is incorrect. A legal minor can be an executor, so C is incorrect, although person 2 would not be able to apply for probate because of their age. This means that all of the people mentioned can act as executors, and A therefore must be incorrect.

Question 3:

The correct answer was B. The brother has been acting throughout as an executor *de son tort* and has intermeddled in the estate. If by doing that he has caused loss to the estate (which the brother has done in this case), then he is liable to repay that loss personally. A is incorrect because the brother has not suffered a loss: the £50,000 loss has been to the estate. It makes no difference to the brother's liability as an executor *de son tort* whether he was insured or not, and C is therefore incorrect, and a genuine belief that the brother was the executor would also not affect his liability, so D is incorrect too. Finally, it is not possible to self-appoint as an executor, even temporarily: the brother cannot be an executor if he was not mentioned in the will, and E is incorrect for this reason.

Question 4:

The correct answer was C. Former spouses are not eligible to be appointed administrators (making B wrong). Nieces and nephews, even of half-siblings, take precedence over grandparents (making A wrong). Here, we have a nephew and niece who are equally entitled. Although the court will prefer to appoint one administrator, it would be possible to appoint both the niece and the nephew as joint administrators because they are equally entitled to the administration. However, in this case the cousins are not speaking to one another, and it is unlikely that they will be able to work together; this makes D incorrect as it is not the most likely solution. As a result, the court is likely to appoint the one who seems most likely to administer the estate well and efficiently. E is incorrect because there are clearly two persons entitled to be appointed as administrator under Rule 22(1) of the NCPR.

Question 5:

The correct answer was B. It is the executor's duty to get in all of the assets prior to distribution, regardless of the person who will receive them on distribution. Only the artist's sister has a right to hold the items prior to distribution, and the person holding the items on the artist's death must not pass them to anyone else. The artist's brother currently has no right to possess any of the items, so A, D and E are incorrect. Neither does the artist's son, so C is incorrect.

■ KEY CASES, RULES, STATUTES AND INSTRUMENTS

The SQE1 Assessment Specification does not require you to be able to cite the specific provisions of the NCPR on this topic, but you are strongly encouraged to learn the principles underpinning the relevant NCPR Rules, including Rules 20, 22 and 46, discussed in this chapter. Although you are not otherwise required to memorise statute sections or cases in relation to this topic, you should also ensure you know:

- s 112 of the Senior Courts Act 1981
- s 5 of the Administration of Estates Act 1925
- ss 2 and 3 of the Mental Capacity Act 2005
- ss 18A and 18C Wills Act 1837.

Interpretation of wills, alterations and amendments

■ MAKE SURE YOU KNOW

In this chapter, we will look at the principles governing the interpretation of wills and the effects of any alterations or amendments. For the SQE1 assessment you will need to be able to classify accurately any gift made in a will and then 'follow through' the effects of that classification if problems have arisen with distribution. You must also be able to decide in a multiple-choice question (MCQ): (i) when (and why) a gift will not take effect and (ii) when an alteration or amendment to an existing will is or is not valid. You must also understand, and be able to explain, codicils.

■ SQE ASSESSMENT ADVICE

As you work through this chapter, remember to pay particular attention in your revision to:
• the definition of all the types of gift made in a will
• how to spot a gift that has failed, and why it has failed
• how s 21 of the Wills Act 1837 is applied
• how to tell the difference between an obliteration and an alteration
• what a codicil is, and the effect it has on an existing will.

■ WHAT DO YOU KNOW ALREADY?

Have a go at these questions before reading this chapter. If you find some difficult or cannot remember the answers, make a note to look more closely at that area during your revision.

1) What is the difference between a 'legacy' and a 'devise' in a will?
   [Interpretation of wills: different types of testamentary gift, page 36]

2) If Person A makes a gift of their antique Cartier wristwatch in their will to Person B, but then Person A sells the Cartier wristwatch before their death, what is Person B entitled to under the will?
   [Failure of testamentary gifts, page 38]

3) Is a beneficiary of a will permitted to be a witness of that will?
   [Failure of testamentary gifts, page 38]

4) True or false? If alterations to a will have been initialled by the testator and both witnesses, those alterations are valid and will be accepted by the probate registry.
[**Alterations and amendments to wills, page 44**]

INTERPRETATION OF WILLS: DIFFERENT TYPES OF TESTAMENTARY GIFT

Imagine for a moment being able to lay out every single item that you own in front of you and surveying everything. There may be some physical objects which have a high value – if you own a car, for example – and some other physical objects which may not be so valuable but which have a particular emotional significance, such as a piece of jewellery which has been passed down to you from a grandparent or great-grandparent. You may be lucky enough to have money saved up in the bank, which could be represented by your savings account passbook or bank card; you may even be lucky enough to own one or more pieces of land, which could be represented by the Land Registry official copy.

Now imagine that you no longer have any use for any of the items in front of you, and that you plan to give them all away. This is essentially what any testator (see **Chapter 1**) is doing when they are making a will: looking, in their imagination, at everything that they own and deciding where all these items will go when they die. Sometimes a testator will have very definite ideas about the person to whom a specific item will go; sometimes their ideas are more general. The way that these ideas are translated into specific provisions of the will is by setting them out as specific types of gift. We are now going to look at the choices that a testator has when making gifts in a will, and the consequences of each choice.

A gift of **personalty** in a will is called a 'legacy' and a gift of land is called a 'devise'.

Key term: personalty
'Personalty' is all property which is not land: it therefore includes all physical objects (which are described as 'chattels'; see **Chapter 5, Personal chattels**), as well as money, interests under a trust (see **Chapter 11**) and any debts owed by other people to the deceased (see **Chapter 8**).

All legacies or devises can be specific, general or residuary (see below).

Let's now look at the definition of each type of gift that may arise in a will and how we identify them. We are going to focus on legacies in each case, though we will also discuss devises where they are relevant.

Specific legacies

The essence of a specific legacy is an item (or a collection of items) that is separated off by the testator from the rest of their personal belongings to be given to a particular person. For example, 'I give my collection of J. R. R. Tolkien first editions to my nephew Caspar' is a specific gift, as is 'I give my VW Golf motor car to my niece Gemma'.

General legacies

The essential difference between specific and general legacies is that specific legacies have to be made of or from a specific item of property, but general legacies can be made from any available part of the estate. So, in the example above, the specific legacy can only be made by the executors taking the books owned by the testator and giving them to Caspar. A general legacy of a sum of money, for example 'I give £1,000 to my nephew Ade', can be paid by the executors from any available money that is in the estate and not necessarily from a specific source.

Exam warning

A specific legacy will generally, though not always, contain the word 'my', but a general legacy will not. So, for example, the gift 'I give *a* first edition of *The Hobbit* to my niece Bella' would normally be a general legacy, and the obligation on the executors would be to purchase a copy of the book for Bella using estate funds and give it to her.

A gift cannot be both specific and general; it must be one or the other.

Pecuniary legacies

These are legacies of money. Pecuniary legacies can be specific: 'The sum of £200 in cash which is kept in the biscuit tin in the kitchen'; or general: 'The sum of £200'. They include straightforward gifts of specific sums, for example, '£2,000 to each of my nephews and nieces', but they also include annuities, which are regular payments made out of the estate to a specific person.

Pecuniary legacies can also be demonstrative.

Demonstrative legacies

Demonstrative legacies are almost always pecuniary. A demonstrative legacy is a legacy which the will directs should be paid primarily out of a particular fund, for example, 'I give my cousin Sharif the sum of £3,000 from my savings account with the Coffers Bank'.

What if, at the time the testator dies, there is less than £3,000 in the testator's Coffers Bank savings account? The principle of a demonstrative legacy is that it is paid primarily, though not necessarily, out of the named fund. This means that if there is less than £3,000 in the account at the time of the testator's death, then the executors (see **Chapter 2**) can make up the shortfall from any other available funds in the estate.

> ### Revision tip
>
> You will have seen that legacies often fall into more than one category. They can be both pecuniary *and* demonstrative (for example), or both pecuniary *and* general.

Residuary legacies

The residue of an estate is what is left after any debts or liabilities of the estate, and any specific, general or demonstrative gifts (be they legacies or devises), have been paid out. If we think back to the image of the testator's belongings spread out in front of them, it is what remains after the specific, general and demonstrative items have been removed.

In fact, in most cases, the residue will form by far the most valuable part of the estate. Whether the residue is large or small, all well-drafted wills contain a clause disposing of the residue of the estate. If this is not done, there is a strong risk that there will be property left over after making the other gifts that the executors do not know what to do with: in other words, there would be a partial intestacy (see **Chapter 5**), which should be avoided if at all possible.

Devises

Although we have focussed on legacies in the sections above, you can see that it is possible to have specific devises of land: 'I give my property 24 Acacia Avenue'; or general ones: 'I give all my land'. It is also possible, and common, to make a residuary devise by placing into residue 'the rest of my land not otherwise disposed of in this will'. As pecuniary gifts can only be money, a devise cannot be pecuniary.

At present, we are only dealing with straightforward gifts of land, by which both the legal and equitable interests are passed on to the same person or persons. However, land can often be given to someone to hold for the benefit of another person: that is, it is handed over as trust property. This is dealt with in more detail at **Chapter 11**.

FAILURE OF TESTAMENTARY GIFTS

You may be wondering why it is important to classify testamentary gifts in this way. The answer is that classification is not so important when gifts are successful, but it becomes vitally important when it looks like they are going to fail (see also **Chapter 5** for more on partial intestacy).

When might a testamentary gift fail?

A gift might fail in the following circumstances.

Disclaimer

Not all testamentary gifts come without strings or are unmixed blessings. Often, there can be inheritance tax to pay (see **Chapter 10**), or associated costs such as transporting or insuring heavy or valuable items, or land may come burdened with mortgages or other secured debts. The general rule is that if the will does not specifically say who is to pay these associated charges, they will be payable by the recipient. Sometimes this makes the gift so burdensome that the recipient may wish to refuse it: to do this, they will *disclaim* the gift by indicating to the executors that they do not want it.

Class gifts

So far, we have discussed testamentary gifts made to a specific individual, but it is also possible to make a gift to a group of individuals, or what is known as a 'class'. The most common example of this is a gift to the testator's descendants (children, grandchildren, etc). Under the general law, the class will 'close' – that is, no more people can become members of the class – at the time of the testator's death. Theoretically, therefore, a person born the day before the testator's death will inherit but a person born the day after will not. To remedy this perceived injustice, and to meet those injustices, the 'class closing rules' may be applied. These rules are beyond the scope of this book but you should be familiar with their broad outlines.

Beneficiaries dying at the same time/in the same incident (commorientes)

Sometimes, the manner of a beneficiary's death can give rise to a particular problem. Let's say, for example, Kobi left everything to his brother Cyril, and Cyril left everything to his partner Marsha. Kobi and Cyril then die together in a car crash. If Kobi died first, Cyril will inherit all of his property and it will then pass on to Marsha under Cyril's will. But if Cyril died first, Marsha will only receive Cyril's estate and not Kobi's.

There may be sound factual evidence (from first responders attending the scene, perhaps) that as a matter of fact, Kobi died before Cyril. However, if there is not, then the *commorientes* rule will be applied (the term means 'persons dying together'). If it is genuinely not possible to tell which person died first, then the presumption is 'oldest person died first'. So in the example above, if Kobi were the oldest brother, then Marsha would inherit both estates; but if Cyril were the oldest brother, she would only inherit Cyril's.

Why might a testamentary gift fail?

Along with the disclaimer of a gift the other main reasons why a testamentary gift may fail are:

• ademption
• abatement
• lapse
• witnessing of a will by a beneficiary
• divorce, dissolution or annulment of marriage
• forfeiture by reason of unlawful killing.

Ademption

Ademption affects specific gifts *only* and has no relevance to general gifts. Make sure you classify a gift before you start applying the rules on ademption to it!

The basic rule of ademption is that if, between making the will and dying, the item that was specifically gifted has gone out of the testator's estate, then that gift completely fails (see **Practice example 3.1**).

Practice example 3.1

Manfred makes a will leaving all of his shares in Dimarmon plc to his stepdaughter Lyra. At the time he made the will, he had 200 Dimarmon shares worth a total of £2,000. The shares then went up in value and he sold them all three years after making the will for the sum of £20,000. However, he did not change his will before he died.

What happens in this situation?

As there were no Dimarmon shares in Manfred's estate when he died, the gift adeems and Lyra receives nothing.

Timing can be all-important because if the item survived to become part of the testator's estate, even if only for a few minutes or hours, but was then destroyed (for example in a fire), then the executors might be liable to pay over any insurance payment for the destroyed item to the disappointed beneficiary. If there is no clear evidence that the item survived the testator, then the gift adeems.

A 'specific gift' means exactly that: if the item named in the will is later replaced by another item, even if it is very similar, then the gift adeems. For example, if the testator leaves to a beneficiary 'my limited-edition Picasso print no. 163', but then sells it and buys another (otherwise almost identical) print numbered 876, the beneficiary will receive nothing.

Abatement

Abatement is the process by which the estate is reduced as the executors pay out all of the debts and liabilities owed by it to third parties. Debts and liabilities are always paid out of the estate first, before any distribution is made: s 33(2) Administration of Estates Act (AEA) 1925. The AEA sets out (at part II of the First Schedule) what property the executors should use to pay these liabilities, and in what order. We take a more detailed look at this duty of the personal representatives (PRs) in **Chapter 8.**

If there is not enough in the estate to pay the liabilities and to make all the gifts, then classification becomes particularly important, because the executors must prioritise paying the liabilities over paying the gifts. If there is a shortage of assets after the liabilities have been paid, then general legacies will abate before specific legacies: in other words, the PRs should pay the specific legacies first, and then pay only those general legacies that can be paid out of the remaining assets. If there is not enough money in the estate, therefore, it is advantageous to be a specific legatee (that is, the recipient of a legacy) because specific legacies will be paid before general legacies (see **Practice example 3.2**). Where they can be paid in full from the specified property, demonstrative legacies are classed as specific legacies for the purposes of abatement.

Practice example 3.2

When Stanislaus died, his estate was valued at £65,000. His will contained a specific legacy to his brother James of 'the sum of £5,000 in cash which is contained in the small safe inside the wardrobe of my home'. He also left a general legacy of £5,000 to his sister Nora. When his executors reviewed his estate, they discovered that Stanislaus' estate had liabilities, on personal loans and credit cards, and on funeral and other expenses, of £57,000.

What happens in this situation?

Under the abatement rules, the executors are obliged to pay the liabilities of £57,000 out of the estate first. This leaves the sum of £8,000 in the estate. This is not enough to pay the full gifts to James and Nora. The executors are directed under the rules of abatement to pay the specific gift first: this is the gift to James, which is paid in full. Nora receives the £3,000, which is the only money remaining in the estate.

Lapse

A gift lapses when there is nobody to give it to: in plain terms, when the recipient of the gift has died before the testator or is otherwise disqualified from receiving it. These disqualifications include being unable to benefit because of a problem with witnessing the will, or subsequent remarriage, or having brought about the death of the testator, all of which we are going to consider in the following sections. A lapsed outright gift will fall back into the residue, unless it is already a residuary gift, in which case it will be given out according to the laws on intestacy (see **Chapter 5**) (so there would be a partial intestacy here). If the gift is of a limited interest, such as a life interest, then lapse means it moves forward to the next person in line (see **Practice example 3.3**).

This may not be what the testator wants: in fact, if it turns out that the rules of intestacy will apply, this may have an effect which the testator would definitely not have wanted. For this reason, a will often contains a fallback provision for what is to happen on a lapse, for example: 'My diamond-set signet ring to my nephew Sylvain, but if he shall predecease me or be otherwise disqualified from taking, to my nephew Mathieu'.

Practice example 3.3

Albert's will leaves a life interest in the sum of £200,000 to Thacker, with the remainder to Copper. At the time that the will is made, Thacker and Copper are both in their 30s and in good health. However, four years later, and while Albert is still alive, Thacker is killed in a car accident. Albert dies a year after Thacker without changing his will.

What happens in this situation?

The gift of the life interest to Thacker has lapsed because Thacker is now dead. The gift immediately passes on to Copper, who receives an absolute interest in the £200,000 (that is, it is his to use as he likes).

Revision tip

There is, however, one extremely important exception to the principle of lapse, and that is where the intended beneficiary was a child (or other descendant) of the testator and has died before the testator but leaves behind a child or children (the testator's grandchildren). In these circumstances, s 33 of the Wills Act 1837 provides that even though the named beneficiary has died, the bequest under the will shall take effect as a devise or bequest to the beneficiary's children. This rule applies to both gifts to individual children and to a child as one of a class (see **Chapter 5**).

Witnessing of a will by a beneficiary

A beneficiary under a will cannot take their gift if either the beneficiary or their spouse/civil partner witnessed the will (see **Chapter 1** for information on witnessing). The gift is treated as 'utterly null and void', which for all practical purposes means that it will lapse (see **Practice example 3.4**).

Practice example 3.4

Fred and Jed are civil partners. Their friend Xanthe made a will in which she left £10,000 to Fred. The witnesses to Xanthe's will were Jed and Alton.

Can Fred receive the gift when Xanthe dies?

Fred cannot take the gift of £10,000 because his civil partner, Jed, witnessed the will. However, Xanthe's will is still valid, and all of the other provisions of the will can be carried out by her executors.

The rule only affects actual spouses and not engaged couples, so in **Practice example 3.4**, if Fred and Jed were fiancés at the time that the will was executed, the rule would not apply even if they went on to marry before the testator died. Note also that if there were three witnesses to the will, of whom the spouse was one (in other words, there was an 'extra' witness), then the will is valid and the gift can be made.

Exam warning

Note that this rule only affects the *gift* – it does not mean that the will itself is improperly witnessed and that it is therefore not valid. Watch out for this point as it is a frequent examination mistake. Candidates also frequently make the mistake of saying that a beneficiary is 'not allowed' to witness a will. There is nothing to prevent a beneficiary witnessing a will; however, the witnessing beneficiary will receive nothing. Watch out for this formulation in MCQs.

This is an area where professional conduct and ethics can loom large. The reason for the rule is to prevent undue pressure being put on the testator by a witness/beneficiary at the very point of executing the will: we have already referred to the dangers of undue influence and duress in this area. You can probably see that if Jed is witnessing a will by which his civil partner is to benefit, he might, if he were unscrupulous, put pressure on Xanthe to leave Fred £10,000, or £100,000. It is very much in Jed's interest to do so. The law tries to prevent this from happening by barring Fred from taking any benefit at all if his civil partner witnessed the will.

The second point is that it is negligent for a solicitor to prepare a will which is then witnessed by a beneficiary or that beneficiary's spouse: see *Ross v Caunters* [1980] Ch. 297. A solicitor must always give very clear advice about who should not witness any particular will.

Please refer to the wills chapter of *Revise SQE: Ethics and Professional Conduct*, where this point is dealt with more fully.

Divorce, dissolution or annulment of marriage

S 18A(1) of the Wills Act 1837 provides that upon divorce, dissolution or annulment of marriage, the provisions of any will which appoints the surviving ex-spouse as an executor, a trustee, or which leaves the ex-spouse property, shall take effect as if the former spouse died on the date of the decree absolute (that is, the day the divorce was finalised). Even if the will is otherwise completely valid, any gift to the former spouse will not take effect.

Forfeiture by reason of unlawful killing

The final main reason for a gift to fail is, to put it simply, that the named beneficiary or recipient has in fact been the unlawful cause of the testator's death. The forfeiture rule applies to both wills and intestacy.

The rule is that a beneficiary who has unlawfully killed the deceased must forfeit their interest under the will or intestacy, because a killer cannot profit from their crime. 'Unlawful killing' includes not just murder of the deceased by the beneficiary, but also manslaughter, death by careless driving and aiding or abetting suicide. Whether the beneficiary has a good and viable defence is not relevant.

Revision tip

In some limited circumstances (though *never* when found guilty of murder), a killer/beneficiary can ask for relief from the forfeiture rule under the Forfeiture Act 1982. Any application under the Forfeiture Act must be brought within three months of the beneficiary's conviction (if a beneficiary misses the three-month deadline, while they can no longer claim that the forfeiture rule should be disapplied, they may still be able to make a claim for financial provision from the estate under the Inheritance (Provision for Family and Dependants) Act 1975): see **Chapter 9**. The detailed provisions of the Forfeiture Act 1982 are outside the scope of this book, but you should ensure that you are familiar with the situations in which forfeiture will apply and when relief may be asked for.

ALTERATIONS AND AMENDMENTS TO WILLS

We have seen how the gift clauses in wills are interpreted: but what happens if, having made a will, there is a change of mind on the part of the testator? Sometimes the change of mind may be so drastic that the testator wants to scrap an existing will and start again. This will require revocation of the existing will, and we will look at that in **Chapter 4**.

However, what if the testator is happy with most of the contents of the existing will but would like to change one or two specific clauses? Or what if the testator is happy with most or all of the existing will but would like to add some extra gifts to the will? In these cases, the rules relating to amendments and alterations, or the rules relating to codicils, will apply. We will look at each in turn.

The basic rule: s 21 of the Wills Act 1837

S 21 of the Wills Act 1837 provides that 'no obliteration, interlineation, or other alteration made in any will after the execution thereof shall be valid or have effect, except so far as the words or effect of the will before such alteration shall not be apparent, unless such alteration shall be executed in like manner as hereinbefore is required for the execution of the will'.

It is not an easy section to untangle when first read, so let's break it down a little. Essentially it is one basic rule with two exceptions.

The basic rule is that obliterations (that is, covering the words of the original will so that they are fully or partly illegible), interlineations (that is, writing between the lines of the original will) or any other alteration made *after* the will has been executed will *not* be valid or have any effect, except for two circumstances:

1) where the obliteration, interlineation or other alteration has been executed in accordance with s 9 of the Wills Act 1837 (see **Chapter 1**); or

2) where it is now impossible to read what was in the original will.

If either of these two circumstances apply, then the alteration will take effect.

Exception 1: alterations executed in accordance with s 9 of the Wills Act 1837

The requirement is that the alteration must be signed by the testator and by two attesting witnesses. The signature can be the full signature of each, but the initials of the testator and the witnesses will be enough to satisfy the exception. One reason for allowing initials is probably that it is more practical, as s 21 also provides that the signatures must appear in the margin or on some other part of the will opposite or near to the alteration. It is also permissible under s 21 to add a memorandum to the will (usually at the end) referring to the alteration, but that must be signed at the foot or end of the memorandum, or opposite it, by the testator and both witnesses. If this is done and duly executed, then there is no need for the signatures to be next to or opposite the alteration. However, the memorandum needs to refer to *all* of the alterations, or the ones which are not mentioned and not signed will be invalid.

You might want to look back briefly at **Chapter 1**, where we looked in detail at the s 9 requirements on signatures. Remember that the testator must sign in person, or if they cannot sign in person for some reason, the alteration must be signed by some other person at the testator's direction and in the testator's presence. The attesting witnesses must also see the testator sign, and it must be clear that they are attesting to the testator's signature to the alteration and not just to the will itself.

Exception 2: the original words underneath the obliteration cannot be read

If the alteration is an 'obliteration' – that is, it has completely covered the original wording so that it cannot be read – then the clause will take effect as if the covered words were blank (see **Practice example 3.5**).

Practice example 3.5

The original wording of Dennis' will was: 'I give the sum of £2,500 to the Irchester Cricket Club'. The will was duly executed and validly witnessed. At a later date, Dennis scribbled over the words 'Irchester Cricket Club' with a ballpoint pen so heavily that it was impossible to read. This alteration was not signed by Dennis, nor was it witnessed.

What happens in this situation upon Dennis' death?

The will is admitted to probate as if the obliterated passage had been left blank: in other words, it is admitted to probate as 'I give the sum of £2,500 to [blank]'. As a result, the gift to Irchester Cricket Club will not be effective, even though the alteration has not been executed according to s 9.

The surprising result of this exception is that if the testator is determined enough to make a section of the will illegible, they will succeed in making it ineffective even if they do not sign it and have it witnessed.

Revision tip

Note that the fact that there may be existing photocopies showing the original will, and therefore revealing what is underneath the obliterations, is irrelevant. It is whether or not the wording is legible on the original which is the deciding factor for the probate registry (see **Chapter 7**).

When is wording illegible, or, to use the words of the section, not 'apparent'? In essence, it is when it is optically apparent: that is, it can be read without the use of any intervening technology.

You should note here that where a testator has obliterated part of a will, then tried to insert substitute wording, but the substitute wording is either not properly executed or is executed but illegible, then what is called the 'conditional revocation' rule will apply (see **Chapter 4**).

Alterations and amendments made before execution

We have already noted that the rule in s 21 applies only to alterations and amendments that are made after the will is executed. In theory, alterations and amendments that are made before the will is executed do not need to fall within either of the exceptions in s 21 to be valid.

However, there is a legal presumption, which the probate registry will apply (see **Chapter 7**), that any alteration or amendment to a will was made after execution unless it can be proved that it was made before.

As a result, it is good practice to ensure that *all* alterations and amendments, even if they are made well before the execution of the will, are witnessed and signed in a way that conforms to s 21.

Alterations made in pencil

We have already seen in **Chapter 1, Table 1.1** that wills written in pencil are assumed to be 'deliberative'; that is, the testator is still thinking them over and they are not the final version (though this can be disproved by evidence). Where, however, the executed will is in ink (whether handwritten, printed or typewritten) and the alterations are made in pencil, it is assumed that they are not intended to be effective even if they are validly executed.

Codicils

Alterations and amendments can also be made using a **codicil**.

> **Key term: codicil**
>
> A codicil is a supplemental or additional document which is made after the will and is intended to be annexed to it and read with it. It can add completely new clauses to an existing will or remove clauses from it. It can also make other changes such as naming new executors or beneficiaries.

The key element of a codicil is that it is entirely dependent on the existing will. In fact, it is customary for a codicil to contain a clause confirming the existing will. It may add to or subtract from the existing will, but it is always intended to be read together with it, and never on its own. While a will and a codicil are not regarded as being the same document, they are regarded as making the same testamentary disposition; that is, taken together, they deal with everything in the testator's estate.

A codicil must be executed in the same way as a will – that is, using the s 9 formalities – and should state clearly on its face that it is a codicil to a specifically identified will, for example: 'This is a codicil to the will of Jane Smith dated 8 February 2022'.

After setting out the provisions of the will that the codicil alters or adds to or removes, the codicil then confirms the other terms of the existing will. This confirmation within the codicil has the effect of 'bringing down' the date of the will: the will is now looked on as having been made at the execution date of the codicil.

In what circumstances would a testator choose to execute a codicil to their will rather than write alterations on the will itself, or simply write a new will? **Practice example 3.6** shows a typical scenario.

Practice example 3.6

Dean, an entrepreneur, made a will in 2018. It included pecuniary legacies of £25,000 each to five of his closest friends and appointed his uncle Jerry and his aunt Norma as his executors. It also contained a full trust over the residue of his estate.

By 2022, Dean wished to make changes to his will. He had decided that he wished to increase the amount of the pecuniary legacies to £40,000 and to add the names of two other friends, who had been particularly loyal to him during some business troubles. In the meantime, also, his uncle Jerry had died and he wished to appoint one of the partners from his solicitors, Minot & Co., as a substitute executor.

Because Dean's will was complex and contained a full trust, and the changes Dean wished to make did not affect the main provisions of the will, Dean decided to execute a codicil rather than make a new will. The codicil made the changes and otherwise confirmed the 2018 will. It was executed and witnessed as per s 9 of the Wills Act 1837.

What is the effect of this 2022 codicil?

The effect of making the 2022 codicil is that the 2018 will and the 2022 codicil will be read together as making one testamentary disposition. The seven friends mentioned by Dean in his original will and in the codicil will all receive pecuniary legacies of £40,000. The executors of the will are now Dean's aunt Norma and one of the partners from Minot & Co. The effect of executing the codicil is that the whole of the will is read as if it had been made in 2022 and not in 2018.

■ KEY POINT CHECKLIST

This chapter has covered the following key knowledge points. You can structure your revision around these, making sure to recall the key details for each point, as covered in this chapter.

• Classifying a testamentary gift.
• Identifying the causes and effects of a failed gift.

- Understanding and applying the technical rules on alterations, obliterations and amendments.
- Understanding what a codicil is and the effect it has on an existing will.

■ KEY TERMS AND CONCEPTS

- personalty (**page 36**)
- codicil (**page 47**)

■ SQE1-STYLE QUESTIONS

QUESTION 1

A testator's will contains a clause giving 'a copy' of a rare first edition of a children's book to his niece. When the testator dies, his executors discover that he owns two copies of the book named in the will: one is signed by the author and the other is unsigned. The signed copy is much more valuable than the unsigned copy.

Which of the following most accurately reflects the legal position in respect of the legacy?

A. The executors must give the niece one of the two books owned by the testator.

B. The executors must give the niece the signed copy of the book owned by the testator.

C. The executors can buy another first edition of the book and give it to the niece.

D. The executors must give the niece the unsigned copy of the book owned by the testator.

E. The clause in the will is invalid because the executors do not know which book they should give to the niece.

QUESTION 2

A testator's will contains a legacy of £30,000 to his daughter, to be paid from the testator's bank account ('the first bank account'). At the time that the testator dies, after the payment of all debts and liabilities, the bank account contains £5,000. The testator's estate also includes an account at a different bank containing £10,000 ('the second bank account') and a residuary estate worth £10,000. The only other provision of the will was that the testator's son should receive the residue.

Which of the following accurately reflects the legal position?

A. The executors can pay the daughter £5,000 from the first bank account and the £10,000 from the second bank account, but not the £10,000 from the residue.

B. The executors can only pay the daughter £5,000 from the first bank account.

C. The gift fails entirely because the estate does not contain a total of £30,000.

D. The executors can pay the daughter the £5,000 from the first bank account and the £10,000 from the second bank account, but not the residue.

E. The executors can pay the daughter all of the money from the first and second bank accounts and the residue.

QUESTION 3

A man and a woman became engaged to marry in March. In April, the pair went to stay for the weekend with the man's stepmother, his only remaining living relative. The stepmother was so pleased to hear of the engagement that she said: 'I am making my will this weekend and I want to make you a present in my will so that you will have something to remember me by when I die'. Later that weekend, the stepmother executed the will, which left £100,000 to her stepson. The stepmother asked the stepson's fiancée and another person to witness her signature.

In September, the stepson and his fiancée married. In November, the stepmother died, without having made another will.

Which one of the following most accurately reflects the position of the stepson's inheritance?

A. The stepson does not inherit the £100,000; the entire will is invalid because the stepson's fiancée witnessed the will.

B. The stepson inherits the £100,000; the stepson's fiancée was able to act as a witness at the time that it was executed.

C. The stepson does not inherit the £100,000; the gift to him is invalid because the stepson's fiancée witnessed the will.

D. The stepson inherits the £100,000; the will fails, but he is the stepmother's next of kin.

E. The stepson does not inherit the £100,000; his marriage in September revokes the gift.

QUESTION 4

A man wanted to make some changes to a will that he had executed three years previously. The man arranged for two witnesses to be present while he made the changes and to attest to any signatures he might make. The change that he made was to cross out the words 'five thousand pounds' in a pecuniary legacy clause on the top line of page 2 and to write the word

'£10,000' immediately above the crossed-out words. The man and the witnesses initialled the bottom of the page.

Which of the following most accurately describes the legal position?

A. The alteration is not valid because there is no memorandum attached to the will to explain it.

B. The alteration is valid because it has been initialled by the testator and the two witnesses.

C. The alteration is not valid because the amendment should have been written 'ten thousand pounds' and not '£10,000'.

D. The alteration is not valid because it is not signed opposite or near to the alteration.

E. The alteration is valid because it has been signed on the same page as the alteration.

QUESTION 5

A woman executes a will in 2016. The woman decides to add further gifts to her will and to do so by way of a codicil. The woman executes a codicil in 2018, making gifts to three more named persons. The 2018 codicil confirms the 2016 will except for the changes made in the codicil.

In 2020, the woman looks at the original will and decides that she would like to make a gift to one further person. In this case, she decides to amend the original will by adding the new gift in handwriting on the original will, writing between the lines. In the presence of two witnesses, the woman initials the amendment and asks them to initial it also, which they do.

Which of the following best describes the legal position of the will?

A. The operative date of the will is 2020.
B. The will is not valid because amendments cannot be made after a codicil.
C. The operative date of the will is 2018.
D. The will is not valid because the codicil confirmed the original will.
E. The operative date of the will is 2016.

■ ANSWERS TO QUESTIONS

Answers to 'What do you know already?' questions at the start of the chapter

1) A 'devise' is a gift of land; a 'legacy' is a gift of any other property, including personal property or money.

2) Person B will receive nothing. This is a specific gift of personalty and if the wristwatch is not in Person A's estate when Person A dies, the gift will adeem.

3) Yes, but the consequences of doing so are very serious for that beneficiary. There is no rule stating that beneficiaries cannot witness the will from which they are to benefit; however, if they do witness the will, they are not allowed to derive any benefit from it, so they would receive nothing.

4) True. If the alterations are executed in compliance with the rules under s 9 of the Wills Act 1837, then they will be valid and will be accepted by the probate registry.

Answers to end-of-chapter SQE1-style questions

Question 1:
    The correct answer was C. This is a general legacy and although the executors could, if they chose to do so, give the niece either one of the books owned by the testator, they are not obliged to do so. Therefore A, B and D are wrong. E is wrong because the clause is clearly able to be implemented as it stands.

Question 2:
    The correct answer was E. The gift of £30,000 is a demonstrative pecuniary legacy which is treated as a specific legacy for the purposes of abatement. Demonstrative legacies can be met from other assets in the estate if the named asset is not sufficient to meet them. As a result, the executors should pay the demonstrative legacy first, even though this exhausts the estate and the son gets nothing. It is for this reason that the other options are incorrect. Note C in particular: the gift is still valid, even though there is not enough money in the estate to pay it in full.

Question 3:
    The correct answer was B. Although gifts (not wills) will fail if the spouse of a beneficiary witnesses the will, that rule does not apply to fiancées even if they subsequently marry before the death of the testator. A is wrong because the whole will is never invalidated even if a spouse witnesses, only the gift. C is wrong because she is his fiancée and not his wife. The will remains valid, so D is incorrect. E is incorrect because there is no rule that any subsequent marriage by a *beneficiary*, as opposed to marriage by a *testator*, revokes any testamentary gift.

Question 4:
    The correct answer was D. The initials must be close enough to the alteration to make it clear what is in fact being altered and attested to. A memorandum is not required for any alteration, so A is incorrect. B is incorrect because the initials are not enough in themselves. C is incorrect because the alterations do not have to duplicate the original form of wording. E incorrectly assumes that any location on the page will do.

Question 5:

The correct answer was C. A codicil republishes the will and the clock therefore re-started in 2018 when the codicil was executed (therefore A and E are incorrect). There is no rule that amendments cannot be made after a codicil, so B is incorrect (although clearly there can be problems if the amendments conflict with the codicil). D is incorrect because the codicil must, in fact, confirm the original will.

■ KEY CASES, RULES, STATUTES AND INSTRUMENTS

The SQE1 Assessment Specification does not require you to know any specific statute sections or case law for this topic. However, you should make sure that you know the contents of the following statute sections and how to apply them:

• ss 9, 21 and 18A of the Wills Act 1837
• Administration of Estates Act 1925 First Schedule Part II.

Revocation of wills

■ MAKE SURE YOU KNOW

This chapter sets out the main principles of how and when an existing valid will can be revoked. Although the basic rules are often straightforward, their effects can be far-reaching, and the results sometimes unexpected. Be sure that you understand the consequences of any revocation that you believe to be valid. This is another area of the wills syllabus where it is vital to understand the definitions *precisely*: for example, to be able to tell the difference between an amendment and a revocation. Matters can become quite complex when you have to decide which one of two (or more) wills is valid, as you may well be asked to do in a multiple-choice question (MCQ).

■ SQE ASSESSMENT ADVICE

As you work through this chapter, remember to pay particular attention in your revision to:
• the difference between an alteration or amendment and a revocation
• what happens to earlier wills when there is an effective revocation
• how express revocation clauses work
• when and how a will can be revoked by marriage
• the difference between express, implied and conditional revocation
• the rules on revocation by destruction.

■ WHAT DO YOU KNOW ALREADY?

Have a go at these questions before reading this chapter. If you find some difficult or cannot remember the answers, make a note to look more closely at that area during your revision.

1) What happens to an existing will if the testator marries after executing it?
   [Revocation by operation of law: marriage or civil partnership, page 56]
2) Can a codicil revoke the provisions of an existing will?
   [Revocation by will/codicil, other writing or destruction, page 58]
3) Is a will still valid if the testator cuts out the signatures of the witnesses?
   [Revocation by will/codicil, other writing or destruction, page 58]

4) True or false? The capacity requirements for revoking a will are identical to the capacity requirements for making a will.
[Revocation by will/codicil, other writing or destruction, page 58]

REVOCATION

It is crucial to understand that wills have two important, but apparently almost contradictory, qualities:

1) A testator (see **Chapter 1**) can have a change of mind about a will right up until the moment of death – although, as we have seen, to make that change of mind effective as an alteration or amendment, the formalities must be observed (see **Chapter 3**).

2) From the moment of death onwards, a properly executed final will is an absolutely immovable and definite document which cannot be changed, except in a very limited set of circumstances which will rarely apply.

This contradiction has important consequences. If, as we have seen, a testator can have a change of mind about how they are going to leave their property at any point up until their death, there need to be clear rules about how that change of mind is going to be manifested and communicated, otherwise chaos would result. We have already seen in **Chapter 3** how that is dealt with as far as 'edits' to the will are concerned: now we will look at what happens if the testator decides to scrap a will altogether and start again. Among other things, there could be a situation where there is more than one will which could be admitted to probate (see **Key term** in **Chapter 1**): which would be the right one? The Wills Act 1837 sets out those rules.

Full revocation: introduction

Revocation occurs when the testator has decided that a previous will they have made should have no effect at all. Although there are exceptions, 'revocation' as a term generally means that the testator wants the entire previous will, and not just parts of it, to have no effect. We have seen in **Chapter 3** that if the testator is generally happy with most of the will, but wants to change some minor parts of it or add further dispositions, that will generally be accomplished by making amendments/alterations to the existing will or adding a codicil.

Revision tip

Generally speaking, all wills are revocable, but mutual wills are a potentially important exception. These are wills made by (usually) two people (let's call them Person A and Person B), in which they agree that their joint property will ultimately be left in an agreed way and to

> agreed beneficiaries X and Y, and therefore write wills which reflect that agreement, and that whichever one of them is the last to die will leave all of their property to Person(s) X and Y. Mutual wills fall outside the scope of this book, but you should be aware that once the first testator has died, it may not be possible for the second person to revoke their will.

Methods of revocation

The only four ways by which a properly executed will can be revoked are:

1) by a marriage or civil partnership (s 18(1) of the Wills Act 1937), as amended
2) by making another will or codicil (s 20 of the Wills Act 1837)
3) by 'some writing' (s 20 of the Wills Act 1837)
4) by destruction (s 20 of the Wills Act 1837).

There is no other possible way by which a testator can revoke an existing will that has complied with the s 9 formalities (see **Chapter 1**). The distinctive difference between the first of these and the other three is that the first type of revocation – that is, by marriage – is automatic and does not require any intention or capacity from the testator at all, while the other three do require the testator to have sufficient capacity to revoke and often to demonstrate sufficient intention also.

Exam warning

Before dealing with the specific detail of any MCQ which appears to be about revocation, ask yourself whether the act specified comes within any of these four broad headings. If it does not, it cannot amount to revocation, no matter how definite it appears to be.

REVOCATION BY OPERATION OF LAW: MARRIAGE OR CIVIL PARTNERSHIP

If the testator enters into a marriage or civil partnership after having made a properly formalised will, that will is automatically revoked by that marriage or civil partnership. This is the effect of s 18 of the Wills Act 1837. This revocation is effected by operation of law and does not depend on any act by the testator: it is unintentional in every sense of the word. Great care must therefore be taken by any solicitor advising a testator in this position that, if the client does not do something about it, they may be left without any valid will after their marriage and are running the risk of intestacy (see **Chapter 5**).

The only exception to this rule is where, after 1982, the testator makes a will before the marriage/civil partnership and that will states (1) that the testator is expecting to be married to a particular person and (2) that the testator does not intend the forthcoming marriage or civil partnership to revoke the will: s 18(3) and 18B(3) of the Wills Act 1837, as amended, the existing will is not revoked.

The rule in s 18(3)/18B(3) is very specific and you must pay attention to all of the relevant parts of it. First of all, the exception will only operate if the will clearly sets out *on its face* that the testator is expecting to be married to a particular person and intending that marriage not to revoke the will. The wording of the will must be clear. It is not enough, for example, to state an intention that the will is not to be revoked by *any* subsequent marriage or civil partnership. It is also not enough simply to put into the will that it is being made 'in contemplation of marriage'; it must be 'in contemplation of marriage to John' (see **Practice example 4.1**). In fact, if the testator then goes on to marry not John but James, then the exception will not work, and the marriage to James will revoke the will!

The expectation of marriage must be plain on the face of the will. If the will is totally silent on the point, it is not possible to 'import' outside evidence into the will to show that the expectation was there. No amount of engagement party photographs, newspaper announcements or ring receipts tells the court anything about whether the testator wanted this will to survive any subsequent marriage.

The will should state in clear terms that the testator is expecting to marry a specific person, but there is in fact no assumption that the expectation must be realistic. For example, a person who is obsessed with a reality TV star could make a will in the deluded expectation that he is going to marry that star, although they have never met. However, as you will have seen, even if his dreams do not come true, that would make no difference to his will, which would remain in force in any case!

Practice example 4.1

Mila, an entrepreneur, is obsessed with Jonnie Chang, the star of a glamorous reality TV show. She has convinced herself that if she can arrange a meeting between herself and Jonnie, he will immediately fall in love with her and propose marriage. She drafts a will, without legal advice, which contains a clause saying that it is made 'in contemplation of my future marriage to Jonnie Chang'. It leaves all of her property to Jonnie.

A friend advises her that it is bad luck to mention Jonnie by name in the will, so she alters the wording to read simply 'in contemplation of my future marriage'. She then executes the will and never makes another.

While on business in Hong Kong she meets Peter Ho and marries him. She does later meet Jonnie Chang, who has fallen on hard times since his show was cancelled, but she discovers that she does not like him after all. Shortly after that, she dies. Jonnie claims that the will in his favour is still valid.

Is he correct?

Because the will did not mention any specific fiancé, it was automatically revoked when Mila married Peter.

Revision tip

Remember also that when a marriage or civil partnership ends in divorce/ dissolution, all testamentary gifts to the former spouse are automatically of no effect under s 18A of the Wills Act 1837 (see **Chapter 3**).

REVOCATION BY WILL/CODICIL, OTHER WRITING OR DESTRUCTION

As we have noted, revocation by marriage will take place whether the testator intends it or not. Positive action is required from the testator in order to prevent revocation by marriage. In our other examples of revocation, which are all set out in s 20 of the Wills Act 1837, positive action is required from the testator in order to revoke at all.

In all three cases where positive action is required – by another will or codicil, by some other writing or by destruction – the testator must have sufficient mental capacity to revoke the will. The standard of mental capacity is the same as the standard for making a will (see **Chapter 1**).

Revocation by making another will or codicil

There are two types of revocation in this case: (1) express revocation and (2) implied revocation. We will look at each in turn.

Express revocation

Every well-drafted will contains an **express revocation** clause.

Key term: express revocation

This clause sets out in plain words that the intention of a new will (let's call it, for the purposes of this chapter, Will 2) is to revoke any previous wills (let's call the previous will, for the purposes of this chapter, Will 1). There can also be wills that were made before Will 1 – we can call them Will 0, Will 1 and so on. If Will 2 contained an express revocation clause, *all* of these wills would be revoked, because that clause revokes *any* earlier will, not just the most recent. For our purposes, though, we will concentrate on Will 2's effect on Will 1.

Revision tip

You should note that it is not enough for a will simply to record that Will 2 is the 'last will and testament'; Will 2 needs to say in express terms that it is revoking any previous wills, for example 'I revoke any previous wills made by me'.

If Will 2 meets all of the formal requirements that we looked at in **Chapter 1**, then this express revocation will mean that Will 1 has no effect whatsoever after Will 2 has been validly executed. It is as if Will 1 had never been written. Note that the formal requirement of knowledge and approval (see **Chapter 1**) applies to the revocation clause in Will 2. It is possible for someone to successfully challenge a revocation clause on the basis that the testator did not have knowledge or approval of it.

If for some reason the revocation clause in Will 2 does not take effect – for example, the testator did not have testamentary capacity at the time of Will 2, or there was a want of knowledge and approval, or some of the s 9 formalities were not complied with – then Will 1 will stand and is able to be submitted to probate (see **Practice example 4.2**).

Practice example 4.2

Kurt executed a will in 2017 in which he left all of his property to his friend Dermot. In 2019 Kurt was diagnosed with Parkinson's disease, which progressively affected his mental capacity. By 2021, Kurt had quarrelled with Dermot. Although his mental capacity was failing, he wrote a new homemade will in which he left all of his property to a charity which promoted the wider use of the Alemannic language. The 2021 will contained a complete revocation clause revoking any previous wills. This would include the 2017 will. Kurt died in 2022.

What course of action could Dermot take?

Dermot could claim that Kurt did not have testamentary capacity at the time of the 2021 will. If his claim is successful, the revocation clause in that will would be ineffective and the 2017 will would be the last valid will left by Kurt. Dermot would then inherit Kurt's estate under that will.

Implied revocation
As well as express revocation, there can also be **implied revocation**.

Key term: implied revocation

Implied revocation typically occurs where a testator has made Will 2 but that will does not contain an express revocation clause. Will 2 contains some provisions which are identical to the previous Will 1, but others that are contradictory to or inconsistent with it. What was the testator's intention? Was Will 2 intended to revoke Will 1, either partly or completely?

It is fair to say that the courts are not enthusiastic about implied revocation and it has been said in at least one decided case that there is a presumption *against* it. However, there are occasions where there is almost no other logical conclusion to come to except that the testator intended Will 2 to revoke parts or all of Will 1 (see **Practice example 4.3**).

Practice example 4.3

Wilbur, a racehorse trainer, made a will in 2016 in which he left his estate in three equal shares to his brother Scott, the Jockey Club and a pony rescue charity. The 2016 will contained a revocation clause. The will also provided that if any of these gifts failed, there should be a gift over to his niece Candice. The will made a gift of £2,500 to Cranborne Chase, a jockey who had won many races as the mount on Wilbur's horses.

Candice came to work for Wilbur in 2017 and they got to know each other well over the next few years. During that period, Wilbur had also disagreed with a number of decisions made by the Jockey Club.

In 2021 Wilbur made another will. He retained the gift of £2,500 to Cranborne Chase but he now also left a gift of £1,000 to the Jockey Club and £1,000 to his brother Scott. He then disposed of the residue of his estate in two equal shares to Candice and the pony charity. There was no revocation clause in the 2021 will. Wilbur died in January 2022. Scott claimed that the 2016 will was still valid because there was no revocation clause in the 2021 will which would have rendered the 2016 will ineffective.

What might happen in this situation?

Although the 2021 will has no revocation clause, it is nevertheless clear that Wilbur, when the wills are read together, intended to dispose of all of his property in a different way from the 2016 will. He intended the 2021 will to stand as his last will and, by making it, to revoke the 2016 will.

Even if Will 2 gets lost or destroyed at some later point in time, if it was validly executed and it either expressly or impliedly revoked Will 1, then Will 1 remains of no effect even if Will 2 has disappeared. As you will understand, the main problem in that scenario will be to prove that Will 2, which is no longer available for inspection, was indeed validly executed. As long as reliable evidence can be produced that Will 2 was executed properly and that all of the formalities set out in **Chapter 1** were met, then the probate registry will assume that Will 1 was revoked: see **Chapter 7**.

Revocation 'by some writing'

It is possible for Will 1 to be revoked by writing even if the testator does not make Will 2. However, s 20 of the Wills Act 1837 makes it clear that the writing, whatever it is (it could be a memorandum or a letter, for example), must be executed in the same manner as a will.

You may wonder why a testator would go to the trouble of drafting a document which was to be executed in the same manner as a will but not go the further few yards and just execute a new will. There have, however, been cases where this has happened, many of them rather mysterious, at least as far as the testator's motives are concerned. One occasion where the rule does help is where time is short and facilities limited, for example, where the testator is very close to death (with minutes or only a few hours to live) and there is no time to organise the drafting of even a basic new will.

However, remember that the piece of writing, whatever it may be, must comply with all of the formalities rules in s 9. For example, if there are no attesting witnesses, then the attempt to revoke Will 1 will fail, and Will 1 can be submitted to probate.

We have already seen that the testator must have sufficient mental capacity to formulate and execute the document in question and that the standard is the same standard used when assessing capacity to make a will.

Revocation by destruction

S 20 of the Wills Act 1837 is in fact fairly specific about some of the methods of destruction: it talks of the 'burning, tearing, or otherwise destroying' of Will 1. In these cases, there is usually no Will 2: the question is whether the testator's attempts to remove the contents (or part of the contents) of Will 1 so effectively from the face of the earth that there is no doubt that the testator intended Will 1 (or parts of Will 1) to be of no effect.

One of the key elements of revocation by destruction is that destruction of the will by itself is not enough: it has to be shown that the testator was *intending* by whatever act they chose to make the will of no effect (and of course that they have capacity to so intend).

Revision tip
Bear in mind that for all forms of revocation except revocation by marriage, the testator must have the same mental capacity to destroy a will as they must have to make it in the first place.

In the specific case of destroying a will, the person destroying must have enough mental capacity to know that as they destroy, 'by destroying this will I am intending to revoke it'. If the testator is destroying the will in a 'red mist' fit of uncontrolled temper, or as a melodramatic gesture, or while drunk or otherwise incapacitated, or even because the testator mistakenly believes that the will is of no effect, that is unlikely in itself to bring about a revocation.

Let's take the two types of destruction specified by s 20 - burning and tearing - and then look more widely at other forms of destruction, which bring in further questions, particularly where not all of Will 1 is destroyed.

Obviously, if the testator has the requisite mental capacity and intent, and Will 1 is burned to a cinder, then there is no practical doubt that it has been revoked by destruction. But if the will is only partly burnt and is still legible, then it has not been 'destroyed' within the meaning of s 20 and remains at least partly effective.

Destruction: essential parts of the will

This leads on to the more general question: if parts of the will have been torn (or cut) off (or burned away), but other parts remain legible, has the will been destroyed (and therefore revoked) or not? If what has been destroyed includes the signature of the testator – that is, the most essential part of the will – then the 'essence' of the will has been destroyed and there will be revocation by destruction. Signatures of the witnesses are also regarded as essential, and the complete removal of both witnesses' signatures by a testator with the required capacity would probably suffice.

What must happen for effective revocation is that the signatures are for all practical purposes completely lost, whatever the method of destruction. Revocation will occur if they have been completely obliterated by being overscored or overwritten with another pen (but in that case, they must be completely illegible). If the testator has destroyed their own signature and the signatures of both witnesses, then there is no realistic doubt that revocation by destruction was intended.

Not all parts of a will are essential, though signatures clearly are. Where parts of the will have been removed by the testator but the provisions of the will make sense and can be carried out without them, then it is more likely that the court will find that the will has been partially, rather than completely, revoked. The key factor is that the will must make sense even with these passages removed, and it must be possible for the executors to implement its provisions (see **Practice example 4.4**).

Practice example 4.4

Morgana died in 2021. When her husband Merlin found her will, which she had made in 2009, he found that a large section of the first page of the will had been cut away with scissors. The will had been properly executed and witnessed in 2009 and contained a revocation clause. It included gifts of £1,000 to each of Morgana's nieces and a gift of all of Morgana's personal chattels to Merlin, and also set up a trust which appointed Merlin and Morgana's solicitor Gawain as trustees. However, the section which detailed the beneficiaries of the trust had been cut away. The trust therefore could not be effective because it offended against the beneficiary principle (see *Revise SQE: Trusts Law* if you need to remind yourself about this).

Morgana's residuary estate was therefore left undisposed of by the will: but did Morgana intend to revoke the whole will by cutting this section away?

The court would find that in cutting a section of the will away, but leaving a will which could be carried into effect, Morgana's intention was not to revoke the will entirely and had intended the existing part to be effective. The gifts would be made and Morgana's residuary estate would pass on intestacy. This is an example of a partial intestacy, which we are going to look at in more detail in Chapter 5.

We have already seen (in **Chapter 3**) that if there has been an unsuccessful attempt to *obliterate* part of a will (usually by overwriting or scoring out or through) but the writing underneath remains legible, the will is admitted to probate using the words that are legible. Unsuccessful obliteration is not 'destruction'.

Note that in spite of the rule that the testator has to intend by destroying the will to revoke it, there is no requirement that there should be any witness of that destruction. That can raise or leave questions about how, and by whom, the destruction was carried out. If all that is left at the end of the testator's life is a will which is torn into pieces, how do we know that it was the testator who tore it up? The lack of a witness can sometimes cause problems here, because the rule in s 20 is that the destruction should be carried out either by the testator in person or by some other person at the testator's direction and in the testator's presence.

There is a legal presumption that, if the evidence shows that the will was in the testator's keeping prior to death, and after the testator's death the will is discovered in a 'mutilated' condition (ie incomplete because of damage), then it was the testator who mutilated it, intending to revoke it. Remember, however, that this is only a presumption, and, like all legal presumptions, it can be displaced by evidence to the contrary. Such evidence could be that the will was in fact damaged by someone else, acting without the testator's authority. If an original will is found with the signature cut out, for example, the first presumption is that the testator removed the signature with the intention of revoking the will: but if evidence is brought forward that someone else removed the signature in an attempt to invalidate the will, the presumption will be displaced.

What about the situation where it is known that there was a will, but that will cannot be found? Again, if the will was known to be in the keeping of the testator up until death but is now lost, there is a legal presumption that the testator has destroyed the will with the intention of revoking it. It follows, however, that if the testator had given the will to a solicitor, bank or family member for safekeeping, the presumption will not apply.

CONDITIONAL REVOCATION

You are not likely to be asked about conditional revocation in any detail, as in practice it is highly dependent on the surrounding factual context, which is difficult to reproduce in an MCQ. However, it is worth being able to understand the basic rule, which is that there are some circumstances, generally when a testator is making Will 2, where it is possible to say that the testator did not intend that Will 2 would revoke parts, or all, of Will 1 unless certain conditions were met. This is a complex concept, so it is easier to consider it by looking at **Practice example 4.5.**

Practice example 4.5
Brandon owned a micro-brewery. He had four cousins: Cliff, Dodie, Emer and Faisal. In 2012 he made a will leaving the micro-brewery to Cliff and Dodie. In 2019 he changed his mind and visited his solicitor to say that he wanted to change his will to leave the brewery to Emer and Faisal. The solicitor could not take instructions for the will that day, but made an appointment to draft the will in two days' time. On the following day, Brandon shredded the original 2012 will in front of his PA, saying, 'I am not going to need this any longer because I'll have a new will by tomorrow night'. However, the PA decided, without telling Brandon, to keep a photocopy of the 2012 will on file. That night, Brandon was killed in a traffic accident. There was no new will and the original 2012 will had been destroyed.
What was the position regarding Brandon's estate?
Brandon appears to have destroyed the original of the 2012 will *only* on the basis that he was going to make a new will, which would revoke it, in the course of the next 24 hours: that is, his revocation (by destruction in this case) was *conditional* on a new will being made. As this condition did not take place, the revocation does not take effect and under the rule of conditional revocation, the 2012 will is still valid. Although the original has been lost, in these circumstances the executors can submit a photocopy of the will to probate (we will learn why, and how, in Chapter 7).

The key question for conditional revocation is: when the testator destroyed Will 1, were they doing so on the basis that something would happen, which in the event did not happen? If that is clear, then conditional revocation will apply. As you can see, however, it is problematic, because if applied here, Cliff and Dodie would inherit the micro-brewery, which does not seem to be what Brandon wanted.

■ KEY POINT CHECKLIST

This chapter has covered the following key knowledge points. You can structure your revision around these, making sure to recall the key details for each point, as covered in this chapter.

- The difference between an alteration or amendment and a revocation.
- What happens to earlier wills when there is an effective revocation.
- How express revocation clauses work.
- When and how a will can be revoked by marriage.
- The difference between express, implied and conditional revocation.
- The rules on revocation by destruction.

■ KEY TERMS AND CONCEPTS

- express revocation (**page 58**)
- implied revocation (**page 59**)

■ SQE1-STYLE QUESTIONS

QUESTION 1

A woman executed a will in 2010 which left all of her property to her husband. At that time, she had testamentary capacity and all relevant formalities were complied with. By 2015, the woman was an alcoholic who regularly had drinking binges during which she did not have testamentary capacity (though she recovered mental capacity when she sobered up).

In 2019, the couple had a serious argument because the husband refused to give the woman money to pay for alcohol. In a fit of temper, and while drunk, the woman took the will from the desk drawer in her home office and tore it into four pieces in front of her husband, telling him, 'You'll get nothing from me when I die'.

When the woman sobered up, she took the torn pieces of the will and kept them together in the desk drawer, intending to tape them back together. However, she had not done so by the time she died in 2022. She had not made any further wills.

Which of the following best describes the validity of the 2010 will?

A. The will is invalid because it is no longer in one piece.
B. The will is valid because the woman lacked testamentary capacity to revoke it.
C. The will is invalid because the woman revoked it by tearing it up.
D. The will is valid because it can be taped back together.
E. The will is invalid because the woman failed to repair it.

QUESTION 2

A woman made a will in 2019 which did not contain a revocation clause. At the time that the woman made the will, she was recovering from a stroke which had affected her ability to speak. The woman had previously made a will in 2017 before she had the stroke. The 2017 will gave gifts of £5,000 each to her four nephews and nieces and divided the rest of her estate equally between her two children. The 2019 will gave £10,000 each to her two nieces, £5,000 each to her two nephews and divided the rest of her estate equally between her two children. The woman has now died and the original of the 2019 will cannot be found.

Which of the following best describes the legal position in respect of the woman's wills?

A. The 2017 will was expressly revoked by the 2019 will.

B. The woman did not have the capacity in 2019 to revoke the 2017 will.

C. The 2019 will cannot revoke the 2017 will because the original has been lost.

D. The 2017 will was not impliedly revoked by the 2019 will.

E. The 2017 will was impliedly revoked by the 2019 will.

QUESTION 3

A man had made a will leaving all of his property to his teenage son. The man was divorced from his ex-wife, his son's mother, and they were not on speaking terms. The man forbade the son from contacting his mother in any way. When the man discovered that his son had been visiting his mother in secret, the man lost his temper. The man confronted his son in a room of their shared home, took his will out of the sideboard drawer and tore it into six pieces in front of the son, saying, 'This will show you what I think of your behaviour'. When the man had calmed down, he put the six pieces of paper back into the sideboard drawer. The man and the son continued to live together and the incident was not mentioned again.

Which of the following best describes the legal position in respect of the man's will?

A. The will was not revoked because the man did not intend to revoke it.

B. The will was revoked because the man destroyed it.

C. The will was revoked because the man was sober when he tore it up.

D. The will was not revoked because tearing it into four pieces was not enough to destroy it.

E. The will was revoked because the words used by the man, together with the act of tearing the will up, were enough to revoke it.

QUESTION 4

An elderly man was angry at the behaviour of his middle-aged daughter, who had left her husband for a man much younger than herself. The elderly man took out his will, which left all of his property to his daughter, and, using a black marker pen, he drew a line through the signature of the first witness of his will so that the signature could not be read. The elderly man then went off to make a cup of tea, leaving the marker pen uncapped on his desk. When he returned, the marker pen had begun to dry up and although he drew a line through the signature of the second witness, that signature remained clearly legible. The elderly man then took a ballpoint and drew a red line through his own signature, but that also remained clearly legible.

Has the man revoked his will?

A. Yes, because he has deleted all three signatures.

B. No, because there is no evidence of any intention to revoke.

C. No, because his own signature remains legible.

D. Yes, because he has attempted to delete all three signatures.

E. No, because deleting signatures cannot revoke a will.

QUESTION 5

A musician had serious substance and alcohol abuse problems. His 2019 will left all of his property to his wife. After crashing his car in an accident, the musician was admitted to a secure rehabilitation treatment centre which he was not allowed to leave without a doctor's permission. While the musician was there, his wife wrote to him to tell him that she was leaving him and taking their children with her. Angered by the letter but unable to get to his will, which was in the safe in his home office, the musician instructed his sister to go to his home and burn the will. The sister did so. Unknown to anyone, the musician's solicitors had retained a photocopy of the will.

The musician died two days later falling from a window at the centre while trying to escape.

Which of the following options best describes the current position regarding the musician's will?

A. The will has been revoked because it has been destroyed.

B. The will has not been revoked because the musician did not have capacity to revoke it while he was receiving treatment at the rehabilitation centre.

C. The will has not been revoked because the musician was not present when the sister destroyed it.

D. The will has been revoked because the musician had capacity to revoke when he instructed the sister to destroy it.

E. The will has not been revoked because the musician cannot legally disinherit his wife and children.

ANSWERS TO QUESTIONS

Answers to 'What do you know already?' questions at the start of the chapter

1) An existing will is automatically revoked by a subsequent marriage of the testator unless the will has expressly been made in anticipation of that marriage.

2) Yes. Although we have already seen that codicils can be used to alter or amend provisions of an existing will, they can also be used to revoke specific clauses or part clauses of existing wills.

3) No. The signatures of the witnesses are part of the 'essence' of the will, so if they are excised from the will, it is no longer valid. However, in some circumstances, a will may be valid if only one of two witness signatures has been cut away.

4) True. There is no qualitative difference between the capacity requirements for making a will and for revoking one.

Answers to end-of-chapter SQE1-style questions

Question 1:

The correct answer was B. Remember that successful revocation by destruction requires not only an act of destruction but also an intention to destroy and the capacity to do so. The damage caused to this will was the result of temper and not a real intention to destroy. Furthermore, the woman was drunk at the time and therefore lacked testamentary capacity. Of the other answers, A is incorrect because a will can be valid even if it has been torn into several pieces; for the same reason, E is also incorrect. D is incorrect because the issue of whether or not the will can be repaired is irrelevant to the issue of whether or not it has been revoked. C is incorrect because the mere act of tearing will not revoke: there must be intention and capacity as well.

Question 2:

The correct answer was E. There is no revocation clause in the 2019 will and therefore there can be no express revocation, making A incorrect. B is incorrect because the woman's mental capacity would not be affected merely by an inability to speak. Loss of the original later will is not a bar to proving revocation, so C is incorrect. The provisions of the 2019 will are similar to the 2017 will to such an extent that the woman's intention can be inferred as revoking the earlier will. This is an implied revocation. D is therefore incorrect.

Question 3:

The correct answer was A. This is the classic example of a testator destroying a will to make a point rather than to revoke, ie with no intention to revoke. B and E are incorrect because destruction of a will does not suffice without an intention to do so and capacity. C is incorrect because the mere fact that the man was not drunk is not conclusive of intention; the testator was in a temper and that affects intention. D is incorrect because although the will remains readable, tearing it into six pieces is technically 'destruction' for the purpose of the question. Remember: revocation requires destruction + intention + capacity!

Question 4:

The correct answer was C. The effect of the elderly man's actions was to delete only one signature, that of a witness: the will may therefore still be valid. A is incorrect because he has only deleted one signature: if a signature remains legible, it has not been 'deleted'. Unsuccessful attempts to delete signatures also do not count as 'deletion', so D is incorrect. E is simply incorrect on the law: there is no rule that deletion of signatures cannot revoke a will. B relates to intention: there is in fact evidence that the testator did have a clear intention to revoke, so this option is incorrect.

Question 5:

The correct answer was C. The musician does not have to destroy the will himself, but he does have to be present when it is destroyed. B is wrong because the mere fact that the musician is an addict receiving treatment does *not* mean that he has lost capacity. A is incorrect because destruction on its own is not enough; there must also be capacity and intention. D is incorrect because as well as having capacity, the musician must also be present during destruction. E is incorrect because there is nothing at all to prevent any person disinheriting their spouse and children (we will look at this again in **Chapter 9** when we consider family provision and the Inheritance Act 1975).

■ KEY CASES, RULES, STATUTES AND INSTRUMENTS

The SQE1 Assessment Specification does not require you to know any specific statute sections or case law for this topic. However, you should make sure that you know the contents of the following statute sections and how to apply them:

• ss 9, 18 and 20 of the Wills Act 1837.

5

The intestacy rules

■ MAKE SURE YOU KNOW

This chapter provides an overview of the intestacy rules. For the SQE1 assessments, this is one of the topics where you are expected to know, and to be able to recognise, statute law: specifically, s 46 of the Administration of Estates Act 1925, including the working of the statutory trusts. You may well be asked to identify a correct rule or subsection in a multiple-choice question (MCQ).

■ SQE ASSESSMENT ADVICE

As you work through this chapter, remember to pay particular attention in your revision to:
- the difference between a total intestacy and a partial intestacy
- the order in which parties are entitled under an intestacy
- the situations in which there is no entitlement at all, eg cohabitees
- the principles of dividing an estate when the intestate deceased leaves behind both a spouse and issue
- how the statutory trusts will work in any given situation, including the proportionate shares which any entitled person will receive.

■ WHAT DO YOU KNOW ALREADY?

Have a go at these questions before reading this chapter. If you find some difficult or cannot remember the answers, make a note to look more closely at that area during your revision.

1) What is the difference between a full and a partial intestacy?
   [Introduction to intestacy and the intestacy rules, page 71]
2) Can a divorced spouse inherit property from their ex-spouse under the intestacy rules?
   [The intestacy rules: the basics, page 72]
3) What are the 'statutory trusts' in intestacy?
   [The intestacy rules: the basics, page 72]
4) True or false? Administrators under a full intestacy have a discretion to distribute the estate in the way that they consider is fair.
   [The intestacy rules: the basics, page 72]

INTRODUCTION TO INTESTACY AND THE INTESTACY RULES

We have now looked in detail at the issues that can arise when a deceased person leaves a will. As we have seen, the deceased person's intention when leaving a will is to control what happens to their assets after death. We have already seen in **Chapter 1** that one of the main reasons why a deceased person made a will may be because that person did not want to die intestate – that is, without a valid will – and they did not want **the intestacy rules** to apply to their property after death.

> ## Key term: the intestacy rules
>
> When lawyers refer to the 'intestacy rules', they are generally referring to the statutory provisions in the Administration of Estates Act (AEA) 1925 which determine (i) who will be the administrator of an intestate estate (see **Chapter 2**) but more commonly (ii) who will be entitled to the property in the intestate estate, as well as to those Non-Contentious Probate Rules 1987 (SI 1987/2024) (NCPR) which relate specifically to intestacy. These rules effectively dictate who will receive the intestate deceased's property.

Therefore, a will is always an intentional act: you cannot make a valid will by accident. The same cannot be said of intestacy: although many people deliberately and intentionally do not make a will because they are happy that the operation of the intestacy rules will pass on their property after death to the appropriate people and in the appropriate way, it is also possible to die intestate unintentionally.

The most common reason for an unintentional intestacy is that people simply put off making a will: for example, because they think they do not need to do so until they are older, and then die unexpectedly and intestate. Unintentional intestacy also occurs where a testator mistakenly believes that they are leaving behind a valid will, but for some reason the will is not valid. We will look at some of those reasons in the course of this chapter. We will also see that it is possible for part of the will to be valid but other parts not. That is a *partial intestacy*, and in this situation also the intestacy rules will come into operation.

> ## Revision tip
>
> The first and main point to understand therefore about the intestacy rules is that they will *always* operate where either there is no will at all or where the will is totally or partially invalid or unenforceable. Therefore, they will apply where the deceased person deliberately leaves no valid will; they will apply where the will is not valid because, for example,

it does not comply with the s 9 of the Wills Act 1837 formalities (see **Chapter 1**); they will apply where the will has been revoked without any further will being made (see **Chapter 4**), whether that happened deliberately or unintentionally (because, for example, the deceased person did not understand that marriage would revoke their existing will); and they will apply where there is a gap in the provisions of the will (see **Chapter 3**) including a partial intestacy.

To this extent, the intestacy rules perform the function of a 'long stop': if there is no specific provision in the will, or there is no will at all, the personal representatives (PRs; see **Chapter 2**) *must* apply the intestacy rules.

You should note that administrators are also appointed trustees 'with a power to sell' under s 33(1) of the AEA 1925. This means that all of the powers and duties of trustees (see *Revise SQE: Trusts Law*) apply to administrators of an intestate estate, just as they do to executors under a will.

Revision tip

Always remember that administrators of an intestate estate are never able simply to give it away on whatever principles seem fair to them. If they do not follow the intestacy rules, then that is a breach of their duty of care as trustees, for which they are personally liable. If the administrator has caused a loss to a person who was entitled under the intestacy, the administrator must make good that loss out of their own pocket.

We shall see in **Chapter 8** that s 33(2) of the AEA 1925 obliges the PRs, including administrators, first of all to pay all of the funerary, testamentary and administration expenses, and all other debts, from the estate. This then leaves them with the residue (see **Chapter 3**), and they are given specific directions about how the residue is to be paid out, which they must follow.

Let's go on now to consider what will happen to the deceased's property under the intestacy rules where there is a total intestacy: that is, where there is no valid will at all.

THE INTESTACY RULES: THE BASICS

The intestacy rules direct the PRs (in a total intestacy and in most cases of partial intestacy, the PRs will be administrators and not executors; see **Chapter 2**) to distribute the estate to specific persons, or classes of persons, and in a specific order. The persons involved are set out at s 46(1) of the AEA 1925, and are outlined in **Table 5.1**.

Table 5.1: Order of entitlement, intestacy rules (s 46(1) AEA 1925)

If there is a surviving spouse or civil partner and no issue (children; but see **Key term** below for a more exact definition)	The spouse or civil partner will receive all of the estate
If there is a child/children but no surviving spouse or civil partner	The children will inherit under the statutory trusts (see **Key term** below)
If there is both a surviving spouse *and* a child or children	(1) The surviving spouse will receive the 'statutory legacy' (currently £270,000; see **Key term** below) plus all of the personal chattels of the deceased, plus 50% of the residue of the estate (2) The children will receive the remaining 50% of the residue of the estate under the statutory trusts
If there is neither a surviving spouse nor any children, then the estate will be distributed to:	
The deceased's parents in equal shares (or the whole estate to the one surviving parent)	If both of the deceased's parents have died, then to:
The deceased's full brothers and sisters (ie siblings with whom the deceased shared both parents) on the statutory trusts	If there are none, then to:
The deceased's half-brother and sisters (ie siblings with whom the deceased shared one parent) on the statutory trusts	If there are none, then to:
The deceased's grandparents in equal shares (or the whole estate to the one surviving grandparent)	If both grandparents have died, then to:
The deceased's uncles and aunts 'of the whole blood' (ie full brothers or sisters of either of the deceased's parents) on the statutory trusts	If there are none, then to:
The deceased's uncles and aunts 'of the half blood' (ie half-brothers or sisters of either of the deceased's parents) on the statutory trusts	If there are none, then to:
The Crown as *bona vacantia* (see **Key term** in **Chapter 2**)	

Exam warning

It is important that candidates can distinguish between the order in which relatives of the deceased must be considered to be administrators (illustrated in **Chapter 2, Table 2.1**) and the order of entitlement (shown in **Table 5.1**).

There is a lot to unpack here, so we are going to look first of all at the most immediate, and the most important, situations which can face the PRs in an intestacy. One of three things has happened: the deceased has left behind a surviving spouse but no children, *or* the deceased has left behind a child or children but no spouse, *or* the deceased has left behind a spouse *and* children. These are by far the three most common situations with which administrators have to deal. After that, we will look at the other categories of entitlement, which are more straightforward.

WHERE THERE IS A SURVIVING SPOUSE AND/OR ISSUE

First, let's clear up what s 46 of the AEA 1925 means when it refers to **spouse** and to **issue**.

Key term: spouse

The term 'spouse' includes anyone who is married to, or in a civil partnership with, the deceased at the time of the deceased's death. It therefore does not include any former husband, wife or civil partner where the marriage or civil partnership has ended in divorce/dissolution. It also does not include any person with whom the deceased is cohabiting without being married. Divorced spouses and cohabitees are therefore not entitled to any property under the intestacy rules. To be entitled, the surviving spouse must outlive their deceased spouse by 28 days: for example, if they die a week after the deceased, they/their estate will not be entitled to anything in the intestacy and the estate will pass to the next entitled person.

Revision tip

If the deceased was separated from their spouse or civil partner at the time of death, then the marriage will still be in existence and that person is entitled to property under the rules, even if the separation has been in place for many years. The one exception to this rule is where a judicial separation order has been made by the Court: this is the one instance where the marriage is still in existence but the spouse cannot claim.

Key term: issue

This includes all 'lineal' descendants of the deceased: that is, all persons to whom the deceased was a genetic/natural parent. That description includes illegitimate as well as legitimate children, and what are called 'legitimated' children, who are children born out of wedlock but whose parents later married. The term 'issue' also includes adopted children. An adopted child is treated as the child of their adoptive parent(s): s 67(1) of the Adoption and Children Act 2002. It includes children of the deceased who were not born by the time the deceased died. Finally, it includes a child carried by its mother even if (as in some kinds of artificial insemination) the child is not genetically related to the deceased at all, for example, where both the egg and the sperm have been donated. One very important factor, however, is that the term 'issue' does *not* include stepchildren or the biological children of stepchildren.

We will explore some of the facets of these definitions as we begin to look at how the rules work in practice in the examples to follow. Let's look first of all at our three most important and immediate scenarios. We are going to call the deceased person 'the intestate' through the rest of these examples, just to keep reminding ourselves that these rules apply only when the deceased died leaving no valid will.

In each case, we are looking at the position if the intestate died after 2014.

Revision tip

From your wider reading, you will be aware that prior to 2014 the rights of a deceased spouse were different, in particular where there was a spouse and issue. This is outside the scope of this book, but you should make sure that you familiarise yourself with the rules for deaths prior to October 2014.

Scenario 1: the intestate leaves a surviving spouse, but no issue

As we have seen from **Table 5.1**, this scenario is relatively straightforward. The spouse gets all of the estate. This is the case even where there are other living relatives of the deceased (see **Practice example 5.1**).

Practice example 5.1

Jackie dies intestate. She is survived by her husband, Anders. They had no children. Jackie's parents are both still living. Jackie's estate is worth £500,000.

Who will inherit Jackie's estate?

Anders inherits all of Jackie's estate under the intestacy rules. Jackie's parents do not receive anything.

Scenario 2: the intestate leaves issue, but no surviving spouse

If you consult **Table 5.1**, you will see that in this scenario, the issue (legitimate, illegitimate, legitimated and adopted children) inherit under the **statutory trusts**.

Key term: statutory trusts

These are trusts that s 46(1) of the AEA 1925 imposes over the estate and also over the PRs/administrators (who are the trustees of the intestate's estate). As trustees, the PRs must follow the terms of these trusts and they have no discretion to alter them in any way.

The first guiding principle of the statutory trusts is that where there is more than one person in a particular category (a child of the deceased, for example), all the persons in that category with a vested interest (see below) will receive equal shares of the estate.

Let's look at how the statutory trusts work in the case of 'issue'. The starting principle, as we know, is equal shares. That is easily understood so long as all of the children are alive when the intestate dies: but what if one or more of the intestate's children has died before the intestate? The statutory trusts provide that if the primary heir has left no children, then their share goes to the survivors. If, however, the predeceased child has left children (these would be the intestate's grandchildren), then those children will take the predeceased child's share in equal shares. This is called the *per stirpes* principle. Note that the statutory trusts do *not* apply to parents or grandparents: see **Table 5.1**.

Let's look at how that will work in **Practice example 5.2**.

Practice example 5.2

Aaron had four children: Ruth, Max, Farren and Agnes. By the time that Aaron died intestate, his wife, Farren and Ruth had already died, so he was survived only by Max and Agnes. Ruth had had two children before she died but Farren had died aged only six, so left no children. Max had one child and Agnes had none.

How was Aaron's estate divided?

Under the statutory trusts, Aaron's estate was divided into three: one-third for each of Ruth, Max and Agnes. Because Farren died before Aaron and left no children, no share is made for him under the statutory trusts. Note that although Ruth also predeceased Aaron, she left behind two children. As a result, note that there is a big difference between Ruth and Farren: the statutory trusts operate to divide what would have been Ruth's share between her two children, but Farren gets nothing.

Because the estate was divided into three, Max and Agnes received one-third each and Ruth's children received one-sixth (that is, one-half of one-third) each.

Note that although Max also has a child, none of Aaron's estate goes to that child because Max is still living. The statutory trusts only operate in favour of grandchildren if their parent (the intestate's son or daughter) has died before the intestate.

Revision tip

The statutory trusts do not just affect gifts to children – they apply to all persons entitled on intestacy other than parents or grandparents – but they generally operate in the way we have illustrated here. So if, for example, the first person entitled is an uncle or aunt, but they have died before the intestate, their share under the trust will pass to their child or children, if any – in other words, the deceased's cousin(s). *Always* remember to consider the statutory trusts where there is a predecease of the intestate!

There are two more points to note before we move on. The first is the general point that no person can acquire a full vested interest under a statutory trust until they attain the age of 18 years. Before that time, their interest is contingent (see **Key term** in **Chapter 11**). The second is that the detailed rules about 'issue' statutory trusts differ in some ways from general statutory trusts, including the 'hotchpot' rule. Those differences are outside the scope of this book, but you should ensure that you know them.

Scenario 3: the intestate dies leaving a spouse and issue

In this scenario, the intestate estate must be divided between the surviving spouse and all of the intestate's issue. First, the surviving spouse will receive the **statutory legacy**.

Key term: statutory legacy

This is a fixed amount from the estate which is currently the sum of £270,000, though the amount can be (and is) altered by statutory instrument from time to time.

The spouse also receives all of the intestate's 'personal chattels' (see **Personal chattels** below) and half of the residue. The other half of the residue goes to the intestate's issue under the statutory trusts.

Again, let's work through this in **Practice example 5.3**.

Practice example 5.3

Keira was the civil partner of Hester and the mother of two children: her adopted son Marley and her natural daughter Iona, both of whom were born during Keira's first marriage to Neil. That marriage ended in divorce which was why Keira was able to enter into a civil partnership with Hester. By the time that Keira died intestate, several years later, Iona had also died, leaving behind a daughter, Skye. Keira was therefore survived by her civil partner Hester, her adopted son Marley and her granddaughter Skye. Keira's estate (excluding her personal chattels) was worth approximately £750,000.

How will Keira's estate be divided?

As well as all of Keira's personal chattels, Hester will receive the first £270,000 of the estate. This will leave a residue of £480,000. The administrators of the estate must divide this sum in half and give £240,000 to Hester. The remaining £240,000 is divided between Keira's issue on the statutory trusts. Half of the £240,000 is given to Marley: as an adopted child, he is entitled as 'issue' under s 46(1). The other half is given to Skye as the only child of Iona – in other words, Skye receives all of what would have been Iona's share if she had lived.

There are two further important points about the position of a surviving spouse in intestacy which we need to consider: appropriation of the matrimonial home to satisfy all or part of the statutory legacy and the question of what is, and what is not, a personal chattel.

The matrimonial home

First, let's look at the question of the surviving spouse's/civil partner's claim over any land owned by the intestate. If, at the time that the intestate died, the intestate owned any interest in any 'dwelling house' in which the surviving spouse was residing, then the surviving spouse can call on the PRs to appropriate that property as part of their statutory legacy. In layman's terms, the spouse is asking the PRs: 'Please give me the house as part or all of my statutory legacy, and if necessary make up the balance in cash'. This ability, to make up part or all of a legacy with some property in the estate, is called a power of appropriation. It does not just apply in intestacy, and we will look at it again in **Chapter 8**.

This right to call for appropriation is given to the surviving spouse in intestacy under para 1(1) of Schedule 2 of the Intestate Estates Act 1952, and if called upon to do this, then the PRs are required to follow that instruction; they cannot refuse to do so. The surviving spouse must give notice to the

PRs within 12 months of the date on which a grant of representation (see **Chapter 7**) is taken out, and if that notice is given, the PRs are prohibited under the Intestate Estates Act from selling or otherwise disposing of the dwelling house. Within that 12 month period, the PRs must not dispose of any interest in the dwelling house.

Personal chattels

The second point to note is what is, and is not, included in the term **personal chattels**.

Key term: personal chattels

Prior to 2014 the definition used was from s 55(1)(x) of the AEA 1925, but this definition is now extremely out of date and included, for example, references to a deceased person's 'horses, stable furniture and effects' but not to cars. In 2014, the definition was amended by the Inheritance and Trustees' Powers Act to mean, for deaths on or after 1 October 2014, 'tangible movable property' – that is, property which you can touch as well as move. The definition does *not,* however, include money (whether cash or in the bank), securities for money or property the deceased used primarily for business purposes or which was held by the deceased at the time of death solely as an investment: these all fall into the main estate. Watch out, therefore, for chattels that have been specifically purchased as investments.

In some cases, the value of the deceased's personal chattels may, when examined, be higher than the value of most or all of the deceased's other assets, and it can make a big difference to the intestate's children and grandchildren whether an item of property is or is not classed as a personal chattel. A person may have died intestate with an estate worth about £100,000 but with house contents worth £2 million. All of the items in the house contents would probably be personal chattels which would automatically pass to their spouse on intestacy. You will see that in these circumstances, because the value of the estate itself is less than the statutory legacy, the surviving spouse would receive £2.1 million and any children of the deceased would receive nothing at all.

WHERE THERE IS NO SURVIVING SPOUSE AND NO ISSUE

We have now examined the position where the intestate deceased has been survived either by a spouse or by issue, or where the intestate has been survived by both a spouse and issue. Where this is not the case, the PRs move through **Table 5.1** until they find a relative of the intestate deceased who fits the bill, and then stop. If they are directed to apply the statutory trusts, then they *must* do so.

Let's have a look at that now in **Practice example 5.4**.

Practice example 5.4

When Halsey died, she was unmarried and childless. Her parents had predeceased her, but she was survived by her half-siblings Chelsey and Lorne; by her aunt Bobbie; and by her grandfather Hugh. Halsey and Chelsey had the same biological mother, and Halsey and Lorne had the same biological father.

Who will inherit Halsey's estate?

You will see if you work through Table 5.1 that if Halsey did not leave a spouse or issue (and we know she did not), then the next category of person to whom her estate could pass is one or both of her parents. However, they predeceased her, so that cannot happen. The next category is brothers and sisters of the full blood, but Halsey had no full brothers or sisters, so that cannot happen either.

The next category is brothers and sisters of the half blood, and Halsey has been survived by one half-sister and one half-brother (it makes no difference to the application of this rule that the half-siblings are from different parents). S 46 obliges the administrators of the estate to stop here, as they have found a category that contains people entitled to the estate. They must now distribute *all* of the estate to the people in this category under the statutory trusts.

Statutory trusts operate for this category, and for all other applicable categories, just as we have seen them operating already. There are two half-siblings in this case who are both still alive. This means that the estate is divided into two equal shares. If Chelsey had died before Halsey, leaving children, then the statutory trusts would operate and the share that would have gone to Chelsey would now go to Chelsey's children in equal shares. If on the other hand Lorne had died before Chelsey, without leaving any children, then Chelsey would take the entire estate.

Note that it does not matter that there are other people – an aunt and a grandparent – who fall into categories lower down in the table. The administrators *must* distribute the estate according to the rules and that means that it must all be distributed to members of the first appropriate class in the table.

PARTIAL INTESTACY

We have already seen that these rules will also operate in the case of a partial intestacy, but we have not yet looked at this in detail. We know that a full intestacy involves a situation where a will does not exist or has totally failed.

A partial intestacy is a situation in which a will exists, and some parts of it can be put into effect, but other parts of it cannot.

Why should this be? Generally, it is because some problem has arisen with a specific gift in the will. We have already seen in **Chapter 3** that there are a number of reasons why a testamentary gift can fail: because it was made to someone who witnessed the will, for example, or because the beneficiary predeceased the testator and the gift has lapsed, or even because the beneficiary does not want the gift and has disclaimed it. Usually, if there is a residuary clause in the will itself, then all of the failed gifts mentioned above would simply fall into residue. That is one reason why a well-drafted will always contain a residuary clause (that is, a clause which disposes of the residuary estate, which we considered in **Chapter 3**).

However, if the will does not contain a residuary clause, or if the residuary clause is itself defective in some way (for example, if any trust of the residue is not set up properly), then there is nowhere for the failed gift to go. Other parts of the will may be perfectly valid and properly executed, but this particular gift cannot be made. In these circumstances, there is a partial intestacy and the PRs must, pursuant to AEA 1925 s 49(1), apply the intestacy rules to that gift, as demonstrated in **Practice example 5.5**.

Practice example 5.5

Sandy's will contained a number of specific gifts but no residuary clause. He died unmarried and childless and his parents had predeceased him. He left the sum of £100,000 to his only sibling, Wilf; his Lexus motor car (value £50,000) to his aunt Janet; all of his stocks and investment bonds (value £250,000) to his long-term partner Kira; and his art collection (value £45,000) to his niece Wendy.

Wilf witnessed the will as he was not advised about the dangers of doing so. He therefore could not inherit the £100,000, although this did not affect the validity of the remainder of the will. Aunt Janet disclaimed the motor car because she said she had no need of it. Wendy predeceased Sandy and the gift to Wendy therefore lapsed.

However, it was still possible for the executors to distribute the testamentary gift to Kira, as this was still valid. Apart from this gift, the executors were left with a partial intestacy of the £100,000 cash, the car, and the art collection.

How should they distribute these?

The items and amounts in the partial intestacy are: the £100,000 which should have gone to Wilf; the Lexus car worth £50,000; and the art collection worth £45,000. What the PRs must now do is look through

> Table 5.1 to find the first category in which there are persons entitled. You will see, if you do that, that the first category in which there are persons entitled is the 'full brother and sister' category. Wilf is a full brother and, as a result, the PRs must stop there and distribute the items in the partial intestacy. As Wilf is the only sibling of the deceased, Wilf will get the £100,000, the car and the art collection.
>
> The statutory trusts do not apply because Wilf is the only person who inherits under his category. Note that Wilf does not get the £250,000 stocks and bonds portfolio, which validly passes to Kira under the will.

This brings us back full circle to the point at which we started this chapter: namely, the reasons why a testator might want to make a will rather than rely on the intestacy rules. If, for example, a person is in a long-term unmarried relationship with another person – particularly if they are living together in a house solely owned by one of them, and/or have children – then it is very likely that the intestacy rules will not distribute the estate in the way they would want.

Note that if a home were in joint names and owned by the cohabitees as beneficial joint tenants, when one person died the property would pass to the other automatically under the rules on beneficial joint tenancies; it would not form part of any intestacy, and the surviving person would therefore have some significant protection. We are going to look in more detail at joint tenancies, and other property which passes outside the estate, in **Chapter 6**.

■ KEY POINT CHECKLIST

This chapter has covered the following key knowledge points. You can structure your revision around these, making sure to recall the key details for each point, as covered in this chapter.
* The basic rules of intestacy.
* The definitions of spouse, issue and personal chattels.
* The specific intestacy rules relating to surviving spouses and issue.
* What happens when an intestate deceased leaves no surviving spouse or issue.
* The circumstances and rules relating to partial intestacy.

■ KEY TERMS AND CONCEPTS

* intestacy rules (**page 71**)
* spouse (**page 74**)
* issue (**page 75**)
* statutory trusts (**page 76**)

- statutory legacy (**page 77**)
- personal chattels (**page 79**)

■ SQE1-STYLE QUESTIONS

QUESTION 1

A man made a will leaving half of his estate to his sister and half to his partner. The will includes a clause that the man does not intend the will to be revoked by his marriage to his partner. The man makes no further wills. Six months later, he marries his partner ('Husband 1'). Three months later, Husband 1 dies. A year later, the man marries Husband 2.

Which of the following best describes who will inherit the man's estate on his death?

A. Husband 1's estate inherits the man's whole estate under the intestacy rules.

B. Half of the man's estate passes to the sister and the other half passes to Husband 1.

C. Husband 2 inherits the man's whole estate under the intestacy rules.

D. The sister inherits the man's whole estate under the intestacy rules.

E. Half of the man's estate passes to the sister and the other half passes to Husband 2.

QUESTION 2

A man was separated from his wife. After the separation, the man bought a rental property with his brother which he and his brother owned as beneficial joint tenants. They rented out the rental property and received an income from it. The value of the house was £350,000. Last year, the wife commenced divorce proceedings against the man. Last month, the man died intestate. The man had savings of £25,000 but no other assets apart from the rental property.

Which of the following most accurately describes the wife's current position under the intestacy rules?

A. The wife is entitled to £25,000 and to the man's share of the rental property.

B. The wife is entitled to £270,000 as the statutory legacy and can ask the administrators to appropriate the rental property to her as part or full payment of that legacy.

C. The wife is not entitled to any cash but is entitled to the man's share of the rental property.

D. The wife is not entitled to any of the man's assets because she has commenced divorce proceedings.

E. The wife is entitled to £25,000 but not entitled to any interest in the rental property because it was held by the man as a beneficial joint tenant.

QUESTION 3

A woman dies intestate, leaving an estate worth £735,000. The woman is survived by her husband. The woman and her husband separated 20 years ago and the husband left to live in another country. They had not met or spoken since the husband's departure. The woman is also survived by her sister, to whom she was very close throughout her life. The sister is currently suffering from a serious illness and is unable to work. In the years before her death, the woman took her sister in as a lodger to her own home, which the woman owned in her sole name.

Which of the following most accurately describes the administrators' powers on intestacy?

A. The administrators have the power to divide the estate equally between the husband and the sister.

B. The administrators have the power to give the husband the first £270,000 of the estate and half of the residue, and the sister the other half.

C. The administrators have the power to give all of the estate to the husband.

D. The administrators have the power to give all of the estate to the sister because her relationship to the woman was closer.

E. The administrators have the power to give the house to the sister because there is an equitable joint tenancy.

QUESTION 4

A man died intestate. In the man's estate were (1) the sum of £135,000 in a savings account; (2) a collection of vintage wines worth £75,000 which he had bought as an investment, but kept locked up in a refrigerated cellar and did not drink; (3) a vintage sailing boat which he bought as an investment, restored himself by hand and sailed every weekend and most holidays, which is worth £785,000 in its current restored condition; (4) a £23,000 mortgage over a house owned by the man's brother. The man was survived by his spouse and by three children from a previous marriage.

Which of the assets are personal chattels which would pass automatically to the man's spouse?

A. The money in the savings account and the collection of vintage wines.

B. The collection of vintage wines and the sailing boat.

C. The mortgage only.

D. The mortgage and the sailing boat.

E. The sailing boat only.

QUESTION 5

A woman died intestate. The woman is survived by her mother's half-sister, her stepson, her stepsister and the biological child of the deceased's aunt (who predeceased the woman) of the full blood.

Who is the first in line to entitlement under the intestacy rules?

A. The woman's mother's half-sister.

B. The woman's stepson.

C. The Crown.

D. The woman's stepsister.

E. The biological child of the woman's aunt (who predeceased the woman) of the full blood.

■ ANSWERS TO QUESTIONS

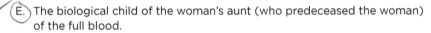

Answers to 'What do you know already?' questions at the start of the chapter

1) In a full intestacy, there is no will at all, either because the deceased never wrote a will or because the will they wrote has completely failed. In partial intestacy, some clauses of the will can still be given effect, but other clauses have failed (for the reasons that we looked at in **Chapter 3**), and the intestacy rules will apply to the items in those failed gifts.

2) No. Once a marriage has been ended by a final decree of divorce, then the ex-spouse has no further personal rights under the intestacy rules.

3) The statutory trusts are trusts imposed on the administrators of the intestate estate by s 46(1) of the AEA 1925. They tell the administrators how to share out the estate, to whom it should be given and in what proportions.

4) False. Administrators in a full or partial intestacy must distribute property within the intestacy exactly as the intestacy rules, including the statutory trusts, provide.

Answers to end-of-chapter SQE1-style questions

Question 1:

The correct answer was C. The testator made a will in anticipation of marriage to Husband 1, and therefore marriage to Husband 1 did not automatically revoke the will. However, the will did not anticipate the marriage to Husband 2, and at the point that the testator married Husband 2, the will was automatically revoked. As there is now no will, Husband 2 can only inherit under the intestacy rules. A is wrong because Husband 1 predeceased the testator and therefore does not fall within the intestacy rules. B is incorrect because those are the provisions of the now-revoked will. D is incorrect because only Husband 2 is entitled to inherit under the intestacy rules. E is incorrect because there is no legal basis upon which the estate could be distributed in this way.

Question 2:

The correct answer was E. Remember that this is a beneficial joint tenancy and the key characteristic of a beneficial joint tenancy is *survivorship*: that is, when the man dies, his interest automatically passes to his brother. A was therefore incorrect because although the wife is entitled to the cash as part of the statutory legacy, she can make no claim on the man's share of the property. B is doubly incorrect, first because although the wife would be entitled to £270,000 if that sum were available, the only available sum is £25,000; and second because even if the property was not jointly owned, the wife still could not demand it as appropriation because she has never lived in it. C is incorrect both because the wife is entitled to the cash and because she is not entitled to the share of the property. D is incorrect because the parties are still married until a final decree of divorce is made: the fact that she has commenced divorce proceedings is not relevant.

Question 3:

The correct answer was C. There is no discretion available to the administrators to distribute the estate in any way other than that provided by the intestacy rules. Where a person dies leaving a spouse and no issue, the rules provide that the estate must be given in its entirety to the surviving spouse (therefore A, B and D are incorrect). E is wrong because the sister lived in the house as a lodger, which means that the sister had not acquired any legal or equitable interest in the property: there could therefore not be an equitable joint tenancy.

Question 4:

The correct answer was E. Although the sailing boat was bought *partly* as an investment, this was a chattel not held solely as an investment at the time of death. The man clearly used it personally, including spending time and money on restoration himself and then sailing the craft during many of his leisure hours. None of the other items are personal chattels, so any option including any of them is incorrect. The wine was bought *primarily* as an investment and never used or enjoyed (therefore both A and B are wrong). Money in the bank and securities for money (including mortgages) are not classed as personal chattels (therefore A, C and D are wrong).

Question 5:

The correct answer was E. The key here, as is very often the case when answering an MCQ, is to be organised in your approach. The first thing to do is to match the options to the classes set out in **Table 5.1**. Go through each one in turn. If you do, this, you will find that B, the deceased's stepson, and D, the deceased's stepsister, do not appear in the table at all. Any option containing these must therefore be incorrect. This then leaves you with three options: an aunt who is the deceased's mother's half-sister (A), the Crown (C) and the biological child of the deceased's aunt (E). Where do these appear in the table? The first to appear is the aunt's child (in fact, the deceased's cousin), so E must be correct. Although A and C also appear in the table, remember that the first person to appear will take all of the estate.

■ KEY CASES, RULES, STATUTES AND INSTRUMENTS

The SQE1 Assessment Specification does not require you to know the specific contents of the statutory sections discussed in this chapter. However, it makes sense that you should be able to identify not only how the intestacy rules operate but also the source of the rules. You should ensure that you are familiar with:

- ss 33(1) and 33(2) and s 46 and s 49(1) of the Administration of Estates Act 1925
- s 1 of the Trustee Act 2000
- Intestate Estates Act 1952 Schedule 2 Part I
- s 67(1) Adoption and Children Act 2002
- s 3(1) Inheritance and Trustees' Powers Act 2014.

6

Property passing outside of the estate

■ MAKE SURE YOU KNOW

This chapter provides an overview of property that passes outside of the deceased's estate. This is an area in which a good working knowledge of fundamental trusts law will be vital (see *Revise SQE: Trusts Law*). More than many other areas of the syllabus, it is essential here to understand whether the deceased owned property beneficially or not. Ensure in particular that you have complete knowledge of equitable tenancies in common and joint tenancies, and especially how and when a joint tenancy can be severed.

■ SQE ASSESSMENT ADVICE

As you work through this chapter, remember to pay particular attention in your revision to:
- which items will not fall within the deceased's estate
- *why* it is important to know which items do not fall into the deceased's estate
- how the law of trusts affects the deceased's estate
- how life insurance policies can be written into trust and why, if they are, they do not form part of the death estate
- the effect of pension nominations on the deceased's estate
- when a gift will be a gift made 'in expectation of death', and the consequences of this.

■ WHAT DO YOU KNOW ALREADY?

Have a go at these questions before reading this chapter. If you find some difficult or cannot remember the answers, make a note to look more closely at that area during your revision.

1) True or false? If the deceased has taken out life insurance, and then dies, the proceeds of the policy are always automatically paid out to the deceased's personal representatives.
   [Proceeds of life insurance policies, page 94]

2) If a person dies owning a half-share in a property under a beneficial tenancy in common, can they pass on that share to another person in their will?
   [Property held in trust, page 91]

3) If a person (A) is granted a life interest in a property, with the remainder to B, can A pass the life interest to B when A dies?

   [Property held in trust, page 91]

4) Is it possible to make a deathbed gift of land to another person by handing over all of the keys to the property?

   [Gifts made in expectation of death: *donatio mortis causa*, page 96]

INTRODUCTION TO PROPERTY PASSING OUTSIDE OF THE ESTATE

We have already looked at the role played by the personal representatives (PRs) in administering and managing the deceased's estate (see **Chapter 2**). Remember that, as always, when we refer to PRs in this chapter, we are referring to both executors and administrators unless otherwise specified.

One of the things that stands out about their role is that the PRs have an absolute obligation to gather in all of the property in the deceased's estate (see **Key term** in **Chapter 1**), and that no other person whatsoever is entitled to deal with the estate. We have already seen that where the person interfering with property has not been properly appointed as a PR, this can constitute intermeddling (**Chapter 2**).

However, it is just as important that properly and duly appointed PRs do not interfere with property which does *not* belong to them. If they do so, they are likely to find that they are personally liable to the true owner of the property for any loss or damage caused.

You will understand, therefore, that it is not only vital for PRs to understand what is in the estate: their duty of care also extends to understanding what is *not* in the estate, so that they do not claim property which in law belongs to someone else.

WHAT ITEMS OF THE DECEASED'S PROPERTY FALL WITHIN THE ESTATE?

Appearances can be deceptive. It may look as if the deceased owned certain items of property, or that their estate should own certain items of property, but on closer inspection that may turn out not to be the case. As a matter of logic, no person can pass on by will something that they do not own. The PRs will normally start with the general rules (statutory for land; common law for personalty (see **Key term** in **Chapter 3**)) and then look for exceptions.

Land

Any interest in real property (ie land) which the deceased owned on death will automatically pass into the estate under s 1(1) of the Administration of Estates Act (AEA) 1925 unless it was an interest which ceased on the deceased's death. This rule applies to both wills and intestacies (see **Chapter 5**).

This important exception includes both life tenancies in land and, more commonly, interests under an equitable joint tenancy (both discussed below). These do not fall within the estate.

Care must be exercised where the deceased was the **bare trustee** of a trust of land.

Key term: bare trustee

This means that the legal title in the land was in the name of the deceased, but all of the equity in the land was owned by someone else. As the deceased did not own any of the equity, none of it can pass into the death estate, because the deceased cannot pass on to their heirs any property they did not own. Where there is a bare trust, the legal title will be held temporarily by the PRs, but usually only while arrangements are made for another bare trustee to be appointed or for the trust to be wound up: it is not possible to inherit a trusteeship.

These are important exceptions. However, as a broad working rule, if the interest in land does not end with the death of the deceased, by s 1(1) of the AEA 1925 it will pass to the PRs.

Personalty

All of the deceased's other property, which will be personalty, will pass under common law to the PRs automatically. 'Personalty' can include incorporeal items such as rights of action under legal disputes and also 'choses in action' (cheques, shares, bonds and so on). It can also include powers to direct what happens in other trusts: these are called 'powers of appointment'.

The PRs need to ask some searching questions when looking at the deceased's personalty. If part or all of that personalty was owned in trust, then what happens to the trust, and to the deceased's interest, when the deceased dies? We will see that there are some very specific questions that they need to ask about life insurance policy payouts and about pensions. Further, did the deceased give any personalty away before dying, but 'in expectation of death'? If the gift meets some technical rules which we will look at towards the end of this chapter, then the subject matter of the gift will not fall into the deceased's estate. These gifts are traditionally called gifts *donatio mortis causa*, which is broadly interpreted as meaning 'gifts made in expectation of death'.

Let's now look in more detail at the items which will *not* fall within the death estate. Just a further reminder: these rules apply whether there is a will or an intestacy.

WHAT ITEMS OF THE DECEASED'S PROPERTY DO NOT FALL WITHIN THE ESTATE?

Some items of property can look, at first glance, as if they did belong to the deceased at death and therefore fall into the estate; but on a more detailed examination, you may find that they did not belong to the deceased at all. We are now going to look at the four main categories of property which you will need to know about, and fully understand, in order to answer SQE1 multiple-choice questions (MCQs). The four categories are:

- property held in trust
- proceeds of life insurance policies
- pension scheme lump sum payments
- Gifts *donatio mortis causa*.

PROPERTY HELD IN TRUST

You will recall that s 1(1) of the AEA 1925 specifically noted that interests in *land* would not pass into a person's estate if the interest ceases on the deceased's death. However, this is also true of a life interest in personalty. Logically, if an interest ceases on death, it cannot be passed on from the deceased into the estate, whether it is in land or personalty. It is the fact that the interest ceases on death which is important, not the type of property involved.

Property owned by the deceased as a beneficial life tenant

If the deceased has a life interest in a particular property (whether land or personalty), that life interest will cease automatically on the deceased's death and will pass on to the next person in line under the terms of the trust: the trust property never becomes part of the deceased's estate.

Property owned by the deceased as a beneficial joint tenant

Note that, for this category of property, you need to make absolutely sure that you understand from your trusts reading what a beneficial **joint tenancy** is. You will find more information on this topic in *Revise SQE: Trusts Law*.

> **Key term: joint tenancy**
>
> In summary, for the purpose of this chapter, we will define this as ownership of an asset in what are called 'undivided shares' (see also *Revise SQE: Land Law*).

The key element that we need to focus on in this context is the principle of survivorship, which applies to beneficial joint tenancies (see **Practice example 6.1**).

Practice example 6.1

Rohit and Angelica own the equity of their home, 'Markvale', as beneficial joint tenants. This means that the law sees them as one composite owner: the equity is owned by 'RohitAngelica' and not by Rohit or Angelica individually. During their lifetimes, neither one of them severs the joint tenancy. Rohit then dies.

What happens to Rohit's interest in the property?

Because of the principle of survivorship, all of his interest in the house passes automatically to Angelica.

Revision tip

Joint tenancy means – as we can see in **Practice example 6.1** – that Rohit does not have a separated 'share' in the equity. This is a common mistake made by candidates, and you need to ensure you understand this.

The other key principle of a joint tenancy is that when one joint tenant dies, their interest in the property automatically passes on to the surviving joint tenant(s) because of the principle of survivorship. It is as if, at the exact moment that the deceased joint tenant dies, their interest in the property is 'snuffed out' and passes on automatically to the survivors: in **Practice example 6.1**, it would pass straight to Angelica.

The interest under a joint tenancy therefore *never becomes part of the deceased's estate*, because it is extinguished at the very moment of death. In this respect it is similar to the life interest discussed above. Just to emphasise that point, a will containing a provision that someone is to inherit an interest under a joint tenancy will be of no effect (see **Practice example 6.2**).

Practice example 6.2

Using the details in **Practice example 6.1**, let's assume that before he died, Rohit and Angelica quarrelled. Rohit then made a will that contained a clause leaving his interest in Markvale to his brother Atem. He did not sever the beneficial joint tenancy at any point before he died.

Can Atem inherit Rohit's interest in the property?

Unfortunately for Atem, the clause in Rohit's will is of no effect and passes nothing to him. Rohit's interest passed automatically to Angelica at the moment of Rohit's death, and there was therefore no interest which could pass to Atem by will.

Practice example 6.2 should have made clear to you how vitally important it is that if a person does not want the principle of survivorship to operate in a joint tenancy, they sever that joint tenancy during their lifetime as soon as their wish becomes clear.

Revision tip

Look back at your trusts textbook and notes on how to sever a joint tenancy and turn it into a **tenancy in common**. You will also find helpful reminders in *Revise SQE: Trusts Law* and *Revise SQE: Land Law*.

The principle of survivorship does *not*, however, apply to a beneficial tenancy in common.

Key term: tenancy in common

Tenants in common own property in what are called 'divided' shares, as opposed to the undivided shares of a joint tenancy.

This means that it is possible to leave a beneficial share under a tenancy in common by will or for it to pass under an intestacy (see **Practice example 6.3**).

Practice example 6.3

Following on from **Practice examples 6.1** and **6.2**, as well as owning Markvale, Rohit and Angelica also owned a beach hut on the Norfolk coast. They owned this beach hut as beneficial tenants in common in equal shares: that is, they each had a half-share in the equity of the beach hut. Before he died, Rohit made a will containing a clause that his interest in the beach hut should pass to his brother Atem.

Will Atem inherit Rohit's interest in the beach hut?

Atem will inherit Rohit's half-share of the beach hut because the principle of survivorship does not apply to a tenancy in common, and Rohit's interest therefore does not pass automatically to Angelica on his death.

This is a complex area of the law, and you will have seen that it is absolutely vital that PRs are sure of whether the deceased's property was held on a beneficial joint tenancy or a tenancy in common, because property held under a tenancy in common will fall within the estate but property held on a joint tenancy will not. Not only is this important because PRs must not claim ownership of assets that are not in the estate, but there are also inheritance tax implications which we will explore further in **Chapter 10**.

PROCEEDS OF LIFE INSURANCE POLICIES

The PRs also need to look very carefully at any policies of life insurance that the deceased took out. The whole purpose of life insurance is that it takes effect after death to look after specified people known to the deceased. The insured person will pay premiums on the insurance policy while they are alive. The crucial part of that life insurance policy is that if the insured event happens – that is, the insured person dies – a lump sum (sometimes a very large lump sum) will be payable by the insurance company in order to meet the needs of the dependants left behind.

Always bear in mind that life insurance, where it is available, is an extremely important part of any estate, particularly where the deceased was a main breadwinner for the family and died unexpectedly or at a young age; even more so where the deceased left infant children. Among other matters, a life insurance policy will normally have been set up to pay off the remainder of any mortgage on the family home. It is literally, therefore, the single element that keeps the roof over the head of the family in these circumstances. It can also amount to a very significant sum of money – in fact, it is often the largest single amount of money left by the deceased. But it is not always an amount of money which falls into the estate, and you therefore need to look at what you are told about any life insurance policy with great care.

If the deceased has made no alternative arrangements for the life insurance policy, then the lump sum payable on the death of the deceased will be paid into the deceased's estate. However, there is always an option for the deceased, during their lifetime, to 'write the policy into trust'. This phrase means that while alive, the deceased created a trust in favour of a particular beneficiary into which any insurance payments would be made (see **Practice example 6.4**).

Practice example 6.4

Mischa, a father of three young children, sets up a life insurance policy which will pay out a six-figure sum if he dies. He writes the policy into a trust in favour of his wife, Giannina. Mischa dies several years later.

What happens to the lump sum payment?

Because the policy was written into trust, the lump sum that is payable on Mischa's death is paid directly to Giannina because she is the beneficiary of the trust set up by Mischa. The lump sum is not paid to the PRs of his estate and does not at any time form part of his death estate.

There are at least two significant advantages of writing a life insurance policy into trust. The first is that it allows the beneficiary to access funds from the policy more quickly than waiting for the estate to be fully administered. This can be extremely important where a mortgage has to be paid and children's needs must be met. We will see in **Chapter 8** that there can be real cash flow problems during the administration for the deceased's dependants. Writing a life policy into trust can generally avoid those problems. The second advantage is that writing a life policy into trust can have significant inheritance tax advantages. Though these are outside the scope of this book, you should take steps to make yourself aware of them.

PENSION SCHEME LUMP SUM PAYOUTS

Like the lump sums payable under life insurance policies, these benefits can often be very substantial sums of money, and also like the life insurance payments, they may not fall within the death estate at all.

First of all, the deceased must have invested in a non-state pension: that is, to have paid into a pension scheme at work (an 'occupational' pension), or to have made regular investments in an independent pension scheme (conventionally called a 'private' pension), or both. In every pension scheme, there is a date upon which the deceased can begin taking the pension as regular income. However, if the deceased dies before the pension can be paid out, the pension scheme will usually provide for what is called a 'death in service benefit' (in an occupation pension) or a lump sum payment (in an independent pension scheme). In either case, this is a specific cash sum which is paid out because the deceased died before getting any other benefit from the pension.

Non-discretionary lump sum and death in service payments

Some pension schemes provide that the deceased (or more correctly, the deceased's estate) will be absolutely entitled to the lump sum if the deceased died before drawing the pension. If this is the case, then it is highly likely that the lump sum will form part of the death estate and be paid directly to the PRs.

However, note that a person can during their lifetime nominate another person to receive the lump sum or death in service payment from their pension, and that if that nomination is made, the lump sum will be paid out directly to that person. A nomination is an instruction to the pension trustees to pay out the lump sum to that particular person and not to the deceased's estate.

Discretionary payments

Not all pension schemes give the deceased's estate an entitlement to a lump sum payment. Often the deceased has no *right* to a lump sum, but the terms of the pension include a term that the pension trustees have the power, or 'discretion', to pay out a lump sum if they consider it appropriate. All pension schemes are trusts, and this is an example of a discretionary power under a pension trust (see *Revise SQE: Trusts Law*). The trustees would be asked, on the deceased's death, whether they are prepared to make a payment out of the pension fund as a lump sum.

You may think that this seems like an uncertain and unpredictable arrangement, but it is in fact very common, and the trustees of the pension scheme will, by convention and under the rules by which they exercise their discretionary power, almost always make a payment out of the pension fund. One important point to bear in mind, though, is that the trustees can choose to whom they make the payment: they can make it directly to the estate, for example, or directly to a person (usually to the deceased's dependants or next of kin). If they make it directly to the estate, then it will form part of the death estate, but note that if they choose to make it directly to the next of kin, it will not.

It is also possible for the insured person to send a letter of wishes or a nomination to the pension trustees, setting out their wishes about any direct payments of lump sums to dependants or other family members. Again, the pension trustees are not bound to follow the letter of wishes or the nomination, but in practice they will probably do so unless they are given good reasons not to. A direct payment made to a family member pursuant to a letter of wishes or a nomination will, again, not form part of the deceased's estate.

If the PRs of the estate are satisfied that one of the above exceptions applies – the deceased only had a life interest in a property, for example, or wrote their life policy into trust, or nominated another person to receive their death in service benefit – they must not touch that property in any way because they are not entitled to do so.

The final category that we are going to consider is different again from all of these. It is property which the deceased gave away, not as a lifetime gift, but on the basis that the recipient would only receive it if the deceased died.

GIFTS MADE IN EXPECTATION OF DEATH: *DONATIO MORTIS CAUSA*

Let us start off with a classic example of a gift made in expectation of death (see **Practice example 6.5**). We can then look at the features which make these gifts unique (and sometimes problematic).

Practice example 6.5

Armand unexpectedly develops a serious heart condition and his doctors tell him that in order to cure it, he must have a long and complex surgical procedure. He is told that his chances of surviving this operation for more than a few days are less than 50% and that if he decides to have the operation, he must have it within the next three days. Armand is therefore in a position where there is a real prospect that he may die within the next few days.

Armand has made a will but he is troubled by the fact that he has not made enough provision in the will for his grandson, Rafe. In particular, he decides now that if he dies within the next few days, he would like Rafe to have the valuable Rolex diver's watch that Armand has worn constantly for the past thirty years and which Rafe has always admired.

When Rafe comes to visit Armand in hospital, Armand takes the watch from his wrist and says to Rafe: 'Here, take the watch; if anything happens to me, I want you to have it'.

Two days later, Armand undergoes the operation but dies on the operating table. Upon investigation, it becomes clear that the Rolex watch is worth no less than £30,000.

Will the watch form part of Armand's estate?

Because the gift complied in all respects with the rules of *donatio mortis causa*, the watch will pass automatically to Rafe on Armand's death, and will never form part of Armand's estate; it therefore cannot pass to anyone else under the will. The PRs cannot (and must not) claim it as part of the estate.

We are now going to look at why, and in what way, the scenario in **Practice example 6.5** complies with all of the rules regarding a gift made in expectation of death. Once we have done that, we will look at some of the common complexities and problems which can arise.

What are the key factors that must be present?

The key factors that must be present in any gift made in expectation of death are:

- 'contemplation' of death; this means that there must be a real prospect of death of which the donor is aware
- an intention that the gift will only take effect if the donor dies (and that if the donor survives, the gift will not take effect at all)
- delivery of the gift; you will have come across the concept of delivery when dealing with formalities and constitution in your study of trusts, so you will find some of the discussion on this point familiar.

Looking at the Armand and Rafe scenario in **Practice example 6.5**, let's go through these elements one by one.

Contemplation of death

First of all, Armand has been told that there is a realistic prospect that he may die within a very short space of time. In Armand's case, he must have the operation within three days and his chances of surviving it for even a short time are poor. He has very little time, for example, in which to alter his will or add a codicil (see **Chapter 3**), particularly as he is extremely unwell.

There is no hard and fast rule in *donatio mortis causa* that says that death must be imminent or very close, but death must be a realistic outcome within a reasonably short timespan: the deceased must be facing some life-threatening prospect in the near future. Armand's case is a classic example of a person suddenly confronted with the prospect of death in the short term and with little time or ability to re-arrange his affairs.

The gift will only operate if the donor dies

Secondly, the intention has to be that the gift will operate only if the giver dies. Two things operate in this example to show that this was Armand's intention. The first is that he made it clear to Rafe that he wanted Rafe to have it only *if* anything happened to him. (Although he has not said in plain words, 'if I die', the implication of his words is clear in the context.) Logically, if he survives the operation, he would want to have the watch back. The second factor is in the context: Armand has worn the watch every day for the past thirty years and the assumption would be that he wishes to continue wearing it for the rest of his life. Certainly, he is not saying anything to Rafe that is inconsistent with that. Intention may have to be gathered not merely from the deceased's words but also from the overall context. It would be convenient for lawyers if everyone who believed that they were in danger of imminent death said in clear words, 'I am giving this to you but you will only own it if I die; if I don't die, I would like it back', but of course they do not. Context is all-important in deciding whether the requisite intention is present.

If Armand had survived the operation and made a good recovery, the gift in expectation of death would automatically have been revoked, and Armand could have demanded that Rafe return the watch to him. It is this 'revocatory' element which makes a gift in expectation of death very different from a straightforward lifetime gift: remember that if the gift is a straightforward lifetime gift, then once it has been made, it cannot be recalled.

Delivery of the gift

Thirdly, and crucially, the subject matter of the gift has to have been delivered to the donee. In this case, the subject matter – that is, the watch – was handed over by Armand to Rafe in the hospital. Note that this is different from lifetime gifts, where delivery of the item will 'perfect' the gift, which means it cannot be taken back. Even though the watch has been 'delivered' to Rafe and he leaves the hospital with it, the watch does not become his property in *donatio mortis causa* unless and until his grandfather dies, after having handed it over to him in the circumstances we have described. In those circumstances, the watch does not become part of the death estate. On the other hand, if his grandfather lives, Rafe is obliged to hand the watch back to him.

Revision tip

So-called 'constructive' delivery will operate in *donatio mortis causa* (see *Revise SQE: Trusts Law*), but 'symbolic' delivery does not.

Gifts of land

This brings us to our final point, which is whether it is possible to make a gift of land in expectation of death. This issue depends crucially on the question of delivery. We have already seen that in order to make an effective gift of this kind, there must be either actual or constructive delivery. Clearly, it is not possible to make an actual gift of land – the donor cannot hand someone a house (and remember that there is no symbolic delivery in *donatio mortis causa*). But constructive delivery of land would require the donor to hand over control of the land to the donee, and that can only be done by handing over the *title*. Handing over the *keys* would never be enough: land is such a valuable asset that the item handed over must be unambiguous. The only item which is not ambiguous would be an item which indicated *ownership*, not merely the right to enter or occupy the property.

It is possible to hand over control of *unregistered* land by giving the donee the title deeds of that land. For that reason, the courts have decided that it is possible for a donor to make a gift of unregistered land in expectation of death as long as all of the relevant title deeds are handed over.

However, the position is not the same in registered land. The only person who has control over registered land is the person named on the Land Register as the registered proprietor; and in order to be recognised as the registered proprietor by the Land Registry, the relevant transfer forms must be correctly completed and lodged. It is not, and never has been, possible to give control of registered land to another person orally. As a result, it is almost certainly not possible to make any gift of registered land in expectation of death.

■ KEY POINT CHECKLIST

This chapter has covered the following key knowledge points. You can structure your revision around these, making sure to recall the key details for each point, as covered in this chapter.

Property which falls outside the estate:
- life interests/joint tenancies
- life insurance policies written into trust
- pension scheme lump sums and nominations
- gifts made in expectation of death.

■ KEY TERMS AND CONCEPTS

- bare trustee (**page 90**)
- joint tenancy (**page 91**)
- tenancy in common (**page 93**)

■ SQE1-STYLE QUESTIONS

QUESTION 1

A woman owned two properties – a cottage and a beach house – together with her spouse. The equity in the cottage was owned by the woman and her spouse as beneficial tenants in common in the shares 65% to the woman and 35% to her spouse. The equity in the beach house was owned by the woman and her spouse as beneficial joint tenants. Two years prior to her death, the woman and her spouse separated and the woman served a valid notice of severance on the spouse with reference to the beach house. The woman died intestate.

Which of the following answers correctly sets out what part of these interests fell into the woman's estate on death?

A. 50% of the interest in the cottage and 50% of the interest in the beach house.

B. 65% of the interest in the cottage and none of the interest in the beach house.

C. 65% of the interest in the cottage and 65% of the interest in the beach house.

D. None of the interest in the cottage and 65% of the interest in the beach house.

E. 65% of the interest in the cottage and 50% of the interest in the beach house.

QUESTION 2

In the five years prior to death, a deceased person acquired a life interest in an overseas investment fund and a beneficial share (as one of three tenants in common in equal shares) of the funds in a UK bank account. Within the same period, the same deceased person made a lifetime gift of a motor car to his nephew.

In the year before his death, the deceased person told his nephew that this nephew was to receive his valuable signet ring on his 21st birthday and that until then, the deceased person was holding the ring for him. He also created a trust of the proceeds of his life insurance policy in favour of his cousin.

The deceased person died leaving a will which did not mention any of these assets specifically.

Which of the following items fall into the deceased person's estate after death?

A. The deceased's share in the UK bank account.

B. The motor car.

C. The deceased's life interest in the overseas fund.

D. The proceeds of his life insurance policy.

E. The signet ring.

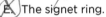

QUESTION 3

A woman is employed as a civilian contractor with a police force and has an occupational pension with that force. Her only living relative is her brother. The woman is, however, very close to her former husband, even though they divorced some time ago. The woman completes a nomination form which she sends to the pension trustees, instructing them to pay any death in service benefit directly to her former husband in the event of the woman's death. The woman dies aged 42 and the lump sum payment due on her death is £150,000. The woman has left a will which was made before her divorce and which leaves all of her estate to her brother and her husband in equal shares.

Which option best describes what will happen to the lump sum payment?

A. The lump sum payment will not fall into the estate but it will pass to the woman's brother on a partial intestacy.

B. The lump sum payment will fall into the estate, but cannot be passed to the woman's former husband because the woman has divorced him since the will was made.

C. The lump sum payment will fall into the estate and be paid to the woman's former husband and the brother in equal shares.

D. No lump sum payment can be made because it is not possible to nominate a former spouse.

E. The lump sum payment will not fall into the estate and will pass directly to the woman's former husband.

QUESTION 4

A farmer is fatally injured by a fall from the roof of a barn. Knowing that he is dying, the farmer takes from his pocket the key to a safe in the farm office and says to his niece, who has worked with him for over ten years, 'Take this key and keep it. Everything inside is yours now'. The farmer loses consciousness and dies shortly afterwards. The farmer dies intestate, leaving a spouse but no children. When the niece opens the safe, she finds inside the title deeds to the farm, which are unregistered, and official copies of the registered title to two large parcels of land which the farmer acquired ten years prior to his death.

Which of the following correctly identifies the legal position in this case?

A. The farmer's niece owns all of the registered and unregistered land through the gift made in contemplation of death and none of it passes into the estate.

B. The farmer's niece does not own any of the land through the gift made in contemplation of death and all of it passes into the estate.

C. The farmer's niece owns the unregistered land through the gift made in contemplation of death but the registered land falls into the estate.

D. The farmer's niece owns the registered land through the gift made in contemplation of death but the unregistered land falls into the estate.

E. Although the gift is valid as it was made in contemplation of death, the farmer's niece cannot inherit anything because under the intestacy rules, all of the farmer's property must pass to his spouse.

QUESTION 5

A solicitor takes will instructions from a client. The client tells the solicitor that she owns two properties jointly with her mother, a house and a villa. The client tells the solicitor that she wants to leave her share in the house to her sister and her share in the villa to her mother. The solicitor does not ask the client whether the client's beneficial interest in either property is a joint tenancy or a tenancy in common, but drafts the will according to the client's instructions. The client then executes the will, which is formally valid. After the client's death, it is discovered that the client owned the house as a beneficial joint tenant with her mother and the villa as a beneficial tenant in common with her mother in equal shares. The client is survived by both her mother and her sister.

How will the property be owned after the client has died and the executed will is put into effect?

A. The clauses in the will respecting the properties are of no effect and there is a partial intestacy of the client's shares.

B. The client's mother acquires all of the equity in the house by survivorship and inherits the client's share of the villa.

C. The client's mother inherits the client's share of the equity in both properties.

D. The client's sister inherits a half-share in the house and in the villa.

E. The client's mother inherits a half-share in the house and acquires all of the equity in the villa by survivorship.

■ ANSWERS TO QUESTIONS

Answers to 'What do you know already?' questions at the start of the chapter

1) False. The proceeds *may* be paid to the PRs, but not 'automatically'. They will only be paid to the PRs if the deceased has not written the policy into trust in favour of another person.

2) Yes. Shares under a tenancy in common can be passed on by way of a will; it is an interest in a joint tenancy which cannot be passed on (it expires on the deceased's death).

3) No. First of all, a 'life interest' means exactly what it says: it comes to an end when the possessor's life comes to an end and is then automatically transferred to the next person. In this example, the property life interest would go automatically to B: so there is, in fact, no need for the interest to be transferred to B by will at all.

4) No. This is an attempt to make a gift of registered land by constructive delivery. The only means by which the ownership of registered land can be changed is by going through the registered transfer procedure. Even giving a person all of the available keys to a property will *not* effect a gift of land if the land is registered.

Answers to end-of-chapter SQE1-style questions

Question 1:
The correct answer was E. As there has been valid severance of the joint tenancy, the beach house has now fallen into equal shares of 50% each. The cottage has always been held as a tenancy in common with the woman owning 65% of the equity. A is incorrect because it gives the wrong figure for the cottage. B is wrong because there was valid severance of the beach house. C is incorrect because on severance, the woman could not obtain more than 50% of the equity in the beach house. D is incorrect because the cottage is capable of being passed on.

Question 2:
The correct answer was A. The deceased's share in the UK bank account is a separate share under a tenancy in common and this will fall into

residue. B is a valid lifetime gift and cannot fall into the estate. C is a life interest which will end on death and therefore cannot fall into the estate. As a valid trust in favour of the cousin has been created, the proceeds of the life insurance policy will be paid directly to the cousin rather than into the estate, and D is therefore incorrect. In E, the ring is the subject of a valid *inter vivos* trust and once the formalities have been complied with, as they have here, the property no longer beneficially belongs to the deceased; he was holding it as a bare trustee and now the estate is holding it on the same terms.

Question 3:

The correct answer was E. The woman is entitled to nominate any person to receive the payment: she does not have to nominate relatives or a current spouse. If there is a nomination, the lump sum cannot fall into the estate, so B and C must be wrong. There is a valid will here and a valid nomination, so there is no possibility of even a partial intestacy; A is therefore wrong. Finally, as this is a nomination and not a will, divorce does not invalidate the gift, so D is wrong.

Question 4:

The correct answer was C. The farmer reasonably believed that death was imminent, made his intention clear and made a constructive delivery of everything in the safe by passing on the key to his niece. As it is possible to make a gift of unregistered land, the niece acquired ownership of the unregistered land (so B and D must be incorrect), but because of the rules on registered land, she could not acquire ownership of that land even though the documents were in the same safe (so A and D must be incorrect). Note that E is also incorrect: the rules of intestacy can only apply to property in the estate, and the whole point of gifts *donatio mortis causa* is that they never become part of the estate.

Question 5:

The correct answer was B. This is because any attempt to will away an interest under a joint tenancy has no effect. As a result, the clause leaving the client's 'share' to her sister was void from the outset. All other options are therefore incorrect.

■ KEY CASES, RULES, STATUTES AND INSTRUMENTS

The SQE1 Assessment Specification does not require you to know any specific statutes or statutory instruments for this topic. However, in addition to the rules set out in this chapter, it is worth making sure that you know how s 1(1) of the AEA 1925 operates to pass land into the deceased's estate.

7

Getting the grant of representation

■ MAKE SURE YOU KNOW

This chapter gives an overview of how personal representatives (PRs) apply for a grant of representation and how they deal with various issues that commonly arise. We do not deal in great detail with the initial application *procedure*, which you will find readily available in your main textbooks, but you are expected to know the practical first steps of applying for a grant. The focus here is on recognising and identifying problems during grant application, and finding the correct solution. This is another topic where you are required to know the relevant Non-Contentious Probate Rules (NCPR): to identify each one by number, to know what is in each relevant rule and to apply it correctly.

■ SQE ASSESSMENT ADVICE

As you work through this chapter, remember to pay particular attention in your revision to:
- the procedure for obtaining a grant, including the circumstances when further affidavit evidence will be required
- how to recognise and define an 'excepted estate'
- how to tell the difference between the various types of limited grant
- the relevant NCPR
- how the inheritance tax liability can or should be paid.

■ WHAT DO YOU KNOW ALREADY?

Have a go at these questions before reading this chapter. If you find some difficult or cannot remember the answers, make a note to look more closely at that area during your revision.

1) What is a grant of representation?

   [A reminder of the key duties of the personal representatives, page 106]

2) Is it possible to obtain a grant of representation if inheritance tax due on the estate has not been paid in full?

   [Applying for the grant, page 96]

3) What action will the probate registry take if an original will is submitted to it with staple marks?

   [Documents to be lodged with the application, page 112]

4) Can a will which has been torn into four pieces be admitted to probate?

   [Documents to be lodged with the application, page 112]

A REMINDER OF THE KEY DUTIES OF THE PERSONAL REPRESENTATIVES

Over the next two chapters, we are going to look in more detail at the duties of the PRs. It's important to remember that when the phrase 'the PRs' is used, we are talking about *both* executors and administrators. However, if the rule we are discussing affects only one type of PR, they will be described as 'the executors' or 'the administrators' as appropriate.

We already looked at the PRs' duties briefly in **Chapter 2**, where we learned that the primary duty of a PR is to collect in all of the assets of the deceased that fall within the will (or, if it is an intestacy (see **Chapter 5**), the administration), pay the liabilities out of them and then distribute them. In this chapter, we are going to focus on the PRs' duty to apply for and obtain a **grant of representation**. In **Chapter 8**, we will look at the other three main duties of a PR: collecting in and managing the estate (defined in **Key term** in **Chapter 1**) assets, paying the debts and other liabilities of the estate, and then distributing the assets of the estate to those entitled to them.

Key term: grant of representation
This is the collective name for either a grant of probate if there is a valid will or a grant of administration if not.

APPLYING FOR THE GRANT

We have already seen in **Chapter 1** that obtaining the grant is vital. If a valid will has been left and the deceased has therefore died testate, then the executors should seek a grant of probate. If no valid will has been left, there is a full intestacy, and the appropriate administrators must apply for a grant of letters of administration. For the remainder of this chapter, we are going to refer to that as a 'grant of administration' for convenience. If there is a valid will but no executor able or willing to act, then the person entitled to be an administrator must apply for a grant of letters of administration with the will annexed (see **Administration** below and **Chapter 2, Administrator with a will**).

Remember that ownership of an intestate deceased's assets does not pass to administrators until the grant of administration has been made. Executors are the legal owners of the deceased's estate under the will from the moment of death, but it is still vital for executors to obtain a grant of probate so that they have evidence that they are in fact able to deal with the deceased's property. Banks and the Land Registry, to name but two, will usually not deal with the executors without sight of a grant of probate.

Common form grants are issued by the Principal Registry of the Family Division or by one of its district registries: s105 Senior Courts Act 1981. In this chapter we will refer to all of these registries collectively as 'the probate registry'. Most grants of probate are made in 'common form', which indicates that there is no dispute associated with the will. If there is a dispute about the will, then the dispute will be dealt with by the Chancery Division of the High Court, which will decide the question and if appropriate make an order for the grant to be made, again by the Family Court, in 'solemn form'.

In order to obtain a grant (whether of probate or administration), the PRs must file evidence showing that they have submitted an inheritance tax return to HM Revenue and Customs (HMRC) and paid any tax due (see **Chapter 10**). If the tax has not been paid, the grant will not be issued. They must also lodge a legal statement verified by a statement of truth with the probate registry confirming:

- that the deceased has in fact died, the date of death and the deceased's domicile (that is, in which country the deceased was habitually living at death)
- whether the deceased died testate or intestate
- in what manner/on what grounds the PRs are entitled to the grant
- how much the estate is worth (gross and net)
- that inheritance tax has been paid (by submitting a receipt from HMRC).

If the application is for a grant of probate, then the whole *original* will (including any codicils; see **Chapter 3**) must also be submitted. Where the original will is still in existence, the probate registry will not accept any copy of the will, though it may accept a copy if there is good sworn evidence that the original has been destroyed. There may sometimes be a need for further evidence, and we will look at that in due course.

If the application is for a grant of administration, the proposed administrator will have to deal in their evidence with '**clearing off**'.

Key term: clearing off

This means that the proposed administrator will explain to the probate registry either that they are the first appropriate person to be administrator under Rule 8(4) of the NCPR 1987 (see **Chapter 2**), or if, for example, they are the second, third or fourth most appropriate person, why the people in front of them are either unable or unwilling to take on the task of administration.

Probate

Most applications for a grant in common form proceed smoothly, but be aware that any person who has suspicions about the will (that it was not validly executed, for example) can '**enter a caveat**': NCPR 1987 r 44. The person doing this is called the 'caveator'.

Key term: enter a caveat

Think of this as raising a red flag with the probate registry: if a caveat is entered, then the probate registry cannot issue a grant of probate until the caveat is either removed or it expires (a caveat lasts for six months, though it can be renewed): r 44(1), 44(3).

If a caveat is entered, the executor(s) will usually respond with a 'warning': NCPR r 44(5). That warning obliges the caveator to do one of two things within eight days.

The caveator can respond by 'entering an appearance': that is, setting out that the caveator has an interest which is contrary to the interest of the person applying for a grant: NCPR Rule 44(10). This could be an interest under the existing will (see **Practice example 7.1**) or under another will which the caveator is seeking to have admitted to probate. In either of these cases, the caveator must state the date of the will on which their contrary interest is based. However, the term 'contrary interest' extends much more widely than this, and can include, for example, a person who believes that they, and not the person making the application, should be entitled to a grant, even though the caveator is not a beneficiary under the will or intestacy.

If the caveator does not have contrary interest, they can still ask for a 'summons for directions' (r 44(6)), which in essence is a request to the court to consider whether the named executor is an appropriate person to act.

If the caveator does not take one of these steps within the eight-day time limit, the caveat can be removed and the probate process will go forward: r 44(12).

Practice example 7.1

Hamble and Theodore were cousins who did not get on. Hamble was an artist who lived a bohemian lifestyle, of which Theodore thoroughly disapproved. Their aunt Jemima left a will in which she appointed Hamble, but not Theodore, as an executor.

After Jemima's death, Hamble applied for a grant of probate in common form. When she applied, the probate registry told her that the grant could not be made because Theodore had already entered a caveat. Hamble then issued a warning to Theodore and Theodore entered an appearance within eight days setting out that his interest was that he was a beneficiary of the estate, and that he objected to the grant being sealed because he believed that for reasons of character, Hamble was not a suitable executor.

Can Hamble still be granted probate in these circumstances?

Hamble cannot now obtain probate of the will until the court has fully heard Theodore's objections (at a full trial), or has dismissed them, or the matter is settled by the parties.

Caveats are used to stop the current executor in their tracks, at least until the concerns raised by the caveator have been resolved. In that respect, they are the mirror image of citation (see **Key term** in **Chapter 2**), where the problem is that there is no executor willing to act.

Administration

Remember that administration applies not just to total intestacy but also to cases where the originally named executor of a will cannot now act: they may be too young, for example, or they may have predeceased the testator, or they may have lost capacity. In such cases, an application for a grant of letters of administration with the will annexed should be made. This will allow an administrator to step in, taking the place of the person who cannot act, but only to carry out the terms of the will: NCPR r 20, and see **Chapter 2**.

Limited grants

Generally, the grant of either probate or administration will cover all of the assets in the deceased's estate without limitation. This is one of the reasons why, as we saw in **Chapter 6**, it is absolutely vital for the PRs to ascertain what is in fact in the estate. However, there are three well-defined scenarios, particularly in administration, where the grant may be more limited (and, at times, temporary). They are:

1) where there are difficulties with the proposed PR and no other PRs are available (this is known as the grant *de bonis non administratis*)

2) where the deceased's property is going to waste or being lost in some way and some immediate steps need to be taken (the grant *ad colligenda bona*)

3) when some or all of the parties interested in the will are fighting about it in court (the grant *pendente lite*).

All of these grants allow someone to act as a PR up to a point, but no further. Let's look at each of these briefly in turn.

Tasks of the PR not completed: de bonis non administratis

This is usually shortened to *de bonis non* (the full phrase in Latin means 'of goods not administered'. This grant generally means that a PR has disappeared from the scene before they could complete (or sometimes, even begin!) administering the estate. It applies, for example, where there were two executors who have both died in the course of administering the estate, or where a single executor or administrator loses mental capacity while still administering the estate. It can even be used where the administrator of an estate has simply vanished. The matter clearly cannot be left like this: *someone* has to finish off administering the estate and dealing with all the matters that the PRs must deal with. To resolve this situation, the grant *de bonis non* allows another person to be appointed as either executor or administrator.

Deceased's property in danger of waste, ruin or destruction: ad colligenda bona

The *de bonis non* grant applies equally to probate and administration, but the grant *ad colligenda bona* (the Latin means 'to collect the assets') is more likely to be used in administration, though it can also be used in probate where there is no current executor (because the named executor is under 18, for example). It can assist in the period between death and the full grant of administration, when the PRs are not empowered to deal with the assets because they do not have title to them. Sometimes this can cause problems because there is a valuable asset in the deceased's estate which must be managed in some way or it will be completely lost (see **Practice example 7.2**).

Practice example 7.2

Dwyr, a fruit farmer, died intestate. The appropriate person to apply for a grant of administration under NCPR Rule 8(4) is his sister Anwen. Until a full grant of administration is made, Anwen does not own any part of Dwyr's estate. She cannot therefore take any action in relation to managing Dwyr's farm or the farming business. (If she did so, she would be intermeddling; see **Chapter 2**.)

At the time that Dwyr died, the main strawberry crop for the year was on the point of ripening. If the strawberries can be sold to a supermarket chain within the next two weeks, the estate will make a profit of £50,000. If the strawberries are not picked and sold by that time, they will not be of an acceptable quality for the supermarket chain and will be left to rot in the field.

What, if anything, can Anwen do?

Anwen could apply for a grant *ad colligenda bona* which, if obtained, would allow her to manage Dwyr's estate to the extent of making arrangements for the strawberry crop to be picked, packed and sold to the supermarket chain. However, she would have to wait for the full grant of administration before she is able to deal any further with the estate.

Ongoing litigation about the estate: grant pendente lite

It may have struck you, when you were looking at the Hamble/Theodore scenario in **Practice example 7.1**, that the effect of a caveat can be to freeze all activity on the estate completely. If Theodore convinces the court that there is substance to his argument that Hamble is not a suitable executor, then there will be no full grant of probate until the litigation arising from Theodore's objections is resolved. But in the meantime, there are still many tasks associated with the estate which have to be done: paying the deceased's debts, for example, or running the deceased's business. The probate registry will therefore often allow a grant of probate or administration to a PR until the litigation is finished (the Latin *pendente lite* means roughly 'while the litigation is going on'): s 117(1) Senior Courts Act 1981. This allows the estate to be properly managed until the court has made a final decision. At that point, another executor may be appointed (or, if the will is invalid and there is no earlier will, an administrator).

If a temporary or limited grant is needed, then if there is a will, it should be applied for by the person who would be entitled to a grant of administration with the will annexed; and if there is no will, by the person next entitled to be appointed under NCPR Rule 22 (see **Chapter 2, Administrators of the estate**).

Once the executor or administrator has the relevant grant, they can move on and deal with their duties.

THE APPLICATION PROCEDURE

An application for a grant of representation, whether it is a grant of probate or of administration, can only be in two ways: (1) personally by the person entitled to the grant or (2) via a 'probate practitioner'.

Revision tip

There are complex rules about who must make an online application for a grant, and who may do so, and further rules about who can make an application on paper. You should refer to your main textbook and ensure you are familiar with these rules.

The matters which are discussed in the remainder of this chapter apply whether the application is made online or on paper.

While there are no time limits to making an application for a grant of representation, the probate registry will not as a general rule issue a grant of probate, or administration with the will annexed, less than 7 days after death, or a grant of administration less than 14 days after death (NCPR Rule 6(2)).

DOCUMENTS TO BE LODGED WITH THE APPLICATION

All applications must be accompanied by the appropriate documents or they will be rejected by the probate registry and no grant will result. We will now look at the most frequently required documents.

Tax

In order to obtain any grant of representation, the applicant must produce evidence that any tax due on the estate has been paid (inheritance tax is dealt with in detail in **Chapter 10**). The evidence of paid tax is a Schedule IHT421 form which has been stamped by HMRC to record that the tax has been paid, unless the estate is an excepted estate (see below).

Tax: excepted estates

What is the exception in an **excepted estate**?

Key term: excepted estate

This is an estate that has an exception from the obligation to make out a full tax return to HMRC under the main tax return form (called an IHT400). If an estate can be classed as an excepted estate, although it still has to file a fairly detailed return with HMRC, the reporting obligations are less arduous. It is therefore important to decide whether or not any given estate falls within the general rules on exceptions.

The rules differ depending on the date of the deceased's death, but we will concentrate on the current position, which affects all deaths occurring after 6 April 2011.

If the deceased was domiciled in the UK *and* the gross value of the deceased's estate was:

(i)   less than the relevant IHT threshold (currently £325,000); *or*
(ii) less than £1,000,000 but no tax is payable because property is passing to the deceased's spouse, or civil partner, or to a charity; *or*
(iii) less than £750,000 and a claim is made to transfer all of an unused nil rate band (NRB)

then the estate may be treated as an excepted estate and the return can be made in form IHT205 instead of IHT400.

You will see that the overall idea behind excepted estates is that they will almost certainly not attract any inheritance tax charges. In the first category, the gross value of the estate simply falls below the current level at which IHT applies; in the second, the gross value of the estate falls above that level, but because the deceased has given away property either to a spouse/civil partner or a charity, these gifts are exempt from IHT and therefore there is probably no inheritance tax to pay. In the third category, the deceased has left a gross estate worth up to twice the current inheritance tax threshold, but if the PRs use an available NR , again there will be no inheritance tax to pay. Further explanation about the inheritance tax limits is set out in **Chapter 10**.

Revision tip

The detailed rules as to the composition of an excepted estate, including rules about jointly owned property, are outside the scope of this book, but you should ensure that you know them.

PRs decide whether or not an estate will qualify as an excepted estate by calculating the tax liabilities and then submitting the appropriate forms to HMRC (IHT205 if excepted, IHT400 if not). They will then receive confirmation of any tax payable, pay the tax and obtain a receipt in form IHT421. *Remember that if there is no proof that all relevant tax has been paid, a grant of representation will not be issued by the probate registry.*

Paying the tax: practical problems

You will remember that the executors' right to deal with estate property arises out of the will, and so technically an executor does not need to wait for a grant of probate in order to, for example, use money in the deceased's bank account to pay any inheritance tax liabilities. In practice, however, the deceased's bank will be extremely reluctant to hand over any assets to the executors until the grant of probate has been obtained. So the executors need access to some of the estate in order to get the grant of probate, but may be refused access to funds in the estate *until* they get grant of probate.

The position for administrators, as we know, is even more difficult as they have no right at all to touch any of the deceased's estate until they have been granted letters of administration.

How is this conundrum solved? The law has provided a number of ways in which it can be.

The Direct Payment Scheme

Where the deceased has left money in a bank or building society account, there is an agreed procedure by which the bank or building society holding the money will electronically transfer to HMRC the amount needed to pay off any inheritance tax liability. A bank or building society must be a member of the British Bankers and Building Societies Association in order to participate in the scheme. The PRs present IHT Form 423 (which sets out the total amount of tax payable) to the relevant bank or building society and the bank then pays this amount directly to HMRC. HMRC then confirms directly with the probate registry that the tax has been paid.

If the deceased has left sufficient money in their bank accounts and there is an inheritance tax charge to be paid, this is clearly the most efficient option in most cases. However, that cannot always happen. What if the deceased's bank was not a member of the Direct Payment Scheme (because it is a foreign-based bank with no UK office, for example)? What if there is no money, or not enough money, in the accounts?

Both of the alternative solutions will involve the estate borrowing money: either from one of the beneficiaries of the estate or, if this is not possible, from a bank or building society.

Borrowing from one of the beneficiaries
One or more of the beneficiaries may have obtained property passing outside of the estate as the beneficiary of a life insurance policy, for example, or as the surviving holder of a joint bank account. It may be very much in the interests of that beneficiary (because they are a beneficiary under the will or intestacy, for example) to lend money to the estate in order to obtain the grant of probate or administration. The beneficiary has a liquid amount of cash at their disposal at a time when the estate has not. A beneficiary may therefore pay an inheritance tax liability from their own resources on the understanding that they are repaid the amount of the loan as well as their other entitlements under the will or the intestacy.

Borrowing from a bank or building society
If all else fails, then it may be possible for the PRs to borrow the inheritance tax payment from a bank or building society, though this is seen as a last resort. If a loan is sought, the PRs will write to the bank concerned setting out a summary of all of the assets in the estate, the net value, the amount of the inheritance tax liability that needs to be paid and the amount of any probate fees, and will ask for a loan account to be opened in the sum that will pay off the tax liability. In return, if the loan request is granted, the bank will usually ask the PRs to give an undertaking that the loan will be repaid from the first assets that become available after the grant.

Statement of truth
All applications for a grant of representation must contain evidence supported by an appropriate statement of truth (NCPR Rule 8(1)).

If the application is for a grant of probate, then the legal statement must identify all testamentary documents left by the deceased (for example, any codicils as well as the will) and confirm the dates of all of those documents. The legal statement must also contain the full name of the testator, any other names by which they held property and their postcode. If the applicant is a substitute executor, it must explain why.

The legal statement must then be signed by all persons making the statement; that is, by all persons who wish to be executors or administrators of the estate.

Will

If the application is for a grant of probate, the *original* will must be lodged with the application (NCPR Rule 11). Wills do sometimes go missing, and if this has happened, then the applicants must make a separate application to the probate registry under NCPR Rule 54(1) for an order that will admit a substitute to probate. This will generally be a copy, but if there is no copy then it may only be possible to ask for a draft to be admitted. All of the relevant circumstances will have to be verified by a statement of truth, including what is known about the will's existence and about the accuracy of the copy or draft.

If the will makes reference to another document which appears to be incorporated in it – for example, 'I give to my cousins one of the items set out in the list which I have given to my executors' – then the original of that document should also be produced and lodged with the probate registry.

When the PRs believe that they have collected together all of the necessary documents, the application should be submitted either on paper or online.

The applicant should also include the appropriate probate fee.

More complex matters: affidavit evidence

In simple grant applications, the evidence in the legal statement of truth is usually all that is required. Where there are specific and more complex problems, the probate registry will require affidavit evidence (that is, written evidence sworn on oath) to be supplied and an *ex parte* application (that is, an application made for one party with minimal or no notice to other parties) to be made. Some of these issues will take us back to points about the formal validity of wills, which we looked at in **Chapter 1**: we can now see how the probate registry deals with these matters when they become problematic at the grant stage.

Due execution

You will remember that if the will does not contain an attestation clause, there is no presumption of due execution (see **Chapter 1**). Even if there is an attestation clause, there may be elements which ring alarm bells, including a will where the testator's signature is not on the final page, for example. In these circumstances, the probate registry will call for an affidavit or witness statement confirming due execution (NCPR Rule 12(1)), preferably from one of the witnesses to the will. If the probate registry is not satisfied that the evidence proves due execution, probate will be refused.

Date

We saw in **Chapter 1** that a will does not have to have a date on it, but that it will usually bear a date. The probate registry must be satisfied that the will submitted for probate is, in fact, the last will of the deceased and not some earlier will. If the original will is undated, therefore, the probate registry will require some affidavit evidence (from an attesting witness if possible, but from some other person present at the execution of the will if not) of the date on which the will was executed (NCPR Rule 14(4)). An affidavit may also be needed if the will bears two inconsistent dates, although as a general rule the probate registry will accept the later of the two as being the date of the will if it is placed at the end of the will.

Knowledge and approval

If the will has been duly executed, there is a presumption that the testator had knowledge and approval of it (see **Chapter 1**). Sometimes, however, the probate registry may not be satisfied that due execution equals knowledge and approval: for example, where it is known that the testator was blind, or illiterate, or could neither read nor write English. If the probate registry has concerns, it can and will require the applicant to file an affidavit that the testator did in fact know all of the contents of the will and therefore understood what they were signing (NCPR Rules 13 and 16).

You will remember that in a well-drafted will, a special attestation clause is inserted in these circumstances to avoid the need for further evidence at the grant stage (see **Chapter 1, Validity of wills: formalities, capacity and intention**).

The physical condition of the will: 'plight and condition'

In **Chapter 4** we looked at the various ways in which a testator may attempt to change or revoke a will, including various methods of altering it or attempting to destroy it. These attempts will leave some trace on the face of the will: words added in or scribbled out; pieces cut out with scissors or torn out; pages actually torn into pieces. What happens if the will is found in this mutilated condition and an application for probate needs to be made?

As far as alterations to the original will are concerned, remember that the basic rule is that all unsigned and unwitnessed alterations are assumed to be made *after* the will has been executed (**Chapter 3**). This means that unless the probate registry has clear evidence that these alterations were made before execution, the alterations concerned will simply be ignored for probate purposes unless evidence is put forward (usually from one of the attesting witnesses) that the alterations were made before the execution of the will: NCPR Rule 14(1) and (2). If that evidence is clear and is accepted, then probate is granted to the full will, including any accepted alterations.

What about a situation where the will has been physically damaged? This includes not just wills with pieces cut or torn out of them, or wills torn into pieces, but also wills which appear to have staple or pin or tape marks, or the impressions of a paperclip which is now missing. In all of these cases, the probate registry will require satisfactory affidavit evidence about the condition of the will when it was executed and the condition after the testator's death.

This is called the evidence of 'plight and condition' and is the basis upon which the probate registry will decide, for example, whether or not the testator had decided to revoke the will by physically destroying it (**Chapter 4**) or (where there is a staple, pin or paperclip mark) whether or not the testator wanted to include another document as part of the will, and that document has now been lost. If it looks as if a part of the will has gone missing, then the probate registry can order a further affidavit to be made detailing the searches that have been undertaken in order to find the missing document, and the results of those searches.

■ KEY POINT CHECKLIST

This chapter has covered the following key knowledge points. You can structure your revision around these, making sure to recall the key details for each point, as covered in this chapter.
- The procedure for obtaining a grant of representation, including the circumstances when further affidavit evidence will be required.
- How to recognise and define an 'excepted estate'.
- How to tell the difference between the various types of limited grant.
- The relevant NCPR rule number.
- How the inheritance tax liability can or should be paid.

■ KEY TERMS AND CONCEPTS

- grant of representation (**page 106**)
- clearing off (**page 107**)
- enter a caveat (**page 108**)
- excepted estate (**page 112**)

■ SQE1-STYLE QUESTIONS

QUESTION 1

A client seeks advice from a solicitor on the 2018 will of their uncle. The will leaves half of the estate to the uncle's live-in carer and the remainder to an animal charity. The client is not a beneficiary under the 2018 will but was a beneficiary under the uncle's previous will made in 2012. The 2018 will contained a revocation clause. The client strongly believes that the uncle did not have testamentary capacity at the time of the 2018 will. The live-in carer was also appointed executor of the will and has now applied for a grant of probate. The client entered a caveat and the caveat has now been warned.

Which of the following is the best advice that the solicitor should give to the client?

A. The client cannot enter an appearance to the warning because the client is not a beneficiary under the 2018 will.

B. The client can enter an appearance to the warning because the live-in carer is not entitled to act as an executor.

C. The client cannot enter an appearance to the warning because the client has no evidence that the uncle lacked testamentary capacity.

D. The client can enter an appearance to the warning because the client has an interest under the revoked 2012 will.

E. The client should not have entered a caveat in the first place and should apply to vacate it.

QUESTION 2

When a woman's will was found after her death, it contained five handwritten alterations. The first and second alterations were initialled by the woman testator herself and by the two witnesses to her will. The third and fourth alterations were initialled only by the testator. The fifth alteration was not initialled at all.

At the request of the probate registry, one of the attesting witnesses filed an affidavit in which he recalled that the fourth alteration had in fact been made prior to the execution of the will. He remembered discussion about that alteration between the testator and another person present before the will was signed. However, he had no recollection of any of the other alterations at all.

Which of the alterations will be admitted to probate?

A. The first, second and fourth alterations only.

B. The first, second, third and fourth alterations only.

C. The first and second alterations only.

D. The first and third alterations only.

E. The first and fourth alterations only.

QUESTION 3

The executors of an estate need to pay an inheritance tax bill of £45,000 in order to obtain a grant of probate. The deceased had an account with an overseas bank which has no branches in the UK and is not a member of the Direct Payment Scheme, and a UK bank account containing £22,500.

The will names two beneficiaries, his 74-year-old stepmother and his infant cousin, aged six years. The deceased had written his life policy into a trust in favour of his stepmother, and the insurer has paid the sum of £50,000 directly into the stepmother's UK bank account.

Which of the following options *cannot* be used by the personal representatives to pay inheritance tax due on the estate?

A. A personal loan from the mother of the infant beneficiary.

B. A direct payment arrangement from the overseas bank.

C. 50% of the amount by a direct payment arrangement with a UK bank and 50% as a loan from the adult beneficiary.

D. A loan arrangement with the overseas bank.

E. A personal loan from the deceased's stepmother.

QUESTION 4

A solicitor is acting as an executor for three separate estates. In the first estate, the deceased's main home was in Scotland ('the Scottish estate') and the estate has a net value of £350,000. In the second estate, the deceased's main home was in France ('the French estate') and the gross value of the estate is £450,000. In the third estate, the deceased's main home was in Northern Ireland ('the Northern Irish estate') and the estate has a gross value of £250,000. The relevant IHT threshold in all cases is £325,000.

Which of the following estates is/are excepted estates?

A. The Northern Irish estate and the Scottish estate only.

B. The Northern Irish estate only.

C. The Scottish estate and the French estate only.

D. The Scottish estate only.

E. The Northern Irish estate and the French estate only.

QUESTION 5

A testatrix appointed two executors of her will. The first executor predeceased the testatrix. The second executor has developed dementia and no longer has sufficient mental capacity to act as executor. There are no provisions in the will for any substitute executors. The will includes some bequests to minors.

Which of the following correctly describes the legal position in the case?

A. As there are no executors able or willing to act, a total intestacy has resulted.

B. As there are no executors able or willing to act, an application must be made for a grant of letters of administration with the will annexed.

C. As there are no executors able or willing to act, the beneficiaries must meet and choose new executors.

D. As there are no executors able or willing to act, the official solicitor must apply for a grant of probate.

E. Although there are no executors able or willing to act, the principal beneficiary under the will is entitled to apply for a grant of probate.

■ ANSWERS TO QUESTIONS

Answers to 'What do you know already?' questions at the start of the chapter

1) A grant of representation is the document which gives the PRs authority to deal with the property in the estate. If there is a will, the grant will be a grant of probate; if there is an intestacy, the grant will be a grant of administration.

2) No. All inheritance tax which is due to be paid must be paid before the grant will be issued. However, inheritance tax on land can be paid by instalments. If this option is chosen, only any instalment payments immediately due need to be paid, and not the whole amount.

3) If an original will is submitted to the probate registry bearing staple marks, the Registry will seek affidavit evidence about whether any document was attached to the will and will not grant probate if the evidence is unsatisfactory.

4) Yes, provided the executors provide satisfactory evidence in the form of an affidavit of plight and condition.

Answers to end-of-chapter SQE1-style questions

Question 1:
   The correct answer was D. The client's interest under the 2012 will, which would be revived if it were to turn out that the 2018 will was made without testamentary capacity, is a contrary interest to the applicant executor. There is no requirement that a caveator should have an interest under the existing will, so A is incorrect. B is incorrect because there is no information within the question that would lead us to believe that the applicant cannot act as an executor: if the will is valid, the appointment of the live-in carer is also valid. C is incorrect because evidence of incapacity would not be required until the matter was fully considered by the court. E is incorrect because the situation – in which the caveator believes that there are good reasons why the will should not be admitted to probate – is suitable for the caveat procedure.

Question 2:

The correct answer was A. As the first and second alterations were properly initialled and witnessed, the presumption that they were added after execution is displaced. Although the fourth alteration was not witnessed, the witness can give clear evidence that it was made prior to execution of the will and it will therefore be accepted by the probate registry. The witness cannot give any such evidence about the third alteration (therefore B, D and E are incorrect). C is incorrect because it does not include the fourth alteration, which the attesting witness can now verify by affidavit.

Question 3:

The correct answer was B. The only one of these arrangements which is not permissible is a direct payment arrangement with the overseas bank which has no UK presence. The Direct Payment Scheme applies only to UK banks named within the scheme and not to foreign banks. They would, however, be able to make a loan arrangement with such a bank, so D is therefore incorrect. A is incorrect as it is possible for the parent of an infant beneficiary to make a personal loan to the estate in order to progress probate; there is in fact no restriction on the category of person who can lend, though clearly for practical purposes it is likely to be a person with an interest in getting on with probate. The stepmother is certainly one such person, and she could make a personal loan to the estate, therefore E is wrong. It is also possible to 'top up' the tax payment with a personal loan from a beneficiary if there are insufficient liquid assets in the bank accounts, therefore C is incorrect.

Question 4:

The correct answer was B. The main home of the deceased must be in the UK, which includes both Scotland and Northern Ireland, but of course excludes France, so neither C nor E can be correct. The gross value of the estate must not exceed £325,000. The net value of the Scottish estate is £350,000 so the gross value must exceed that amount: A, C and D cannot be correct.

Question 5:

The correct answer was B. Where there is a valid will but no able or willing executors, an application must be made for a grant of letters of administration with the will annexed. A is incorrect because the lack of executors does not affect the validity of the will and does not cause intestacy. C is incorrect because the beneficiaries do not have the power to choose new executors. D is incorrect because the official solicitor will not be involved in applying for a grant of administration unless there is no person at all within the intestacy rules who can apply for administration: we are not told that this is the case here. E is incorrect for the same reasons as C. No matter how much any beneficiary receives from the estate – even if the beneficiary receives 100% of the estate – there is no automatic entitlement to act as executor (though the beneficiary could of course apply for a grant of administration).

■ KEY CASES, RULES, STATUTES AND INSTRUMENTS

The SQE1 Assessment Specification requires that you know any relevant provisions of the NCPR related to this topic. It is likely that you will be required to identify the rules by number, explain the contents of each rule and apply them. In this chapter, those are: Rules 8(1), 8(4), 12, 14(2) and (2), 44(10), and 54(1). You should also be able to identify and describe how s 115 Senior Courts Act 1981 operates.

8

Administration of the estate

■ MAKE SURE YOU KNOW

This chapter provides an overview of the administration of the estate after the personal representatives (PRs) have obtained the necessary grant. Again, it is practical knowledge which is most important here.

■ SQE ASSESSMENT ADVICE

As you work through this chapter, remember to pay particular attention in your revision to:

- how the PRs must perform their duties in getting in the estate assets and managing them prior to distribution
- the PRs' specific powers and duties in relation to personalty, land and businesses
- how and when the PRs can sell off estate assets
- the rules on abatement
- distribution where there are missing beneficiaries or minors
- the rules on appropriation and assent.

■ WHAT DO YOU KNOW ALREADY?

Have a go at these questions before reading this chapter. If you find some difficult or cannot remember the answers, make a note to look more closely at that area during your revision.

1) True or false? After a person dies, any debts owed *to* them by another person are wiped clean and do not have to be repaid.
   [Getting in/collecting the estate: debts owed to the deceased, page 126]

2) Do the PRs have to wind up the estate within a specific time, and if so, what is the time limit?
   [Managing the assets, page 126]

3) What powers do the PRs have over any land that is in the estate?
   [Managing the assets, page 126]

4) What should the PRs do if they cannot trace a beneficiary under either a will or intestacy?
   [Uncertainty about specific beneficiaries, page 134]

INTRODUCTION TO THE ADMINISTRATION OF THE ESTATE

In **Chapter 7** we looked at how the PRs (see **Chapter 2**) successfully apply for a grant of representation. However, getting the grant of representation is only the first step. Once they are entitled to administer the estate (see **Key term** in **Chapter 1**), they must actively do so and they are not expected to delay. Section 44 of the Administration of Estates Act (AEA) 1925 provides that PRs are not bound to distribute the estate before the expiry of a year after the deceased has died. This has given rise to the informal expectation, known as the 'executor's year', by which PRs are expected to obtain the grant and get all of the administrative tasks in the estate completed within a year of the death, so that they are ready to distribute at the end of that time. While it is more of an ambition than a regularly achieved goal, it does remind us that PRs are always expected to carry out their work efficiently and without undue delay.

In this chapter, we will first look at the liabilities and duties of care of the PRs, and then the three other key duties of the PRs: (1) collecting/getting in the estate assets, (2) paying the estate debts and liabilities and (3) distributing the remaining assets to the persons entitled to them.

As in our previous chapters, when we refer to 'the PRs' we are referring to both executors and administrators unless the context indicates otherwise.

LIABILITIES OF PERSONAL REPRESENTATIVES AND THEIR PROTECTION

Section 25(a) of the AEA 1925 obliges the PRs to 'administer' the estate. This word takes in two essential functions: the first is to manage the estate responsibly until distribution (including getting in the assets and paying the debts), and the second is distribution itself. In other words, while the estate is in the hands of the PRs, they must look after it and they certainly must not do anything which would reduce the value of the estate or any of its assets; and at the earliest reasonable moment they must hand out the estate to those who are legally entitled to it, either under the will or the intestacy rules (see **Chapter 5**).

While they carry out those administrative duties, the PRs are held to at least two, and often three, overriding *duties of care* or *fiduciary duties*. Because that means we have two sets of duties (administrative and care/fiduciary), both operating at the same time, we are going to refer to the **duties of care** as the *standards* to which the PRs must perform the administrative duties. If they fall below or breach these standards, then the PRs will be liable to the estate and to the beneficiaries.

Key term: duties of care

These duties of care/standards are:

- the common law duty not to commit an act of waste, known as a *devastavit*
- for some administrative actions, the statutory duty of care under s 1 of the Trustee Act 2000
- the fiduciary duty to the estate and the beneficiaries.

Where executors are also will trustees (see **Chapter 11**), they may have further duties relating to their exercise of the trust powers. Let's look at each of these in a little more detail.

Common law duty not to commit waste

There is a common law duty on all PRs to duly administer the estate assets and distribute them to those who are rightly entitled to them. In order not to breach this main duty, the PRs will need to preserve the assets in the estate and not allow them to come to any harm or to waste away; to deal with them responsibly, for example by making sure that they are sold at an appropriate time if they need to be sold; and to make sure that the right assets go to the right people. If a PR breaches any of these duties, they commit what is called a *devastavit*, which is Latin for 'he has wasted'. If a PR is found liable on a *devastavit*, then they are personally liable to make good any loss caused to the estate: that is, they must pay that loss out of their own pocket.

Statutory duty of care under s 35/s 1 of the Trustee Act 2000

If the deceased died after 1 February 2000, then s 35(1) of the Trustee Act 2000 applies the provisions of that Act (including the duty of care under s 1 of the Act) to the PRs when they are (among other things) exercising a power of investment (see **Chapter 11**), acquiring land for the estate, or insuring estate assets. It also applies a higher standard to professionally qualified persons (see *Revise SQE: Trusts Law*). Again, a PR found to be in breach of this statutory duty of care will be personally liable for any loss caused to the estate by breach of that duty. This duty runs concurrently with the common law duty and with the PR's fiduciary duty (see below).

Revision tip

It is also worth noting that the application of the Trustee Act 2000 to post-February 2000 estates means that all PRs during the course of administration have the powers set out in the Trustee Act, including the powers of investment at ss 3–5 and the power to acquire land in the UK under s 8 (unless the will, if there is one, has expressly excluded those powers).

Fiduciary duty

A further extremely important duty of the PR is their fiduciary duty. The key element of a fiduciary duty is that it extends not just to loss but to any unauthorised profit made by the fiduciary (see *Revise SQE: Trusts Law*). PRs who are found to be in breach of fiduciary duty must repay any profits they have made from that breach, whether they have caused loss to the estate or not.

Protection from liability

Although these concurrent duties are heavy, it is possible to exclude liability in a will if it contains express wording which limits or excludes liability on the part of the executors (clearly this would not apply to administrators). If there is no express exclusion of liability, all PRs can also argue under s 61 of the Trustee Act 1925 that they have acted honestly and reasonably and therefore ought to be excused liability.

Let's now take a look at each of the specific administrative duties: collecting/ getting in the estate assets, paying the estate debts and distributing the remaining assets to the persons entitled to them.

GETTING IN/COLLECTING THE ESTATE: DEBTS OWED *TO* THE DECEASED

Section 25(a) of the AEA 1925 provides that the PRs must 'collect and get in the real and personal estate of the deceased and administer it according to law'. One factor which can cause complications are debts owed by other people to the deceased (these are classed as personalty; see **Chapters 3** and **6**). It is an absolute duty of the PRs to call for repayment of those debts and to collect in that repayment. They must further make sure that they have possession of any items which give control over the deceased's assets: bank or building society passbooks, debit or credit cards, and, if appropriate, passwords and other security details. Not to do this is a *devastavit* (particularly if it results in the loss or removal of property out of the estate) and a breach of their fiduciary duty to the beneficiaries.

Revision tip

Note that it is possible for testators to set out in the will that they 'forgive' a debt – that is, an instruction to the executors not to ask for repayment – but unless that instruction is expressly present in a will, then the borrower must pay back the money to the PRs. The death of the lender does not wipe the debt-slate clean.

Managing the assets

We have already seen that under the common law duty not to waste estate property (*devastavit*), PRs must be extremely careful to preserve and where possible enhance the value of assets in the estate. We have also seen that the statutory duty of care under s 1 of the Trustee Act 2000 applies where PRs are carrying out specific administrative tasks for the estate, including the acquisition of land. On the other hand, PRs must not personally profit from their position as PRs, even if they cause no loss to the estate by doing so, as this is a breach of their fiduciary duty.

Let's look first of all at the two broad headings of property that will fall into the estate – personalty and realty (land) – and then we will look at some of the issues that face PRs in administration.

Personalty

As well as the chattels (see **Chapter 5**) which formerly belonged to the deceased (including valuable chattels like jewellery, watches and motor vehicles), PRs may also have investments and money on deposit in their hands for an extended period of time while the estate is administered. We have seen that the PRs have the investment powers given to trustees under ss 3 and 4 of the Trustee Act 2000, which they must exercise subject to the duty of care in s 1. Remember that this duty/standard of care applies to *all* PRs when exercising a power of investment, even if they are not trustees of a will trust (we will look at will trusts in **Chapter 11**). To refresh your memory on these duties, see *Revise SQE: Trusts Law*.

It is worth emphasising the following aspects of ss 3 and 4 (again, see *Revise SQE: Trusts Law* for more detail):
- PRs have the power to invest under s 3 as if they were the absolute owner of the assets
- they must always consider the standard investment criteria under s 4 and review the investments from time to time (s 4(2))
- they should obtain proper advice from a person suitably qualified to give that advice before exercising any of these powers: s 5.

PRs cannot therefore simply gather up the deceased's property and omit to check whether the investments that have been made are suitable and meet the standard investment criteria: they must also review them. There is an overall statutory duty to take care, which includes making sure that the investments retain as much of their value as possible. Being a PR is always an active job and never a passive one. If the PR has professional qualifications or claims to have professional qualifications – as a lawyer, accountant or investment manager, for example – then the s 1 standard will be the higher one (see **Practice example 8.1**).

Practice example 8.1

Hasibah and Jatinder are the executors of Flinders' estate. At his death, Flinders had the sum of £55,000 invested in a high-interest fixed-term bond. Flinders could not access the bond for 10 years. Two months after Flinders died, the bond matured and paid out £75,000. Hasibah and

Jatinder paid the money into Flinders' current account at the Mammon Bank, which pays out no interest at all, and left it there for a further 18 months while they administered the rest of the estate.

By way of background, Hasibah was a family friend of Flinders and was not professionally qualified; Jatinder was an accountant.

Have they breached any of their duties as PRs, and if so, how?

This is a breach of the PRs' s 1 duty of care in relation to their powers of investing. By their actions, the PRs have lost any interest which would have accrued on the sum of £75,000 over a period of 18 months. Even in a basic savings account paying 1%, this sum would have earned over £1200, which is the loss that they have caused to the estate. Note that because this is a breach of the duty of care, the PRs are personally liable for that loss.

Jatinder, being professionally qualified, will be held to the higher standard of duty, and Hasibah to the basic standard.

As Hasibah and Jatinder have also wasted estate property, they have also committed a *devastavit*.

Land

If the estate contains any land at all, then s 1 of the Trusts of Land and Appointment of Trustees Act 1996 (TLATA) states that a *trust of land* is automatically imposed on that land (see also **Chapter 11**). This makes the PRs trustees of land, and the statute gives them some very wide powers, which again are the powers of an absolute owner (s 6(1)). They can, for example, manage the land if it is rented out; they can rent it out themselves and put the rental income back into the estate; and they can sell it.

Remember, however, that if there is a will, the executors of a will must do exactly what the will tells them to do. If a will specifies that a person is to be able to occupy a house for life, then the executors cannot simply decide that the life interest is burdensome or inconvenient: they must give effect to that instruction from the testator. Their general powers are always limited by the express words of the testator.

Businesses

The deceased may have owned and run their own business (you may like to read this section in conjunction with *Revise SQE: Business Law and Practice*). If they ran it together with one or more other people as a partnership, or as a limited company in which the deceased was a director, the partnership agreement or the company articles will usually set out what happens to the business when the deceased dies.

Matters can be more complicated if the deceased ran a business alone as a sole trader. You will recall that the PRs must not waste any estate assets. If the deceased left a business, therefore, the PRs cannot simply refuse to have anything to do with that business and leave it to fail. If they did this, they would significantly reduce the value of the business and possibly take it into insolvency, which would be an obvious act of waste. They must, therefore, make sure that any business contracts are fulfilled. There is one exception to this, and that is where the contract was for personal services to be carried out by the deceased: a contract for personal services cannot now be fulfilled and the PRs are under no obligation to do so.

Unless the will expressly gives executors the power to carry on the deceased's business indefinitely, the PRs should attempt to either sell or wind up the business within the 'executor's year'. Their objective within that time is to sell the business as a going concern or to wind it up. Where the will, if there is one, has not authorised them to carry on the business indefinitely, any liabilities that a PR incurs while carrying on a business are the personal responsibility of that PR. So, for example, if an administrator running the deceased's printing business under the general rule orders a crate of paper for that business, it is the administrator's personal responsibility to pay. PRs can, in some circumstances, claim an indemnity from the estate – that is, they can claim that the estate should pay them back the money they have spent.

If the PR is able to claim that the liability/debt was taken out either because the PR has specific authority to run the business (usually under the will) or because the PR is in the course of realising the assets during administration, then the claim for indemnity is likely to be successful. They can also claim an indemnity if the creditor knew the position and assented to it.

PAYING THE ESTATE LIABILITIES: SELLING ESTATE ASSETS

The PRs have a general power to sell. This is particularly significant where there are debts owed *by* the deceased which have to be paid: these debts will also survive the deceased's death.

You will remember that before the estate can be distributed, the PRs must identify all of the liabilities and debts owed by the estate and pay them. Only once that has been done can the final distribution of the estate assets be made. The PRs' duty is to pay the debts with 'due diligence', and all well-advised PRs will attempt to pay the debts within the first year after the grant is made.

Revision tip

You should note that PRs *must* pay off all the deceased's debts first before they can start to distribute the property to the beneficiaries. This may mean that by the time the debts have been paid off, there is not enough in the estate to make all of the gifts intended by the testator; if this is the case, then those gifts cannot be made. Debts must be paid first before any part of the estate is distributed.

Estate debts and PRs' liability

As well as any debts owed by the deceased during their lifetime (including personal loans, mortgages and even household matters like gas and phone bills), the PRs must pay debts that have arisen after death, including any tax due on the estate, the costs of the funeral and the costs of administering the estate. These include professional fees, and a well-drafted will generally includes a charging clause allowing any solicitor executor to charge fees for their work on the estate.

All of these liabilities can add up to a considerable sum. Sometimes they add up to more than the estate is worth: in this case, the estate will be insolvent. This presents new problems for the PRs, but that is not a topic that we deal with in SQE.

The PRs are responsible for payment of all of the deceased's debts after death and they can be asked to pay those debts personally, even years after all of the rest of the estate has been distributed. To avoid this risk, the PRs may decide to advertise for creditors under s 27 of the Trustee Act 1925, saying that the PRs are intending to distribute the estate and asking any creditor with a claim to come forward. If this is done, and no creditors come forward, the PRs have no personal liability to creditors who appear later.

Liquidity

Even if the estate is worth more than the liabilities, however, the PRs may face the specific issue that there is not enough cash in the bank to pay off the debts; in other words, there is not sufficient liquidity in the estate. The issues that arise can be seen in **Practice example 8.2**.

Practice example 8.2

Danny and Jeff are the administrators of the estate of Liz, who died intestate. On investigating the liabilities and assets, Danny and Jeff have established that the total amount of the liabilities, including inheritance tax, personal loans, funeral expenses and costs of administration, is £83,500.

Most of Liz's estate is made up of her home, which is worth £365,000 free of mortgage. Apart from this, the estate comprises the sum of £40,000 in a savings account with Whitehorse Bank, a stocks and investment portfolio worth £35,000 and a car worth £15,000. The assets therefore total £455,000.

Can Danny and Jeff pay the estate liabilities in these circumstances?

There is certainly enough in the estate (£455,000) to pay the liabilities (£83,500), but the problem for Danny and Jeff is that most of it is

> tied up and therefore illiquid. Only £40,000 is available as cash. The remainder is either in the house, or in the stocks and investment portfolio, or in the car.
>
> In order to pay off the liabilities and get to the position where they can distribute the estate, Danny and Jeff will have to sell at least two of the three remaining assets. But have they the power to do so?

The short answer to this last question in **Practice example 8.2** is yes, though there may still be issues for Danny and Jeff. However, first of all, let's look at the power to sell.

PRs are given the power to sell personalty under s 39(1)(i) of the AEA 1925. The crucial factor about s 39(1)(i) is that it confirms that any PR selling an estate asset can give good title to that asset: that is, they can pass on legal ownership to another person. This is vital, as buyers in good faith from a PR need to know that an aggrieved beneficiary of the deceased, or creditor, cannot pursue them for the return of the item. The power extends to items that have been specifically bequeathed: even if the testator wanted an item to go to a particular individual, if it is needed to satisfy the liabilities of the estate, the PRs can take it and sell it (see **abatement**, below).

All of the deceased's interests in real property pass to the PRs under s 1(1) of the AEA 1925, though the PRs' power to sell now arises because s 39(1)(ii) of the AEA gives them 'as respects the real estate, all the functions conferred on them by Part I of the Trusts of Land and Appointment of Trustees Act 1996', which include the ability to deal with the land as an absolute owner under TLATA s 6(1). The fundamental power of an absolute owner is the power to sell, although you may want to note that it also includes the power to mortgage or lease.

These powers, which combined together amount to an ability on the part of the PRs to sell any part of the personal or real estate of the deceased, can be used to realise assets and raise money to pay off any debts or meet other liabilities.

Abatement

However, the PRs are not able simply to pick the assets which they think are most suitable for paying off the liabilities. Section 34(3) of the AEA 1925 obliges them to go through the assets in a particular order (see **Table 8.1** and **Practice example 8.3**). Although these provisions apply in the case of all estates, whether intestate or testate, you will see that their main relevance is to estates where there is a valid will. This order, and the process of working through the order to pay the liabilities, is known as abatement.

Table 8.1: Order of assets to pay liabilities under s 34(3) of the AEA 1925

Property which was not bequeathed or devised in the will: the classic example is property which was in a lapsed gift and which did not fall into residue (see **Chapter 3**) though the PRs can retain an amount to pay any pecuniary legacies	If none or not enough, then:
Residue though again, the PRs can retain an amount to pay any pecuniary legacies	If none or not enough, then:
Any money specifically set aside by the deceased to pay debts	If none or not enough, then:
Any legacy or devise to any beneficiary charged with the payment of debts	If none or not enough, then:
Money retained to pay pecuniary legacies (see **Chapter 3**)	If none or not enough, then:
Property specifically bequeathed (eg specific gifts of valuable chattels or land)	Sold off in order of value, greatest to smallest if none or not enough, then:
Property over which the PRs have a general power	Beyond the scope of this book, but check your wider reading

Revision tip

Remember, the PRs cannot start distributing the estate until they have paid off all of the liabilities. This duty takes precedence over any express instructions in the will, or the rules of intestacy. If money given in a pecuniary legacy is required to pay a debt, then it must be used for that purpose and not given to the legatee.

Practice example 8.3

Pippa and Rory are the executors of Brian's estate. They have calculated that the liabilities of the estate total £215,000 and the gross value of the assets is £780,000.

They must first look to see whether there is any property in Brian's estate which was not disposed of by will; for example, lapsed or disclaimed gifts which did not fall into residue. As there are none of these in Brian's estate, they move on to consider whether there is sufficient property in the residue. At this stage, they are allowed to set aside a fund which will pay out any specific pecuniary legacies in the will. The residue has a total value of £165,000 but Pippa and Rory are allowed to set aside £25,000 of that to pay specific pecuniary legacies, leaving a balance of £140,000. This sum can be used to part pay the liabilities, but as it is not enough, Pippa and Rory must continue to work through the list.

Next, they must consider whether the deceased left a sum of money which was specifically to be used to pay his debts. Brian did leave the sum of £50,000 in his will to do this, so Pippa and Rory can use this sum, which means they now have a total of £190,000 to pay the debts of the estate, but they are still £25,000 short, so they must continue to work through the list. The next class of property is any property which was bequeathed under the will but specifically charged with the payment of debts, or simply charged with those payments. There is no such property in this estate, so they pass on to the next item in the list, which is the money set aside for pecuniary legacies. In this case, that is £25,000 and that money does in fact take the total amount available for payment of the estate's debts to £215,000.

Will the beneficiaries of the will still receive their gifts in these circumstances?

In the circumstances outlined above, no beneficiary who was left a pecuniary legacy will get that money because Pippa and Rory must use it to pay off the liabilities first. You will see that if this still had not been enough, the next item on the list would have been other property (that is, not sums of money) specifically bequeathed or devised. That would include, for example, a devise of land under the will, so beneficiaries who get sums of money under the will are more likely to have their gifts taken away than beneficiaries who receive valuable chattels or land.

Revision tip

Although the order outlined in **Table 8.1** and **Practice example 8.3** is known as the 'statutory order' and will be followed unless there is a direction in the will to the contrary, you should note that a testator can in fact vary this order in their will.

DISTRIBUTING THE ASSETS

Once the PRs have calculated the total amount of the estate's liabilities and worked out exactly how they are to be paid, their next duty is to take action and pay them.

After this has been done, the PRs are finally in a position to distribute the assets, either according to the provisions of the will if there is one or according to the intestacy rules if there is a full intestacy. If there is a partial intestacy, the provisions of the will are carried out to the extent that they are effective, and the intestacy rules are applied to any ineffective provisions.

Revision tip

Note that for their own protection, the PRs should obtain a receipt from every beneficiary to acknowledge that the legacy has been paid or property transferred. This causes particular issues with minors – beneficiaries under the age of 18 – who under the general law cannot give a good receipt. The rules on this point are complex and outside the scope of this book, but you should ensure that you are aware of them.

Although distribution is a relatively straightforward exercise for the PRs, there are a few issues which are more complex.

Uncertainty about specific beneficiaries

Sometimes the PRs know who a beneficiary is – whether under a will or an intestacy – but not where they are (or even if they are still alive). If the PRs are instructed to divide the property in equal shares, eg between all living nieces, this can cause problems. If there are three nieces but the PRs can only find two of them, what should they do in this situation? Should the two nieces they have found receive one-half each, or one-third?

In these circumstances, the PRs may do three things. They can for one thing advertise their intention to distribute the estate. If no person comes forward making a claim on part of the estate, then the PRs are absolved from any personal liability under s 27 of the Trustee Act 1925.

They may also make an application to the court for what is called a 'Benjamin' order, after the case of *Re Benjamin* [1902] 1 Ch 723. The application asks the court to order that the PRs should distribute the estate on the basis that the missing beneficiary predeceased the deceased.

If the Benjamin order is made, it completely protects the executors from liability if the missing beneficiary does return after the estate has been distributed. However, it does not mean that the missing beneficiary has lost their entitlement to their share of the estate, and, in the event they reappear, they could in those circumstances seek payment from the other beneficiaries of their share. A Benjamin order is therefore not a complete answer to the missing beneficiary problem, because although it protects the PRs, it does not completely protect the beneficiaries themselves.

The final option for the PRs would be to take out an insurance policy in case the missing beneficiary turns up: this missing beneficiary insurance policy is a more complete protection because it covers the beneficiaries as well as the PRs and it is an allowable administration expense, so can be paid for out of the estate. These days, it is much more likely where there is a missing beneficiary that the PRs will take out an insurance policy, perhaps combined with one or both of the other courses of action.

Passing the property on: appropriations and assents

We had a brief look at **appropriations** in **Chapter 5** in the context of intestacy, but they also apply where there is a will. In this section, we will also look at **assents**.

Key term: appropriation

An appropriation is a power by which PRs can give a specific item within the estate to a beneficiary as part of that beneficiary's entitlement: it is a sort of part payment and payment in kind.

Key term: assent

An assent is a straightforward transfer of a chattel or an interest in land from the ownership of the PRs to the ownership of a beneficiary.

Let's look at these by way of **Practice example 8.4**.

Practice example 8.4

Barry and Vanessa are the PRs of Bryn, a widower who died intestate. Under the intestacy rules, Bryn's children Cariad and Lloyd inherit his estate in equal shares. The total value of the estate is £80,000 and the estate comprises (1) the sum of £20,000 in the bank; (2) Bryn's vintage Land Rover car, valued at £20,000; and (3) a plot of land valued at £40,000.

Barry and Vanessa have the power to sell the car and the land in order to pay Cariad and Lloyd their entitlements in cash. However, Cariad and Lloyd have discussed the matter between them and would like the distribution of the estate to be that Cariad will take the £20,000 in cash and the Land Rover car, and Lloyd will take the plot of land. Each of them is getting the exact value of their interest. They ask the administrators to distribute the estate in this way.

Is this possible?

Under s 41 of the AEA 1925, all PRs have the power to appropriate items in the estate in or towards satisfaction of any legacy left by the deceased or any interest or share in the deceased's property though they must obtain the consent of any person beneficially entitled to the appropriated property or any income from it (s 41(1)(ii)). The administrators therefore have the power to make up part of Cariad's £40,000 entitlement by passing the Land Rover car on to her. Under s 41(1)(ii), Lloyd's consent will be required, but that will be forthcoming, as Lloyd has already agreed to dividing the estate in this way. This is an intestacy, but you should note that most wills specifically vary the statutory power of appropriation to dispense with the need for the consent of other beneficiaries.

The administrators must now consider how they can make a straight transfer of the Land Rover to Cariad and the land to Lloyd. The method

of transfer out of the hands of the PRs (remember that until distribution, the PRs own all of the assets) and into the hands of the beneficiaries is the assent.

As the Land Rover is personalty, all that is required of the administrators is to indicate that the chattel is not required for the administration of the estate and that it can pass to Cariad. They can do that in writing, or orally, or even by way of conduct: although express wording will make things clear, it is not required.

The position with the land is different, however, and an assent of land must be in writing and must name the person who is to receive the land (s 36(4) of the AEA 1925), in this case Lloyd.

■ KEY POINT CHECKLIST

This chapter has covered the following key knowledge points. You can structure your revision around these, making sure to recall the key details for each point, as covered in this chapter.

- PRs' duties of care: common law, statutory, fiduciary.
- Protection from liability.
- Getting in/collecting the estate.
- Managing the assets.
- Paying the estate liabilities and selling estate assets.
- Abatement.
- Distributing the assets.
- Appropriations and assents.

■ KEY TERMS AND CONCEPTS

- duties of care (**page 125**)
- appropriation (**page 135**)
- assent (**page 135**)

■ SQE1-STYLE QUESTIONS

QUESTION 1

A man was appointed as an administrator of an intestate estate. The estate included a valuable antique wristwatch worth £50,000. The man failed to make arrangements for storing the watch correctly and it sustained damage which reduced its value to £25,000. The man then delayed selling the watch for a further two years, by which time its market value had dropped to £20,000. In the meantime, the man fulfilled a contract for the supply of goods at the price of £40,000 which the deceased (a sole trader) had signed shortly before he died, but made an unauthorised personal commission of £12,500 for himself in the process. However, the man also negotiated to reduce the sale price from £40,000 to £35,000. Finally, the man neglected to pursue a debtor of the deceased until the debt was no longer legally enforceable.

Which of the man's actions was not an act of waste?

A. Causing damage to the wristwatch by failing to store it adequately.

B. Making an unauthorised personal commission out of estate assets.

C. Delaying the sale of an estate asset until the value of the asset had been reduced by £5,000.

D. Negotiating to reduce the sale price of the goods supplied under the contract.

E. Failing to collect the money under the debt.

QUESTION 2

A woman ran a computer consultancy business as a sole trader. The woman had two revenue streams: one was providing her services as a programmer and consultant to businesses seeking advice on banking software; the other was the supply of mainframe computers and their associated hardware. The woman died intestate. Letters of administration were granted to the woman's husband as PR.

At the time of the woman's death, she had two contracts which she was due to fulfil the following month. The first was to work in-house at a city of London bank as a consultant and advisor on the bank's current banking software ('the consultancy work'). The second was to deliver a mainframe computer to a bank in Paris. The woman had ordered the computer hardware and had paid a deposit for it at the time of her death, but still had to pay the balance and arrange for the transportation of the computer to the Paris client.

The PR has no knowledge of, or expertise in, computing or finance. There is not enough money in the estate to pay the balance due on the computer.

Which of the following best describes the PR's position?

A. The PR must not involve himself in the business at all as the business does not fall into the estate and therefore this would be intermeddling.

B. The PR does not have to perform either contract because both contracts ended automatically with the woman's death.

C. The PR does not have to pay the balance due on the computer, or deliver it to the client, because there is not enough money in the estate to do so.

D. The PR must arrange for the consultancy work to be done by a third party because this contract did not end with the woman's death.

E. The PR must pay the balance due on the computer and deliver it to the Paris client, but does not have to arrange for the consultancy work to be done.

QUESTION 3

Three beneficiaries under a will have asked for advice about whether they have a claim against the executors. The residuary estate under the will contained a portfolio of shares in a private company which is held by the executors as trustees and which gives the trust a controlling interest in the company. The trust is for the benefit of one of the beneficiaries for life, then the remainder to be divided equally between the two remaining beneficiaries. The executors used the voting rights attached to the shares to be appointed as managing director and financial director respectively of the company, telling the beneficiaries that they had done this in order to manage the company for the benefit of the estate. The shares have doubled in value since the executors were appointed as directors. The executors themselves have each received a salary for acting as directors of the company.

Which of the following is the best advice that can be given to the beneficiaries?

A. The executors have committed a *devastavit* in that they have caused loss and damage to the estate for which they are personally liable.

B. The executors are in breach of their duty of care in that they have not diversified the estate's investment in the shares.

C. The executors are in breach of the fiduciary duty to the beneficiaries in that they have made an unauthorised profit.

D. The executors are in breach of their duty of care in that they have failed to get in the assets of the estate in a reasonable time.

E. The executors are not in breach of any duty.

QUESTION 4

Two executors of a will have sought advice from a solicitor. The executors need to apply the assets of the estate to pay off the total liabilities of the estate, which amount to £43,000. There is no residuary gift in the will.

Which of the following assets must the executors use first to pay the debts?

A. A bequest of an investment portfolio valued at £60,000 'subject to the payment of all of my debts and funeral and testamentary expenses'.

B. The sum of £75,000 which the executors have set aside to pay all of the specific pecuniary legacies.

C. A specific devise of a 100-year lease in a commercial property.

D. A failed pecuniary legacy of £40,000 to the deceased's brother, who died two years before the deceased.

E. The sum of £35,000 which the deceased specifically set aside in the will for payment of all debts and other liabilities of the estate.

QUESTION 5

Under her will, an aunt left a sum of £10,000 to each of her nieces. She also left a collection of antique jewellery which forms part of the residue. This jewellery collection includes a diamond ring which has been valued at £2,500. Both of the nieces have asked the executors if they can have the diamond ring as part of their legacy under the will. There is only one diamond ring. The first niece requested the ring from the executors three weeks before the second niece. The second niece says that her aunt repeatedly told her that she could have the ring when the aunt died. The will contains a clause which varies the statutory power of appropriation to dispense with any obligation on the part of the executors to obtain the consent of the beneficiaries.

Which of the following options best sets out the executors' position?

A. The executors have no power to give the ring to either the first niece or the second niece because their legacies are pecuniary only.

B. The executors have no power to give the ring to either the first niece or the second great-niece because the agreement of both nieces is required for a gift of the ring.

C. The executors must give the ring to the first niece as she requested the ring earlier than the second niece.

D. The executors must give the ring to the second niece because it was promised to her by her aunt.

E. The executors have the power to give the ring to either niece or to neither of them.

■ ANSWERS TO QUESTIONS

Answers to 'What do you know already?' questions at the start of the chapter

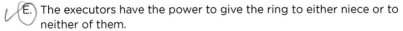

1) False. Debts outlive the creditor unless the creditor expressly 'forgives' them. They must be repaid to the estate.

2) The PRs are not given a time limit within which to wind up and distribute the estate, but they should bear in mind the 'executor's year' and attempt to distribute the estate within a reasonable time.

3) Unless there is a will which restricts their powers in some way, the PRs have all the powers of an absolute owner and can sell, mortgage or rent out any land in the estate.

4) They should advertise for the missing beneficiary under s 27 of the Trustee Act 1925 and they should also take out a missing beneficiary insurance policy. They may also wish to apply for a Benjamin order.

Answers to end-of-chapter SQE1-style questions

Question 1:
The correct answer was B. It is possible for a PR to make a personal profit out of estate assets without causing any loss or damage to the assets themselves. If no loss or damage is caused, then the default is not a *devastavit*. As the other options all involve mismanagement of the estate causing loss to all beneficiaries, they are all examples of *devastavit*. B, however, is an example of a breach of fiduciary duty, not an act of waste, and the PR would be liable to account to the estate and the beneficiaries for any unauthorised profit.

Question 2:
The correct answer was E. The contract to carry out the consultancy work was a contract for personal services, so it automatically came to an end on the woman's death; the contract to deliver the mainframe computer was not, and did not. A is incorrect because the woman was a sole trader and therefore her business did fall into the estate. B is incorrect because although the consultancy contract came to an end, the supply contract did not. C is incorrect because the PR should pay the balance out of his own pocket and then claim an indemnity from the estate; this would be available from the profits made as a result of the supply contract. D is incorrect because the personal services contract came to an end on the woman's death.

Question 3:
The correct answer was C. The executors have obtained a profit by virtue of their position as executors. As fiduciaries, they must avoid conflicts of interest and in particular must avoid making unauthorised profits. The executors have not caused any loss or damage to the estate, whether as administrators or trustees – on the contrary, they have doubled the value of the estate's interest. For that reason, A is incorrect. We are not told what the total investment portfolio is, but we are told that it includes the shares in the private company and not that it is composed entirely of those shares; there does not therefore seem to be a diversification problem and B would appear to be incorrect. The duty to get the estate in within a reasonable time does not apply to the assets in a will trust

(see **Chapter 11**), which continues (in this case) for the life of the life tenant, so D is incorrect. E cannot be correct because there clearly is a breach of a fiduciary duty.

Question 4:

The correct answer was D. This is because when paying debts, failed gifts come out of the estate first (see **Table 8.1**). You will note that this would not be quite enough to pay off all the debts, and a balance of £3,000 would have to come from the second item in line, which (as there is no residue in this case) would be money specifically set aside for payment of debts (E). Although this would in fact fully pay off the debt, the next item would be property charged with payment of debts (A), then sums set aside to pay pecuniary legacies (B), followed by the specific devise of land (C), which is the lowest on the list.

Question 5:

The correct answer was E. This is because the executors always have a power to appropriate a part of the estate in satisfaction or part satisfaction of a legacy (A is therefore incorrect in principle). The statutory power requires the executors to obtain the consent of all beneficiaries, but that requirement has been dispensed with under the will, so agreement of both the nieces is not required (therefore B is incorrect). The timing of the requests, or the fact that there was some informal discussion about the ring by the deceased before death, does not oblige the executors to exercise their power of appropriation one way or the other (therefore C and D are incorrect).

■ KEY CASES, RULES, STATUTES AND INSTRUMENTS

The SQE1 Assessment Specification does not require you to know specific statute sections or case names for this topic. However, we recommend that you can recognise and define the following, which have all appeared in this chapter:

- Administration of Estates Act ss 2(1), 25, 34(3), 36(4), 39(1), 41, 44
- Trustee Act 1925 ss 27, 61
- Trusts of Land and Appointment of Trustees Act 1996 ss 1, 6(1)
- Trustee Act 2000 ss 1, 3, 4, 5
- *Re Benjamin* [1902] 1 Ch 723.

9

Claims under the Inheritance (Provision for Family and Dependants) Act 1975

■ MAKE SURE YOU KNOW

This chapter provides an overview of claims under the Inheritance (Provision for Family and Dependants) Act 1975 (although the Act is sometimes known for short as I(PFD)A, we are going to refer to it as 'the Inheritance Act' in this chapter). As with all topics for the SQE1 wills assessment, pay particular attention not just to the definition of the rules but also how they work in practice. This is one of the statutes you are expected to know for the SQE1 assessment, so ensure that you can not only identify the important sections by number but also explain their meanings and apply them. In particular, you are expected to be able to identify who is and who is not entitled to be an applicant, the grounds for any application and the relevant time limits (with clear reference to the relevant sections).

■ SQE ASSESSMENT ADVICE

As you work through this chapter, remember to pay particular attention in your revision to:
- the meaning of the correct 'reasonable financial provision' test
- the two standards of financial provision, the 'maintenance standard' and the 'spousal standard'
- all of the categories of possible claimants under s 1(1) of the Inheritance Act
- all of the factors which the court must consider under s 3 of the Inheritance Act
- how to conduct the 'balancing exercise' by which the court reaches its decision.

■ WHAT DO YOU KNOW ALREADY?

Have a go at these questions before reading this chapter. If you find some difficult or cannot remember the answers, make a note to look more closely at that area during your revision.

1) Can a beneficiary under a valid will make an application under the
    Inheritance Act?

    [What are Inheritance Act claims and why are they important?, page 143]

2) True or false? The sister or brother of a deceased person has an
    automatic right to claim under the Inheritance Act.

    [The basic machinery of the Inheritance Act, page 144]

3) True or false? When deciding whether or not to make an Inheritance Act
    award to an applicant, the court cannot consider any amount received
    by any other beneficiary of the estate.

    [The basic machinery of the Inheritance Act, page 144]

4) Can a person who has inherited under the intestacy rules make an
    Inheritance Act claim on a deceased's estate?

    [The basic machinery of the Inheritance Act, page 144]

WHAT ARE INHERITANCE ACT CLAIMS AND WHY ARE THEY IMPORTANT?

In this chapter we are going to look at claims made under the Inheritance
Act 1975. In brief, these are claims made by persons who can argue that they
have not received 'reasonable provision' under either the will or the rules of
intestacy (see **Chapter 5**), or (if applicable) the combination of the two.

The Act therefore represents an important opportunity for the courts to
correct matters if a person who could reasonably have been expected to
receive adequate financial support from the deceased's estate has not done so.
If that person falls within certain categories and can argue that the deceased
should have made more financial provision for them, that person can make a
claim. From now on, we are going to call this person 'the applicant'.

The cause of this failure to provide can either be a deliberate decision by the
deceased – to cut the applicant out of the will completely, for example – or the
accidental result of poor planning or no planning (including an unintended
total or partial intestacy, which we looked at briefly in **Chapter 5**). Both
of these situations can give rise to an Inheritance Act claim (see **Practice
example 9.1**).

Practice example 9.1

Ramon died intestate as a result of a car accident. At the time of his
death, he had been living with his partner, Lulu, for ten years and they
had two children, aged four and nine years old when Ramon died.
However, Ramon had never divorced his wife Mimi. Ramon had always
intended to make a new will, but had never done so. His estate was
worth £240,000.

What happens in this situation?

As the amount of Ramon's estate was less than the amount of the statutory legacy, and as Mimi was Ramon's spouse at the time of his death, Mimi receives all of the £240,000 and Lulu and the children receive nothing. Ramon has unintentionally disinherited his partner and children. Lulu should therefore consider submitting a claim under the Inheritance Act on her own behalf and on behalf of the children.

In **Practice example 9.1**, you will see that Lulu and the two infant children have been left without a home and with no financial support, while on the other hand Mimi has received all of Ramon's money and property. You may immediately have a reaction about whether or not these outcomes are 'fair' in a general, non-legal sense. *One of the first, and most difficult, things to learn about Inheritance Act applications are that they are not about 'fairness' in the sense that a non-lawyer might use the term.* The only question for the court is whether the financial *provision* made by the intestacy for the applicant – and no provision at all has been made for Lulu – is *reasonable* provision.

Revision tip

Keep at the forefront of your mind that the question in Inheritance Act claims is *never* 'Was the deceased acting reasonably?' or 'Was the deceased being fair?' These are always the wrong questions. The right question is instead 'Was the *financial result* of the decision(s) made by the deceased reasonable?' The two things are very different.

THE BASIC MACHINERY OF THE INHERITANCE ACT

We are now going to look at how the Act works in practice by setting out in overview the six steps the court will go through in each case when deciding whether or not an applicant has made a good claim for financial provision. Keep these steps, *and the order in which we are approaching them*, in mind as we go through the remainder of the chapter:

1) *Standing*: In order to make a claim under the Inheritance Act, a potential applicant must first fall within one of the categories set out at s 1(1) of the Act, or they cannot make any claim at all.

2) *Timing*: The application must be made no later than six months after the grant of probate or letters of administration (see **Chapter 7**), unless the circumstances are very exceptional.

3) *What the applicant received from the estate*: Have they been left any money or property?

4) *The relevant standard of financial provision*: If the applicant is not a spouse/civil partner of the deceased (we are going to describe all such people as 'spouses'), how much does the applicant need for their maintenance? If the applicant is a spouse of the deceased, what would

the applicant have received if the marriage/civil partnership had ended in divorce rather than death?

5) Bearing this latter figure in mind, was the *financial provision* made by the deceased *reasonable* (using the balancing exercise under s 3 of the Act)? If it was reasonable, then the applicant will receive nothing.

6) If it was not reasonable, then the court will exercise its *powers* under s 2 of the Act to redistribute the estate to assist the applicant.

Let's now look at each of these steps in more detail.

STEP 1: STANDING

Only the following persons have standing to make an application under s 1(1) of the Inheritance Act:

1) the current spouse or civil partner of the deceased (*not*, under this heading, ex-spouses and civil partners from whom the deceased is divorced) (s 1(1)(a))

2) a former spouse or former civil partner of the deceased, provided that person has not entered into a new marriage or civil partnership (s 1(1)(b))

3) a cohabitee of the deceased (defined in s 1(a) of the Act as a person who was living in the same household as the deceased as a spouse or civil partner for the 'whole of the period of two years ending immediately before the date when the deceased died') (the 'cohabitee' category) (s 1(1)(ba))

4) a child of the deceased (see explanation below) (s 1(1)(c))

5) any person who was treated as a 'child of the family' by the deceased (this includes stepchildren but also any other person who is not a stepchild but was treated by the deceased in the same way that the deceased would have treated any child of the family (s 1(1)(d))

6) any person (not being a person included in the foregoing paragraphs of this subsection) who was being maintained, either wholly or partly, by the deceased immediately before the deceased died (the 'dependant' category) (s 1(1)(e)).

Note that there are, therefore, some very close relatives of the deceased who do not have an automatic right to make an application under the Act, including brothers or sisters, parents, grandparents and cousins. These persons may be able to bring their claim as part of one of the other categories (for example, as dependants), but if they cannot do so, then they cannot claim.

While a detailed examination of all of the categories is beyond the scope of this book, it is worth taking a closer look at four of them in particular: children; those treated as children of the family; cohabitees; and dependants. These are the categories which can cause the most problems at Step 1.

Children: s 1(4)

All biological children of the deceased automatically have standing to make an application under s 1(4), whether they are legitimate or not, including any illegitimate children that the deceased had not acknowledged. Children adopted by the deceased also have automatic standing under s 1(4). 'Child' does not exclusively mean 'infant': an adult child can also make an application. However, an adult child may have significant difficulties at Steps 2 and 3 of the process. As a general rule, an adult child who is capable of earning their own living will find it difficult to claim that a parent's estate has not made reasonable provision for them, even if that estate has left them nothing (see **Financial needs and resources of the applicant** below).

It is sometimes said that adult children can only succeed where there is a 'moral obligation' of some kind (*Re Coventry* [1980] Ch 461), but that is a wide class and can include, for example, children who have been promised by a parent that property, or a particular item of property, will be left to them; situations in which the deceased was a stepparent and the bulk of the estate comes from the adult child's biological parent; and of course situations where the child is still not financially independent for some reason, including children still in full-time study and adult children who cannot work because they are ill.

Bear in mind that there is no absolute rule that an adult child cannot make a claim for reasonable financial provision even if they are working; and also bear in mind, once again, that the test is *not* whether the parent acted reasonably in leaving nothing, or very little, to that child.

Children of the family: s 1(5)

It is tempting to consider that the category 'treated as a child of the family' (s 1(5)) is intended for purely stepchildren, but this is not the case. What is important here is not how the applicant is defined but how the deceased treated them. Some stepchildren are very closely woven into the deceased's blended family and there is no doubt that the deceased, for example, paid for all of their school expenses and for their holidays, and so on; some stepchildren spend most of their time with their other family, and the deceased does not have a great deal of interaction with them. It is not sufficient for an applicant to say only, 'I was the deceased's stepchild and therefore I was a child of the family'. The key question is *treatment*.

Cohabitees: s 1(3)

To be a 'cohabitee', the applicant must do more than live under the same roof as the deceased: the two must be living together in the style of spouses, even though they are not married/in a civil partnership. In broad terms, the question for the court is whether or not the two are regarded generally, by those who know them, as 'a couple'. If the answer is 'no', then the applicant will not have standing.

Being part of the same 'household' implies a sense of sharing more than just a mere roof. If two persons live in two separate flats in the same building, but do not, for example, share their household goods such as cooking utensils, bedding or furniture, and operate separate budgets for cooking, cleaning and repairs, the court is likely to see them as making up two small independent households rather than one single household.

> ## Revision tip
> Note that parties can live in the style of spouses without any evidence that they have a sexual or intimate relationship: it is *not* essential for a claim under s 1(3) to prove that the parties were in a sexual relationship, only that they formed the same household.

The cohabitation period must be for two years immediately prior to the date of death: in other words, if the deceased died on 25 March 2021, then the applicant must prove that they were living with the deceased by at least 25 March 2019. If they moved in with the deceased on 25 April 2019, then they are not a cohabitee for these purposes and do not have standing.

Temporary absences from home, however, will not stop the clock running on a cohabitation period. This point quite often arises because the deceased has had to go in to hospital for a period prior to death, but can sometimes also arise where one or other of the cohabitees has had to spend time away on vacation or on business.

Dependants

This is undoubtedly the most complex category. We have seen that the basic requirement is that the applicant must have been 'maintained, wholly or partly' by the deceased 'immediately' before the deceased died. Applicants have sometimes found it hard to prove either that the deceased was in fact financially supporting them, or that the financial support was happening right up until the point that the deceased died, or both.

> ## Revision tip
> A person is not being 'maintained' by the deceased if the deceased was paying the person a proper wage under a contract for services or employment. So, for example, a carer who looked after the deceased, but was paid the market rate for their services by the deceased, cannot claim to have been 'maintained' by the deceased: s 1(3). To put it another way, the person must not have given 'full valuable consideration' for the money paid over by the deceased (that is, the deceased paid the person roughly what the services were worth).

Bear in mind also that 'maintenance' generally means several payments made over a period of time, even if not at regular intervals, rather than a one-off payment. The court is looking for a payment pattern which has been going on for some time and has continued right up until the deceased's death.

STEP 2: TIMING

The application must be made not later than six months after 'the date on which representation with respect to the estate of the deceased is first taken out' (s 4), unless the court gives permission. This means that the application should wherever possible be made no later than six months after the grant of probate or letters of administration. However, it is possible for an application to be made *before* a grant of representation is taken out. In very exceptional circumstances, the time limit may be extended by an order of the court.

STEP 3: WHAT THE APPLICANT RECEIVED FROM THE ESTATE

If the applicant has standing, they must then prove what financial provision has been made for them out of the estate under the will, or the intestacy, or the will and the intestacy combined if there has been a partial intestacy. This part of the exercise is a matter of fact and generally quite straightforward. No conclusions at all are drawn by the court at this stage, even if the applicant received nothing at all from the will or intestacy, because it might be reasonable provision for this applicant to receive nothing at all.

> **Revision tip**
>
> Remember that only the value of 'the *net estate*' is considered: s 25(1). This excludes assets such as insurance policies or nominated payments out of pensions which will have been paid directly to a nominated beneficiary outside of the will or intestacy because, as we saw in **Chapter 6**, these do not fall into the estate.

The joint tenancy exception

We saw in **Chapter 6** that, as a general rule, there can be no severance of a joint tenancy after death. There is one exception only: s 9 of the Inheritance Act allows the court to include the deceased's interest under a joint tenancy as part of the deceased's estate. This power is often of considerable assistance to applicants, particularly where almost the only substantial asset owned by the deceased before death was an undivided share in a beneficial joint tenancy (see **Practice example 9.2**).

Practice example 9.2

Tom and his friend Marcus owned Christie Cottage as beneficial joint tenants. Tom died intestate and his wife Rita made a claim under the Inheritance Act. Although Marcus would in the usual way have acquired all of the equity in the property as the surviving joint tenant, Rita successfully applied for Tom's interest in Christie Cottage to be included as part of his estate. The cottage was worth £250,000 immediately before the deceased's death.

How much of the equity in the property will now be included in Tom's estate?

The court can treat Tom's share as being worth £125,000 and could add this sum to the estate. Marcus still has his share worth £125,000, but Rita can now make a claim on Tom's share.

STEP 4: THE RELEVANT STANDARD OF FINANCIAL PROVISION

There are two standards of financial provision: the '**maintenance standard**' and the '**spousal standard**'.

The 'maintenance standard' (all applicants except spouses/civil partners)

Now that we know that the applicant has standing, and what the applicant in fact received out of the estate, we need to establish the relevant standard of reasonable financial provision. Bear in mind that we are not yet deciding whether or not the applicant has a claim under the Act; we are simply looking at the figures.

Key term: maintenance standard

In every application except those made by spouses or civil partners, the court must consider 'such financial provision as it would be reasonable in all the circumstances of the case for the applicant to receive for his maintenance' (s 1(2)(b)), which is known as the 'maintenance standard'. Bear in mind that this question is very specific. It is not: what would any person in the position of the applicant receive from any person in the position of the deceased? It is: what was reasonable for *this* applicant to receive from *this* deceased as part or all of their maintenance?

The key question on the maintenance standard, for any applicant, is: what does this applicant *reasonably* require in order to live 'decently and comfortably according to his or her station in life'? (The phrase comes from a Canadian case, *Re Duranceau* [1952] 3 DLR 714, but it is often quoted in Inheritance Act cases.) In other words, an applicant with a modest lifestyle cannot claim that it is 'reasonable provision' to be provided with a luxury lifestyle.

The 'spousal standard' (all married/civil partnership applicants)

Let's now look at the 'spousal standard'.

> **Key term: spousal standard**
>
> Where the applicant was married to the deceased or was the deceased's civil partner (again, we are going to describe all such people as 'spouses'), the court must have regard to 'such financial provision as it would be reasonable in all the circumstances of the case for a husband or wife [or civil partner] to receive, *whether or not* that provision is required for his or her maintenance' (ss 1(2)(a) and (aa)). Section 3(2) explains this a little further by saying that the relevant standard should be the share that the spouse would have received if instead of ending by the death of the spouse, the marriage had ended by divorce or dissolution.

As you will know from your studies in family law, since *White v White* [2000] UKHL 54, the usual starting point for division of assets on divorce/dissolution is that the assets should be divided in equal shares. This is not an obligatory or automatic starting point, but it is a helpful benchmark for the court. A spouse can ask for more than half of the estate in an Inheritance Act claim, given that there is now only one living party in the marriage, and the estate therefore does not need to support two people.

By this stage, we know (1) how much the applicant received from the estate and (2) what the applicant's reasonable financial provision is; in other words, how much the applicant needs either for their maintenance or (if they are a spouse) how much they would have received on divorce. The amount left by the deceased to the applicant may look very small, but that does not mean that the applicant has a good Inheritance Act claim against the deceased's estate. In order to decide that, we have to carry out the s 3 balancing exercise.

STEP 5: IS THE FINANCIAL PROVISION REASONABLE (USING THE BALANCING EXERCISE UNDER S 3)?

The next question to be addressed is, using the factors set out in s 3 of the Inheritance Act, did the disposition of *this* estate make reasonable financial provision for *this* applicant? The words are emphasised because the most important point to grasp about the Inheritance Act is that every decision will be different depending on the personal circumstances of each applicant.

The court must consider *all* of the factors in s 3, though there will of course be times when one or more of the factors simply do not apply to the case before the court, so the item is considered simply to be dismissed. Those factors are:

(a) the *financial resources and financial needs* which the *applicant* has or is likely to have in the foreseeable future

(b) the *financial resources and financial needs* which *any other applicant* for an order under s 2 of this Act has or is likely to have in the foreseeable future

(c) the *financial resources and financial needs* which *any beneficiary of the estate* of the deceased has or is likely to have in the foreseeable future

(d) any *obligations and responsibilities which the deceased* had towards any *applicant* for an order under the said s 2 or towards any *beneficiary* of the estate of the deceased

(e) the *size and nature of the net estate of the deceased*

(f) any *physical or mental disability of any applicant* for an order under the said s 2 or any *beneficiary* of the estate of the deceased

(g) *any other matter*, including the *conduct* of the applicant or any other person, which in the circumstances of the case the court may consider relevant.

Because the court must look at every one of these factors, the result is that the court will get a complete picture of all of the relevant circumstances in this estate. All of these factors must then be put into the scales by the court, and only after weighing them all up can the court decide whether, in the circumstances of this particular case, the estate has made reasonable financial provision for the applicant. There is no rule that the applicant's financial needs and resources are the most important factor: sometimes they will be the least important factor, depending on the circumstances.

The court is conducting a complex balancing exercise in every single case. Let's look at some of the typical issues that can arise under the headings of s 3, and at some examples of how the section is used in practice.

Financial needs and resources of the applicant

These are normally fairly self-explanatory. As far as resources are concerned, the court will look at what property or savings the applicant has, what the applicant's income is and so on (see **Practice example 9.3**).

Practice example 9.3

Gethin received a lump sum of £25,000 from his mother's estate. Gethin's lifestyle (he owns two properties in the UK and drives a top-of-the-range 4x4 car) means that he requires income of about £65,000 per year (after tax) for his maintenance. There is therefore a very large shortfall between the financial provision made for Gethin in his mother's will and what he needs to support his lifestyle. However, Gethin earns a basic salary of £275,000 per year in his job as a futures trader at a City bank.

Has the disposition of Gethin's mother's estate made reasonable provision for Gethin?

Although the disposition of his mother's estate does not really assist with his maintenance, Gethin has a very healthy income and is able to meet all his maintenance needs from that income without any need for income from his mother's estate. This is taken into account in deciding whether or not the sum that he was left under his mother's will was reasonable or not. His mother's will therefore did make reasonable financial provision for Gethin. *Please note, once again, that an Inheritance Act claim does not decide whether or not his mother was reasonable when she decided not to leave him any more money.*

Financial needs and resources of any other applicant, or of any beneficiary of the estate (s 3(1)(b) and (c))

The court cannot look only at the financial needs and resources of the applicant; it must also look at the needs and resources of any other person who has applied under the Inheritance Act (note that more than one person can apply) and also the needs and resources of any beneficiary under the estate. It may well be that the applicant has an arguable case that reasonable financial provision has not been made for them, but if there are also other applicants and beneficiaries in need, their needs may rank higher than the applicant's (see **Practice example 9.4**).

Practice example 9.4

Brenton has made a claim for reasonable financial provision from the estate of his late father, Stefan. Brenton is the child of Stefan's first marriage. He is 19 years old and studying full-time at university. His only income is from a part-time job and his student loan.

Stefan's estate is worth £275,000, all in cash. Stefan left all of his estate by will to his second wife, Bridget, who is now the sole carer for their three-year-old daughter. Bridget is able to work part-time but does not receive much more than the minimum wage.

How is the court likely to view Brenton's claim?

The court will consider not just Brenton's financial needs and resources but also Bridget's. It is obliged to do so because it must consider the financial needs and resources of all beneficiaries of the estate under s 3(1)(c). It is likely to consider that Bridget's financial needs are much greater than Brenton's because Bridget has to look after the deceased's infant child. The estate is comparatively small, and will have to support Bridget and her child until the child is no longer a minor. In these circumstances, even if the court considers that the estate did not make reasonable financial provision for Brenton, it will prioritise the beneficiary's financial needs over the applicant's.

Obligations and responsibilities of the deceased to any applicant or any beneficiary (s 3(1)(d))

Looking at **Practice example 9.4**, you may have seen that this consideration would also apply. Stefan had a legal responsibility to maintain his spouse and his infant child. These obligations are likely to carry very considerable weight in the scales when the court is conducting its balancing exercise. It is true that Stefan also had a moral obligation to assist Brenton, who, although he has attained the age of legal majority, is not financially independent because he is still in full-time education. However, it is unlikely that this very limited estate can support both Brendan and his infant half-sister. In general, where there are legal obligations to support either a beneficiary of the estate or another applicant, those obligations will carry great weight, particularly where the obligation is to support an infant child, and will almost always outweigh any moral obligations.

The size and nature of the net estate (s 3(1)(e))

The court considers not only the total value of the net estate but also how that estate is made up, particularly if it contains land or other assets which the personal representatives (see **Chapter 2**) would need to sell in order to pay the applicant's claim. It is often when considering the size and nature of the net estate that it becomes apparent that the applicant's claim is simply not realistic, either because the assets of the estate are insufficient to meet it or because some asset in the estate (often a piece of land) is needed by a beneficiary or another applicant, and cannot be sold. This is another area where liquidity in the estate, which we considered in **Chapter 8**, can be significant. Remember that throughout the balancing exercise, the court has to consider the needs and resources of any beneficiary and any other applicant (see **Practice example 9.5**).

Practice example 9.5

Claude's net estate has been valued at £375,000, and £350,000 of that value is in the property, 'Bonnybank', which he owned in his sole name and in which he lived with his partner (but not spouse) Maisie. Claude left all of his property by will to Maisie. Maisie has been diagnosed with motor neurone disease and is no longer able to work. She has lived in Bonnybank for the past 12 years. Maisie's only income is from state benefits.

Claude's nephew, Alfie, has made a claim against the estate as a person who was partially maintained by the deceased. While Claude was alive, he paid the sum of £10,000 per year to help with educational expenses for Alfie at his private school. Alfie is now in his final year of school and is intending to study for a medical degree, which will take five years, and then to go on to postgraduate study. He is claiming the sum of £75,000 from the estate.

How is the court likely to view Alfie's claim?

The only way in which Alfie's claim could be met in full or in part would be for 'Bonnybank' to be sold. 'Bonnybank' has been Maisie's home for a long time; she would find it extremely difficult to move to another property in her current state of health; and it might well not be possible, if money were deducted from the proceeds of sale and paid to Alfie, for Maisie to find a suitable alternative property in which to live. As a result, the size of the net estate (which is not sufficient to make provision for both Maisie and Alfie) and the nature of the net estate (more than 93% of it is tied up in land) mean that the court is likely to prioritise the needs of Maisie (a beneficiary) over Alfie (an Inheritance Act applicant), to the extent that it is unlikely that Alfie would receive anything at all, or at least more than a very small amount, from the estate.

Any physical or mental disability of the applicant or of any beneficiary or other applicant (s 3(1)(f))

In **Practice example 9.5**, the court would have considered Maisie's serious illness as another factor under s 3(1)(f) which would persuade it that all or almost all of this estate should go to Maisie. Where any person, whether they are an applicant under the Inheritance Act or a beneficiary of the estate, is suffering from an illness (including a mental illness) or a disability, that illness or disability will weigh very heavily in the scales. Any person who has standing has a strong claim to financial provision from the deceased's estate if they are now ill or disabled, particularly if their illness or disability means that they are now financially compromised through lack of earning power.

Any other matters, including conduct (s 3(1)(g))

Although s 3(1)(g) includes any other relevant evidence, we will focus on the mention of 'conduct'.

> **Revision tip**
>
> Candidates very often mistakenly assume that s 3(1)(g) is there to deal with the supposed 'bad behaviour' of an applicant. In fact, that is not primarily what 'conduct' is referring to here. The purpose of the s 3 balancing exercise is not to punish any applicant for behaving badly to, or disappointing, the deceased; nor is it for giving out awards to applicants who have behaved particularly well to the deceased, for example by caring selflessly for the deceased over a long period of time.

In fact, the 'conduct' referred to at s 3(1)(g) is more likely to be the conduct of the deceased, and in particular any information that the deceased has given (possibly in the will, but also elsewhere) about why the deceased has chosen to leave their property in the way that they have. One factor which can be highly material is a letter or other document written by the deceased that sets out the financial support given by the deceased to an applicant during the deceased's lifetime. The court will pay a great deal of attention to such a document, but it remains only one factor in the overall balancing process.

However, such information can only assist the court; it cannot be conclusive. No one is allowed to avoid the provisions and effect of the Inheritance Act, and whatever the deceased's reasons for not providing for an applicant, the court must still look objectively at whether or not the disposition of the estate makes reasonable provision for that applicant.

STEP 6: EXERCISING THE COURT'S POWERS UNDER S 2

If the court decides, having conducted the balancing exercise under s 3, that the disposition of the estate has not made reasonable provision for the applicant, its powers to remedy the position are set out in s 2 of the Act. The most important of these are the powers at s 2(1) (a)–(c) to order the estate to make periodical payments to the applicant, to make a lump sum payment to the applicant or to transfer property to the applicant. There are further powers at s 2(1) (d)–(h) allowing the court to settle property on an applicant, or to vary an existing settlement in favour of an applicant, or to order or permit the estate to acquire property for an applicant's use.

As a matter of logic, you will see that if an Inheritance Act applicant succeeds in their application, the money or property used to satisfy their claim must come from a beneficiary of the estate. The court is therefore given the power at s 2(4) to make any consequential or supplemental orders which are required to give effect to the satisfaction of the applicant's claim. The overall effect is that the court can reorganise the distribution of the estate under the will or intestacy in order to give effect to the applicant's claim.

■ KEY POINT CHECKLIST

This chapter has covered the following key knowledge points. You can structure your revision around these, making sure to recall the key details for each point, as covered in this chapter.

- The meaning of the correct 'reasonable financial provision' test.
- The two standards of financial provision: the 'maintenance standard' and the 'spousal standard'.
- All of the categories of possible claimants under s 1(1) of the Inheritance Act.
- All of the factors the court must consider under s 3 of the Inheritance Act.
- How to conduct the 'balancing exercise' by which the court reaches its decision.

■ KEY TERMS AND CONCEPTS

- maintenance standard (**page 149**)
- spousal standard (**page 150**)

■ SQE1-STYLE QUESTIONS

QUESTION 1

A client seeks advice about the estate of his deceased civil partner. They lived a modest lifestyle together, taking only one holiday per year and driving a second-hand saloon car. The client believed that his civil partner's estate was worth no more than £250,000. The client has now discovered that the estate is worth more than £3 million. The civil partner left a will which made no provision at all for the client and left all of his estate to a distant relative. In the last year of his life, the client's civil partner left the matrimonial home and commenced proceedings to dissolve the civil partnership. There was no decree of dissolution by the time the client's civil partner died.

Which of the following best describes the claim which can be made by the client under the Inheritance (Provision for Family and Dependants) Act 1975?

A. The client can make a claim with a starting point of £1.5 million.

B. The client cannot make a claim because dissolution proceedings had been commenced.

C. The client can make a claim with a starting point of £125,000.

D. The client can only claim an amount which will allow him to continue to live his current modest lifestyle.

E. The client cannot make a claim because he was not living with his civil partner at the time of the civil partner's death.

QUESTION 2

A father fell ill and persuaded his adult daughter to give up her university studies to look after him. The daughter gave up her studies without graduating and became her father's full-time carer for over five years. The daughter later became romantically involved with a man to whom she became engaged, though she continued to live with her father and care for him. The father demanded that the daughter should terminate the relationship and break off her engagement, but the daughter refused to do this.

The father then revoked his existing will, which left all of his estate to his daughter, and wrote a valid new will leaving all of his estate to a local charity. When the father died, his daughter received nothing from his estate but did receive the sum of £10,000 from a life insurance policy that he had forgotten to cancel.

After the father's death, his daughter was homeless and, because she had not studied or been employed, could only obtain minimum-wage employment. The daughter now seeks advice.

Which of the following best describes the daughter's current legal position under the Inheritance (Provision for Family and Dependants) Act 1975 ('the Act')?

A. The daughter cannot make a claim under the Act because her father intentionally disinherited her.

B. The daughter can make a claim under the Act because her father intentionally disinherited her.

C. The daughter cannot make a claim under the Act because she received £10,000 from the estate.

D. The daughter can make a claim under the Act because the distribution of her father's estate is not fair to her.

E. The daughter can make a claim under the Act because the father's estate has not made reasonable provision for her.

QUESTION 3

A sister gave up her job in November 2019 to care full-time for her elderly brother, moving in with him in order to do so. For the next three years, the brother paid his sister a monthly sum which was slightly lower than the market rate for care services and did not charge her any rent for living at his property. Although the sister retained her own property, she had lived with the brother for a period of three years by the time that he died.

The brother died intestate in November 2022. He was survived by his sister and his daughter.

Which of the following best describes the woman's legal position after the brother's death?

A. The sister has standing to make an application under s 1(1)(e) of the Inheritance (Provision for Family and Dependants) Act 1975 as she was being maintained by her brother immediately before his death.

B. The sister has standing to make an application under s 1(1)(ba) of the Inheritance (Provision for Family and Dependants) Act 1975 as she lived in the same household as her brother for a period of two years preceding his death.

C. The sister has standing to make an application under both s 1(1)(e) and s 1(1)(ba) of the Inheritance (Provision for Family and Dependants) Act 1975 as she lived in the same household as her brother for a period of two years preceding his death and was also being maintained by her brother immediately before his death.

D. The sister has no standing to make an application under the Inheritance (Provision for Family and Dependants) Act 1975 and no rights of inheritance in intestacy.

E. The sister will inherit the brother's estate by reason of s 46(1) Administration of Estates Act 1925.

QUESTION 4

A woman died intestate, leaving an estate worth £54,000, all of it cash deposited in a building society account. The one person entitled on her intestacy was her daughter. The woman had, however, financially maintained her seriously ill sister, who therefore had standing to make a claim under the Inheritance (Provision for Family and Dependants) Act 1975. Upon the woman's death, the proceeds of a life insurance policy, which she had written into trust and forgotten about, amounting to £150,000, were paid out to the woman's ex-husband, who had been the named beneficiary on the policy.

Which of the following statements best describes the sister's position?

A. The sister cannot make a claim on any of the money because the woman died intestate.

B. The sister can make a claim on both the £54,000 and the £150,000 on the basis that the £150,000 was paid to the ex-husband by mistake.

C. The sister can make a claim only on the £150,000 on the basis that the estate did not make reasonable provision for her.

D. The sister can make a claim only on the £54,000 on the basis that the estate did not make reasonable provision for her.

E. The sister can make a claim on both the £54,000 and the £150,000 on the basis that the estate did not make reasonable provision for her.

QUESTION 5

A man died, leaving an estate of £75,000 in cash. He also owned a house as a beneficial joint tenant with his current partner, which passed to that partner on his death. At the man's death, the house was worth £360,000 in total. The partner also received death in service benefits worth £550,000 as the man's named beneficiary under his occupational pension.

The man had an infant daughter (from a previous relationship) who had standing to make a claim under the Inheritance (Provision for Family and Dependants) Act 1975.

Which is the best description of the total amount of the estate against which the infant daughter may make a claim?

A. £75,000.

B. £435,000.

C. £255,000.

D. £805,000.

E. £360,000.

■ ANSWERS TO QUESTIONS

Answers to 'What do you know already?' questions at the start of the chapter

1) Yes. The question is not whether a person received nothing from the estate: the question is whether what the person received was reasonable financial provision. If a beneficiary received a fixed sum from the estate but this was not reasonable financial provision for that beneficiary, the beneficiary can make an Inheritance Act claim.

2) False. There is no category at s 1(1) of the Act for 'siblings of the deceased', so a brother or sister has no standing to make an application unless they fall into one of the other categories in s 1.

3) False. The court *must* consider the amounts received by other beneficiaries of the estate, but can decide what weight to give this when conducting its overall balancing exercise under s 3 of the Act.

4) Yes. The key question is not whether the person inherited under a will or under an intestacy, but whether the distribution of the deceased's estate resulted in reasonable financial provision for the applicant.

Answers to end-of-chapter SQE1-style questions

Question 1:

The correct answer was A. These two parties were in a civil partnership and the client therefore has standing to make the claim under the 1975 Act. The correct standard of financial provision is the spousal standard, which expressly refers to what the client would have expected to receive on dissolution of the civil partnership. The starting point would be 50% or £1.5 million. The fact that dissolution proceedings have been commenced does not remove the client's standing: only a decree of dissolution would do so (therefore B is wrong). The fact that the client mistakenly believed that the estate was worth only £250,000 is not relevant, so C is wrong. D is incorrect because it refers to the wrong standard of provision: spouses are not limited to the maintenance standard. E applies only to cohabitees: where the parties are married or living in a civil partnership, it is not relevant whether they were cohabiting at the time of death.

Question 2:

The correct answer was E. A and B are wrong because the question is not whether the father intentionally disinherited his daughter; it is whether the result of that disinheritance caused unreasonable financial provision. C is wrong because the £10,000 did not come from the father's estate – it came from an asset which was never part of the estate. Although all of these answers are incorrect, it is D that you should be most aware of and avoid. The question in an Inheritance Act case is never whether the distribution of the estate is 'fair'. It is whether or not the distribution of the estate has made 'reasonable financial provision' for *this* applicant, which is why E is, in this case, the correct answer.

Question 3:

The correct answer was D. A is incorrect because although the brother paid the sister a monthly sum, she was giving full valuable consideration for it in the form of her caring services. B is incorrect because even though the siblings were arguably living in the same household, they were not doing so as a married couple or civil partners. As these two options are incorrect, then C must also be incorrect. E is incorrect because the brother left a child, namely his daughter, who will inherit all of the estate on his intestacy.

Question 4:

The correct answer was D. Remember that Inheritance Act claims can only be made on the deceased's estate. The insurance policy proceeds were paid directly to the ex-husband as the named beneficiary. Any option which says that the sister can make a claim against the £150,000 (B, C or E) is clearly incorrect. It makes no difference to an Inheritance Act claim whether the woman dies testate or intestate (therefore, A is incorrect). B is further incorrect because it does not matter whether the money was paid 'by mistake' or not: the £150,000 never falls into the estate.

Question 5:

The correct answer was C. The sum of £255,000 comprises the £75,000 in the estate plus one-half of the value of the property (£180,000). This is a case in which the infant daughter may apply to sever the beneficial joint tenancy under the Inheritance Act and the value of the man's half-share would therefore be included in the estate. A is incorrect because it does not take this into account. B is incorrect because it includes the full value of the property rather than simply the man's share. D is incorrect because it includes the death in service benefit, which was never part of the estate. E is incorrect because it only takes account of the value of the property, half of which cannot come into the estate in any event, and does not include the £75,000 which is definitely within the estate.

■ KEY CASES, RULES, STATUTES AND INSTRUMENTS

The SQE1 Assessment Specification requires you to know and be able to cite the Inheritance (Provision for Family and Dependants) Act 1975. You will need to understand the principles that underpin this Act. You are therefore advised to ensure that you are able to identify, explain and apply ss 1, 2, 3, 6 and 9 of the Act.

10

Inheritance tax

■ MAKE SURE YOU KNOW

This chapter provides an overview of how inheritance tax (IHT) affects the estate. You may well be asked, as part of the IHT topic, to identify a correct tax calculation in a multiple-choice question (MCQ). To do this, you will need to understand the rules thoroughly and to have practised 'walking through' sample calculations such as the ones set out in this chapter.

You will also need to know how capital gains tax (CGT) and income tax impact on a death estate, but we do not deal with what you need to know about either CGT or income tax within the scope of this guide.

■ SQE ASSESSMENT ADVICE

As you work through this chapter, remember to pay particular attention in your revision to:
- when IHT will be charged, during lifetime and after death
- how to identify a potentially exempt transfer (PET) and a lifetime chargeable transfer (LCT)
- when a transfer will be exempt from IHT and when it will attract relief (and understand the difference between exemption and relief)
- how to define and apply the standard, transferable and residence nil rate bands
- how to calculate the cumulative total
- how to correctly apply the lifetime and death rates of IHT.

■ WHAT DO YOU KNOW ALREADY?

Have a go at these questions before reading this chapter. If you find some difficult or cannot remember the answers, make a note to look more closely at that area during your revision.

1) True or false? IHT is only charged when someone inherits a deceased person's estate.

   [Inheritance tax is charged at three different times, page 163]

2) When is IHT payable on gifts made during a person's lifetime?

   [Lifetime transfers, page 164]

3) If a person dies owning an undivided share in a beneficial joint tenancy of a property, is IHT charged on that undivided share after death?
[**Inheritance tax on the death estate, page 176**]

4) True or false? The beneficiaries are responsible for paying IHT on the testator's estate after death.
[**Inheritance tax on the death estate, page 176**]

THE SCOPE OF THIS CHAPTER

This chapter is going to look in detail at some aspects of how IHT operates. The functioning legal knowledge specifically required for this section of the SQE1 assessment has been set out as:
- IHT on lifetime transfers that are immediately chargeable and those that are potentially exempt
- IHT on transfers on death
- exemptions and reliefs from IHT
- the scope of anti-avoidance provisions.

You are also required to know a limited amount about CGT in the wills environment, specifically when the personal representatives (PRs; see **Chapter 2**) or the beneficiaries may be required to pay it, and also know when the PRs may have to pay some income tax on the estate. There are, as you will be aware from your main reading and study, complex rules around these taxes, and further complexities around how those complex rules work together and are implemented.

What we are going to do in this chapter, though, is to focus on a fundamental understanding of the rules on how IHT specifically is charged on lifetime transfers and on death. If you understand the rules on specific points and can apply them, you will be better placed to start to combine the rules when you are faced with more complicated questions. This chapter therefore does not take you through more complex tax calculations, for which you should refer to your wider reading, but focuses on a full understanding of the basics.

INHERITANCE TAX IS CHARGED AT THREE DIFFERENT TIMES

One of the key concepts to grasp about IHT is that it can arise, and be charged, on three separate occasions: (1) at the time that a transfer made during a person's lifetime (a 'lifetime transfer'), is made (from now on we will call the person making the transfer 'the transferor'); (2) on the *same* lifetime transfer if the transferor dies within seven years of making the transfer; and (3) on the transferor's *estate* (see **Key term** in **Chapter 1**) after the transferor has died.

It is first of all essential, therefore, to be able to identify the two kinds of lifetime transfers, and the very different ways in which they are treated during the lifetime of the transferor and after the transferor's death.

LIFETIME TRANSFERS

Let's start by looking at the two fundamental concepts in IHT lifetime transfers: the **lifetime chargeable transfer (LCT)** and the **potentially exempt transfer (PET)** s 3 IHTA 1984.

Key term: lifetime chargeable transfer (LCT)

This transfer is:
- made while the transferor is still alive
- made to any natural person or legal entity which is not an individual or a trust in favour of a disabled person (so, for example, to a company, a discretionary trust or an unincorporated association)
- a transfer for value (see below)
- charged to tax at 0% if it falls within the nil rate band (see **The nil rate band (NRB) and the cumulative total** below)
- charged to tax at the lifetime rate (currently 20%) when made, if it falls outside the nil rate band
- if the transferor dies within seven years of the transfer, possibly charged to tax a second time at 40% (the 'death rate')
- subject to taper relief (see **Taper relief** below) if the transferor dies between three and seven years after making the transfer.

Key term: potentially exempt transfer (PET)

This transfer is:
- made while the transferor is still alive
- made only to an individual, or to trustees of either a bare trust (see **Chapter 6**) in favour of an individual or a trust in favour of a disabled person ('disabled trust')
- a transfer for value
- is not charged to tax at all if the transferor survives for seven years after the transfer is made
- is charged to tax at the death rate (currently 40%) if the transferor fails to survive for seven years
- subject to taper relief (see below) if the transferor dies between three and seven years after making the transfer.

We can see immediately that LCTs and PETs have two things in common – they are always transfers for value, and they are always made during the lifetime of the transferor – and one major defining difference: PETs can only be made to individual persons, bare trusts in favour of individual persons or trustees of a disabled trust. Everything else *must* be an LCT (s 2 of the IHTA 1984).

Revision tip

Remember that every time we talk about a transfer to a trust, we are in fact referring to a transfer to the trustees of that trust: only the trustees can receive any gifts that the transferor makes (see also **Chapter 11** for more on will trusts).

'Transfer for value'

In order for the rules to apply, the transfer must be a transfer for value. If the transferor is making a gift of money, that is quite easy to determine: for example, if the transferor gives £10,000, then the value of the transfer is £10,000. If the transferor gives away an item of property, however, the rule is that the value transferred is the amount by which the transferor's estate is reduced by the disposition. So if, for example, the transferor gives away a diamond ring worth £5,000, the value of the transfer is the market value of that ring.

Where a person is making a straight gift of money or property to another person, there is no problem. However, sometimes a person will try to get around the rules by not making a straightforward gift, but pretending that they are selling to another person. The pretence is that the sale is at market value when in fact it is at a bargain price (see **Practice example 10.1**).

Practice example 10.1

Clarice wants to make a gift of an expensive item of jewellery to her cousin Patrice. The jewellery is worth £35,000 but Clarice can save a substantial amount of IHT by selling it to Patrice for the sum of £5,000. Patrice pays the sum of £5,000 to Clarice and is given the jewellery.

Will the tax to Clarice's estate be impacted by this transaction?

This is called a 'sale at an undervalue' and, as you can see, what Clarice has in fact done is make a gift of £30,000 to Patrice. However, the amount by which Clarice's estate has been reduced is also £30,000. This 'sale', therefore, is considered as a transfer for value of £30,000 and will be taxed on that basis.

There are a couple of important exceptions to the transfer for value rules, both connected with the rule that the transferor must be intending to make a 'gratuitous disposition' – a gift, in other words. If the transfer is not intended to be a gift, then it does not attract IHT. So if the transfer is being made to fulfil an obligation to maintain a spouse, a civil partner, a child or a dependant relative, that is not a transfer for value. The other exception is where the transferor has sold on an open market at an undervalue without knowing that they were doing so. An accidental 'bad bargain' is not a transfer for value.

Exempt transfers

Some transfers for value, even though they fall within the class of LCTs, are exempt from IHT.

Revision tip

Please note the difference between 'exemptions' and 'reliefs'; we are going to consider 'reliefs' shortly. If a transfer is exempt or part exempt, then we do not consider the exempt part for IHT purposes at all; we ignore it. We do *not* ignore transfers which attract reliefs.

• *Gifts to a spouse, charity, political party or national institution*

If a transferor makes a transfer to their spouse or civil partner which is intended to take effect immediately (s 18 IHTA), or makes a transfer to a charity or political party, or makes a gift to an important national institution (the Victoria and Albert Museum, for example), those transfers are *never* considered to be LCTs or PETs. There are also exemptions for transfers to entities which do not make a profit, even if they are not charities (local community organisations are good examples): ss 23–25 IHTA. These exemptions apply to lifetime transfers and also to transfers made out of the death estate.

• *Annual exemption*

Every taxpayer can make lifetime transfers up to a limited amount in each tax year without paying IHT: currently, that limit is £3,000 per year in total (which can be split across as many people as you choose). This is called the 'annual exemption'. It is possible to carry forward the unused amount of an annual exemption from one tax year to another, but only for one tax year. If, for example, a taxpayer does not use their annual exemption in tax year 1 or tax year 2, they can only carry forward their exemption from tax year 2 into tax year 3. The tax year 1 exemption has been lost. Annual exemptions do not apply to the death estate.

• *Presents, including wedding and engagement presents and small gifts*

There are also some limited exemptions for wedding or engagement presents. The parent of a bride or groom can give them up to £5,000 free of IHT, a grandparent can give £2,500 and a person not related to the bride or groom can give £1,000: s 22 IHTA 1984. This of course includes not just gifts of money but also gifts of other property up to those values. Any amount given in excess of these values will be charged to tax at the appropriate rate.

One final exemption at s 20 IHTA relates to small gifts: any gift to an individual not exceeding £250 will be disregarded. These small gifts cannot be added together either, and therefore will not count towards a person's cumulative total. The rules on small gifts are complex and outside the scope of this revision guide.

Annual exemptions and the exemptions for wedding, engagement and other small presents apply *to lifetime gifts only*.

Practice example 10.2 works through what we now know about transfers for value.

Practice example 10.2

Ghyslain would like to make some gifts to friends, family and associates. He decides to do the following:

- give £5,000 to his 20-year-old niece Sancha
- give his collection of antique silver yachting trophies (valued at £35,000) to the local sailing club of which he is a member (the sailing club is a profit-making institution)
- give £25,000 to the trustees of a trust set up to help his friend Bogdan, who was severely injured in a motorbike accident
- give £15,000 to the Pantheist Party, a political party which supports green and ecological causes
- add a codicil to his will giving the sum of £7,500 to his uncle Yannick.

Are these gifts an LCT, a PET or neither? In each case, if you decide it is a transfer for value, what is the value of the transfer?

- **The gift to Sancha is made during Ghyslain's lifetime and is to an individual. It has a value of £5,000 and it is therefore a PET of £5,000**
- **the gift to the sailing club is made during his lifetime, but is not to an individual or to a bare/disabled trust (it is in fact to an unincorporated association) and is therefore an LCT; because the club makes a profit, the transfer is not exempt; the value of the transfer will be £35,000**
- **the £25,000 is a gift during his lifetime to a trust, which would normally be an LCT, but as this is a disabled trust, it is a PET; the value is £25,000**
- **the £15,000 is a gift to a political party and is therefore automatically exempt from IHT**
- **the gift made in a codicil is not a lifetime gift; it takes effect only when the will takes effect. It therefore does not qualify as either an LCT or a PET.**

TAXATION OF GIFTS AT THE POINT OF TRANSFER

We are now going to build on this to look at how these transfer types are taxed during the transferor's lifetime. We will look at the basic rules first, and then we will add in the more complex concepts of the nil rate band (NRB) and cumulative totals.

Taxation of PETs

Using Ghyslain's gift of £5,000 to Sancha in **Practice example 10.2**, let's see how this might be taxed in **Practice example 10.3**. We already know that this is a PET. It is sometimes helpful to think of a PET as a 'wait and see' transfer – we literally 'wait and see' whether the transferor survives for seven years after the transfer or not. If the transferor survives seven years, then no IHT is ever payable. However, if the transferor dies, then tax will be payable at the appropriate full IHT rate, unless taper relief applies.

Practice example 10.3

Ghyslain makes the £5,000 PET to Sancha in December 2016 when he is 35 years old. If he survives until December 2023, then no IHT will be payable. In fact, Ghyslain contracts Covid-19 in March 2021 and dies.

How much IHT is now payable?

If the gift falls outside the NRB, IHT is now payable at 40% on the entire gift. However, this is a case in which taper relief will apply. If a transferor dies between four and five years after making a gift, the tax payable will be 60% of the total IHT liability on that gift. The total tax payable without taper relief would be £2,000; with taper relief of 60%, the total tax payable is £1,200.

We will come across taper relief again when we look at LCTs. For the moment, concentrate on how taper relief works and how the calculation of the tax is arrived at. The main point here is that no tax is payable on a PET at all unless the transferor dies within seven years of the transfer.

Taxation of LCTs

The position is a little more complicated here. Using Ghyslain's gift of the trophy collection to the sailing club in **Practice example 10.2**, let's see how this might be taxed in **Practice example 10.4**. The collection was valued at £35,000, so this is an LCT of £35,000. Again, to keep things simple, let's assume for the moment that no exemptions or reliefs could be applied to this gift.

This time, there is no 'wait and see'. An LCT attracts IHT as soon as it is made. If the gift falls within the NRB, IHT is charged at 0%. If it falls above the NRB, it is payable at the 'lifetime rate' of 20% as opposed to the 'death rate' of 40%.

Practice example 10.4

Ghyslain's gift to the sailing club is made in January 2017. The value of the gift is £35,000. Ghyslain dies in March 2021 having used up all of his NRB.

How much IHT is payable on this LCT?

As the gift falls above the NRB, the tax is charged at the lifetime rate: 20% of £35,000 is £7,000, and this is the amount that must be paid in IHT straight away.

If Ghyslain had survived for seven years, there would be no further tax to pay. However, as he died in March 2021, he survived for only four years and two months after making the gift. Therefore, following Ghyslain's death, the gift will be reviewed and IHT will then be charged at the death rate: 40% of £35,000 is £14,000, and this further amount will be payable subject to deductions. *This means that the same gift can be taxed twice: once when it is made, and again if the transferor fails to survive for seven years.*

Revision tip

Strictly speaking, it is the transferor (the giver of the gift) who is responsible for paying the IHT, but it usually the transferee (the recipient) who actually hands the money over to HMRC. This can cause issues with the value of the transfer, so transferors often prefer to pay the gift to the recipient and pay any tax due to HMRC. To calculate what the correct transfer value should be, the 'grossing up' rules are used. These are outside the scope of this book but you should ensure that you revise and know them.

HOW TO CALCULATE INHERITANCE TAX: THE ORDER IN WHICH TO CALCULATE

We will now look at the order in which you must put together all of the rules that we have considered so far, add in any appropriate reliefs and then apply the cumulative total and the NRB to the resulting total. It is vital to apply the rules in a strict order to establish the correct amount of tax, and *you must not deviate from this order in any way*: if you do, you will go wrong!

We use this same order whether we are calculating tax at the time of the gift, tax on lifetime gifts after the transferor has died or tax on the death estate. In other words: same batting order, used at different times. You will see, however, that this can result in very different outcomes.

Let's look now at this order, with some explanations as we go.

For every transfer, lifetime and on the death estate, you need to perform a calculation as follows:

1) What is the value of the transfer?
2) Deduct any available *exemptions* from that value.
3) Deduct any available *reliefs* from that value.
4) Calculate the *cumulative total* of all of the transfers to date.
5) Calculate whether there is anything remaining in the *NRB*.
6) Apply IHT to the new transfer value at the applicable rate.
7) Where you can, apply *taper relief.*

We have not yet looked at some of these concepts, so let's do so now before we take them back to our calculation.

Exemptions

Annual exemptions are the most relevant here. The maximum amount of annual exemption that can ever be claimed is the maximum exemption for the tax year in which the gift is made, plus (if it has not been used) the exemption for the previous tax year. As the current maximum per tax year is £3,000, this means that currently, total annual exemptions can never exceed £6,000 – but they will often be much less than that. Remember that annual exemptions are not included in a death estate calculation.

Reliefs

There are two main types of tax reliefs on IHT: business property relief (BPR; see also **Revise SQE: Business Law and Practice**) and agricultural property relief (APR). Where a chargeable transfer has been made within four years of the transferor's death, taper relief may also reduce the amount of tax payable.

In each case, the rules are complex and outside the scope of this revision guide. The following is a brief summary.

BPR (IHTA 1984 Pt V Chapter I)

BPR will be available at 100% (that is, all of the transfer will be free of IHT) if the transferor is selling a business or an interest in a business (including a partnership), and the transferor has owned the business as sole proprietor for at least two years/has been a partner for the same length of time; or if the transfer is of shares in an unquoted ('private') company (that is, a company whose shares are not traded on any public stock market). In very broad terms, a limited company which is not a public limited company (plc) is likely to be a private company.

BPR is available at 50% (that is, half of the applicable IHT rate will be charged) if the transferor has control of a *public* company (that is, a plc) and is transferring shares of that company, or if the transferor is transferring specified assets (including land, buildings, plant or machinery) of a company (private or public) that is controlled by the transferor, or a partnership in which the transferor was a partner.

APR (IHTA 1984 Part V Chapter II)

APR is available at 100% if the transferor occupied the transferred property for agricultural purposes for at least two years prior to the transfer, or it was owned by the transferor for at least seven years prior to the transfer but was occupied during that time by someone else who was using the property for agricultural purposes. So a transfer by a farmer of a working farm that she has owned for over two years will attract 100% relief from IHT, and so will a transfer by a landlord who has rented the property out to a tenant farmer, provided the landlord has owned the land for at least seven years and the tenant has worked it as a farm during that time. APR is also available at 50% in other specified circumstances.

Revision tip

In addition, there are specific rules which apply to both BPR and APR on lifetime transfers. These relate, in summary, to whether the property is still owned by the transferee if the transferor has died within seven years of the transfer being made. They are outside the scope of this book but you should ensure that you know these rules.

Taper relief

We have already seen that if a transferor dies within seven years of making an LCT or PET, there will be a further charge to tax. However, if the transferor has died within six to seven years of the transfer, then only 20% of that charge is payable. If the death is within five to six years of the transfer, then 40% of the charge is payable; if within four to five years, 60%; and if within three to four years, 80%. If the death is within three years of the transfer, there is no taper relief. See **Practice example 10.5**. Taper relief is also only chargeable on lifetime transfers: it never applies to calculations on the death estate.

Practice example 10.5

Mikaela died in October 2021. She had made a lifetime transfer of £200,000 in May 2017 which, after calculation of her cumulative total and NRB, was all chargeable to IHT at the death rate of 40%. The basic amount of IHT payable was therefore £80,000. However, Mikaela died within four to five years of making the transfer.

How much IHT is payable?

Taper relief meant that only 60% of the £80,000 was payable: the total amount of IHT was therefore £48,000.

The nil rate band (NRB) and the cumulative total

As well as the annual exemptions of £3,000, which can be made in each tax year free of any tax at all, each taxpayer can transfer up to £325,000 over a total period of seven years at a tax rate of 0%: this is the so-called 'standard' NRB. Note that this is tax charged at 0% and is *not* an exemption.

There are two further NRBs which are only relevant on death.

Transferable NRB (s 8A IHTA 1984)

Spouses (including civil partners) have the benefit of what is called the 'transferable' NRB. If a married person dies with part of their NRB unused, that unused portion can be transferred to their widow(er), subject to complex rules which are outside the scope of this guide. This can be a very significant advantage in dealing with estates of married couples.

Residence NRB (IHTA 1984 ss 8D–8M)

The 'residence' NRB of £175,000 is available where after 6 April 2017 a residential property in the deceased's estate is being transferred to a direct descendant either of the deceased (including grandchildren or great-grandchildren) or direct descendants of the deceased's spouse. Again, this can be a very significant advantage, particularly where, as with most estates in the UK, the single biggest asset is the deceased's former home. The NRB limit on death is in effect lifted by a further £175,000. However, if an estate is worth over £2 million, the residence NRB is reduced by £1 for every £2 over the £2 million limit.

We are going to concentrate next on the standard NRB and its effect on lifetime transfers. First of all, let's look at taxation at the point that the transfer is made.

Taxation on the gift at the point of transfer: the cumulative total

In order to work out how much is in the NRB, we look back seven years from the date of a lifetime transfer and work out how much the transferor has gifted over that seven-year period. If the transferor is still alive, PETs are ignored. The resulting figure is the cumulative total. If the amount exceeds £325,000, then the transferor has used up all of their NRB and tax on lifetime transfers above the £325,000 limit is now payable at 20%. This is the 'lifetime rate'. **Practice example 10.6** illustrates how this might work.

Practice example 10.6

Park makes a gift of £10,000 to a discretionary trust, the Haviland Trust, in January 2019. This is an LCT. To calculate if he must pay tax on that transfer, we first need to establish whether he has exhausted his NRB or still has part of it remaining. We must therefore look back at all the transfers he has made in the seven-year period between January 2012 and January 2019. We do not include any PETs made while Park is still alive (which he currently is) because we 'wait and see' whether these will become chargeable transfers. It turns out that Park made the following transfers in that period:

February 2014	£125,000 to his business
October 2017	£75,000 to another discretionary trust
December 2017	£150,000 to his partner Suki
June 2018	£85,000 to a family trust with a life interest for his father
November 2018	£30,000 to the alumni fund of his old university (not a charity)
January 2019	£10,000 to the Haviland Trust

To simplify the point, we have shown the *net* values of all of these transfers – that is, that all available exemptions and reliefs have been deducted. Remember that in practice, you will first have to apply these to the gross value of each transfer, and calculate the correct net figure.

Including the transfer of January 2019 in your calculation, has Park used up all of his NRB or not?

The answer is that he has not – but only just. Over the past seven years, he has used up all £325,000 of his NRB; in other words, his cumulative total over those seven years is £325,000. If you thought that he had used it up because he has transferred a total of £475,000, you have made the mistake of counting the transfer to Suki. That transfer is to an individual, so it is a PET and it is not counted: we 'wait and see', remember. This means that the gift to the Haviland Trust would just fall within the NRB. (There may be further exemptions or reliefs which could be deducted: see below.) Remember that any transfer that falls within the NRB is not exempt from tax: it is taxed at 0%. The result is that Park has no IHT to pay.

Please note that we have only considered the question of the cumulative total in this example – we would also have to go on to consider exemptions and reliefs before calculating IHT. We will do this in the examples which follow.

Tax chargeable on LCT when the gift is made

What would happen if the cumulative total exceeded the NRB? Then, for LCTs, tax is payable at the lifetime rate, which we know is 20%. Let's look again at Park, this time in **Practice example 10.7.**

Practice example 10.7

Park makes a very large gift of £250,000 to his nephew's IT company in May 2021. This is an LCT. We must look back over the previous seven years: that is, from May 2014 to May 2021. Here is the picture now:

October 2017   £75,000 to a discretionary trust
December 2017   £150,000 to his partner Suki
June 2018   £85,000 to a family trust with a life interest for his father
November 2018   £30,000 to the alumni fund of his old university
January 2019   £10,000 to the Haviland Trust
May 2021   £250,000 to the IT company

Note that the seven-year period has changed: you always count back seven years from the date of the most recent transfer. This means that the gift made in February 2014 is no longer included for cumulative total or NRB purposes. What is the cumulative total including this new gift and is any IHT payable? Remember, again, that to simplify matters, all of the figures given from October 2017 to January 2019 are shown *net* of any applicable reliefs and exemptions. However, in practice you would first have to apply these to the gross value of the transfer to give the correct net value.

First of all, let's consider the transfer of £250,000 itself. When it was made, you will note that two annual exemptions of £3,000 were available: one for the tax year ending 5 April 2021, and another for the

tax year ending 5 April 2022. This sum of £6,000 can be deducted from the total amount of the transfer: the total *taxable* transfer in May 2021 was therefore £244,000.

Now let's look at the new cumulative total. It is £450,000. Before the May 2021 gift is made, the cumulative total is £200,000 (that is, there is £125,000 of the NRB left). That means that £125,000 of the taxable May 2021 transfer of £244,000 is taxed at 0% but the remaining £119,000 that falls outside the NRB is taxable at the lifetime rate of 20%. The tax payable will be 20% of £119,000 = £23,800. This is payable immediately.

Tax chargeable on LCT if the transferor dies within seven years

If the transferor dies within seven years of making an LCT, the inheritance tax must be recalculated at the death rate. **Practice example 10.8** shows this calculation.

Practice example 10.8

When a transferor dies, we must re-calculate the inheritance tax due, looking at each individual transaction which took place in the 7 year period prior to death. In this next example, Fela died in May 2022, so the relevant 7 year period is May 2015–May 2022. He made no transfers before November 2015. After that, he made the following transfers (in all cases, we are again using the net values, after deductions of any applicable exemptions and reliefs):

November 2015	£80,000 to his sister's limited company
January 2016	£75,000 to a discretionary trust for his nieces and nephews
March 2018	£225,000 to the Baxis Foundation, a profit-making association
May 2022	Fela dies

Fela paid all chargeable inheritance tax on these gifts at the time they were made. What further inheritance tax is payable after his death?

We must now take each individual chargeable transfer, from the earliest to the latest, and work out the post-death inheritance tax for each one. In each case, we look back seven years from the transfer in question to see how much of the relevant NRB has been used. In the seven-year period prior to November 2015, Fela had the full NRB of £325,000 available. His transfer of £80,000 was therefore within that NRB and is now charged to tax at 0%. In January 2016, when he transferred the net sum of £75,000, he had used up £80,000 of his NRB within the past 7 years, and therefore still had £245,000 of it available. His transfer of £75,000 was well within that band, and is again charged to tax at 0%. However, by March 2018, when he transferred the £225,000 to the Baxis Foundation, he had only £170,000 of his NRB available. The first £170,000 of the March 2018 £225,000 transfer is therefore charged to inheritance tax at 0%, but the balance of £55,000 is now charged at the death rate of 40%, a total of £22,000. As the March 2018 transfer was made between four and five years of Fela's death, taper relief is available at 60%, so the chargeable total is £13,200. HMRC will take account of any tax paid on this transfer during Fela's lifetime (that is, at the lifetime rate).

The effect of death on PETs

As you have seen, the death of the transferor within seven years of an LCT causes a big impact. It causes an even bigger impact to a PET because the 'potentially exempt' transfer is no longer exempt from tax at all. Let's look at the effect of this in **Practice example 10.9.**

Practice example 10.9

In September 2019, Maisie makes a gift of £75,000 to her sister Purdie. It is the first transfer for value she has ever made. At the time it is made, it is a potentially exempt transfer and would attract annual exemptions of £3,000 for the tax years ending April 2019 and April 2020, meaning that the total taxable value of the gift is £69,000.

We then 'wait and see' whether Maisie will survive seven years. We know therefore that at the time it is made, the transfer is not liable for any inheritance tax. If Maisie survives until September 2026, then no IHT is ever payable on that gift. However, Maisie dies in June 2023. Assuming she made no other transfers before she died, how much IHT is now payable on that gift?

Although no tax was payable in September 2019, IHT will now be payable. Just as we did in the previous examples relating to Fela, we have to look back at the seven-year period between June 2016 and June 2023 to calculate the cumulative total. In this case, that is simple: the cumulative total is £69,000 (because Maisie had made no other transfers) and therefore the NRB has not been used up. The gift is therefore taxed at 0% and no tax is payable on the lifetime transfer.

What would the position be, though, if Maisie had made an LCT of £300,000 (after deductions of exemptions and reliefs) in July 2016, and then the gift to Purdie, and then died in June 2023?

In this case, the cumulative total from June 2016 to June 2023 would be £369,000, and £44,000 of the gift to Purdie would exceed the NRB. This would now be chargeable to tax at the death rate of 40% and therefore £17,600 would be payable in tax. As Maisie died within three to four years of the September 2019 gift, taper relief is available at 40%, which makes the total amount of tax payable £7,040.

INHERITANCE TAX ON THE DEATH ESTATE

We have now looked at the basics of IHT on lifetime transfers. There is one further occasion on which IHT is payable, and that is on the whole of the estate upon death. In summary, having looked at the taxation of what the deceased gave away during their lifetime, we are now looking at the taxation of the property and money they did not give away, but kept until they died. In fact, the law looks on what then happens as a further transfer: all of the deceased's property passes from their hands into the hands of their PRs (s 4 of the IHTA 1984). When that happens, there is another taxable transfer. In a very real sense, the passing of the estate to the PRs is the deceased's last ever gift.

Tax is chargeable at the death rate on all of the estate which falls above the NRB. Yes – we must calculate for a third time! See **Practice example 10.10**.

Practice example 10.10

Madox dies, leaving an estate worth £425,000. Within seven years of his death, he had made an LCT of £100,000 after deduction of all applicable reliefs and exemptions. He made no other transfers during his lifetime.

How much IHT is payable on the estate?

When Madox died, he had £225,000 of the NRB remaining and this passed to his estate. This means that IHT is due on £200,000 of his estate at the death rate of 40%. No taper relief is available on the death estate; taper relief applies to lifetime transfers only. The tax due is £80,000.

When calculating the amount of IHT payable on death, you move through the applicable rules in the same strict order that you move through them in relation to lifetime transfers.

What is the 'death estate' for inheritance tax purposes?

As well as all of the items that we looked at in **Chapter 6**, there are some further items which are not included in the death estate for administrative purposes, but are included for tax purposes. The most important of these is an interest in an equitable/beneficial joint tenancy.

Joint tenancies

We know that the principle of survivorship applies to joint tenancies and that the deceased's interest in the property, whatever it is, will immediately pass to the other co-owners on death and does not form part of the inheritable estate (see **Chapter 6**). However, the deceased's interest in the joint tenancy is in fact included in the death estate *for tax purposes only*. For example, if the deceased owned a property worth £250,000 jointly with a business partner, the property would pass entirely to the business partner on the deceased's death, but the estate would be liable for tax on the deceased's 'share' of £125,000.

The rule does not change if the deceased shared the joint tenancy with a spouse or civil partner, but the effects of the rule in that case are generally very different because, as we have seen, transfers to spouses or civil partners are always exempt from IHT.

Donatio mortis causa *gifts and interest in settled property*

Donatio mortis causa gifts (see **Chapter 6**) are also included in the death estate for IHT purposes, because the deceased owned them at the moment of death – they only pass to the donee in the seconds after death.

There are complex rules about inclusion in the death estate if the deceased had a life or a limited interest in settled property. If the interest was created before 2006, it may be valued as if the deceased owned all of the capital in the trust fund. The subject is too complex to be dealt with in the scope of this book.

Gifts with a reservation are also included in the death estate for tax purposes (see **Anti-avoidance: gifts subject to a reservation** below).

Property ignored

IHT can only apply to property owned by the deceased at the time of death. This means that many of the assets that we looked at in **Chapter 6** as property passing outside of the estate will not be liable to IHT, including life insurance policies written into trust and pension scheme nominations. If the benefits are discretionary (see **Chapter 6, Proceeds of life insurance policies**), even if they might be payable to the deceased, the deceased had no right to them at the time of death. You should now be able to see why, for example, well-advised testators will want to write their life insurance policies into trust: otherwise, 40% of the payout could be spent on IHT when it might be desperately needed by the family they leave behind.

All of the assets in the estate have to be valued in order for a correct calculation to be made. If there are particularly valuable assets, including land and antiques, specialist valuers will be called on to give a market valuation.

ANTI-AVOIDANCE: GIFTS SUBJECT TO A RESERVATION

The most commonly used stratagem to attempt to defeat the effects of IHT is the 'gift subject to a reservation' (s 102 Finance Act 1986). A typical example is given in **Practice example 10.11**.

Practice example 10.11

Mitzi owns a London flat worth £575,000. She has decided to retire to her cottage in Dorset. In order to minimise her IHT liabilities, she decides to make a lifetime gift of the flat to her nephew, Rowan. However, Mitzi tells Rowan that although she is transferring the flat to him, she wants to be able to live there rent-free for at least two months in the summer and one month in the winter.

Can Mitzi claim that this gift is a PET?

What Mitzi has done is to *reserve* some of the benefit of the property to herself: she has given Rowan a gift 'with strings', the string specifically being that Mitzi wants to carry on getting use and benefit from the property while appearing to give it away. This means that Mitzi cannot claim that this is a PET. If she tried to do so, and she was still using the flat at the time that she died, then the entire transfer would be ignored and the flat would be treated as part of her death estate. Note that if Mitzi died within seven years of this attempted PET, not only would the value of the flat be added to her estate but IHT may also be charged on the failed exempt transfer: in other words, the transfer would be taxed as if it had succeeded and also as if it had failed. This means that the same property would be taxed twice. The consequences of such an outcome are, as you will understand, potentially disastrous for the estate and therefore for all of the beneficiaries, and very strong efforts have to be made to avoid such an outcome.

In **Practice example 10.11**, the gift would not be subject to a reservation if Mitzi decided to pay the market rent for staying in the flat, or if she decided that she would not stay in the flat at all. The gift would then not be subject to the reservation after the date of her decision; it would become a PET. However, as you will have seen, any potential gifts with reservations are best avoided because the sanction of double taxation is particularly severe.

There are other anti-avoidance rules which are outside the scope of this guide: these are very closely based on fiscal statutes and it is less likely that you will be required to know them or their effects in detail for the purpose of the SQE1 assessments.

LIABILITY TO OTHER TAXES DURING ADMINISTRATION OF THE ESTATE

For SQE1, you also need to be aware of the rules concerning the liabilities of PRs and beneficiaries to CGT and income tax. We have given you the absolute basics here which you must reinforce by further reading.

Capital gains tax

The main rules relating to CGT are dealt with in *Revise SQE: Business Law and Practice*, and we are not going to look at them in detail here. However, we will look at the principal ways in which they impact PRs and beneficiaries.

Personal representatives

If the deceased died owing CGT on a taxable gain, then the PRs must obviously pay that as part of their duty to administer the estate. One thing to note, however, is that although for IHT purposes death is a 'transfer' (see above), for capital gains purposes death is not a 'disposal'. This means that there is no CGT chargeable as the death estate passes into the hands of the PRs. Instead, the PRs take on the assets with the (market) value they have at the date of death. They will in due course have to distribute those assets to the beneficiaries and no CGT arises when they do so (even if values have risen in the meantime). This includes transfers to non-natural persons such as trusts.

However, PRs may have to, or choose to, sell assets of the deceased's estate once it is in their hands. If they do, and the proceeds of sale exceed the market value on death, there is a chargeable gain on which they must pay CGT. There are exceptions and exemptions to this general rule which are outside the scope of this guide.

Beneficiaries

We have already seen that for CGT purposes assets come into the estate and are passed out to beneficiaries at their market value on the date of death: therefore, no CGT is payable. However, there is an area in which beneficiaries can be caught out. This is where they sell the inherited asset on at a higher value. For example, if a beneficiary receives an asset worth £15,000 but then decides to sell it the following year for £25,000, they will be liable for CGT on that gain (although they may be able to use their personal CGT allowance to reduce or extinguish their liability).

Exam warning

Of course, for both PRs and beneficiaries, you must always check that the disposal you are being asked about has indeed resulted in a gain! Where there is a loss, no CGT is payable.

Income tax

As with CGT, let's look at the main ways in which income tax impacts PRs and beneficiaries.

Personal representatives

While the estate is being wound up, investments (building society accounts, investment accounts and so on) may be earning some income in the way of interest. If the income earned is less than £100 and is only from interest on savings accounts, the PRs do not need to pay income tax on it. However, if it is larger than £100 and comes from other sources, then income tax will arise and it is the PRs who are responsible for paying it. While most estates only earn a small amount of interest and almost wholly from savings accounts, watch out for the anomalies, which will include income tax on rent paid to the estate for a property which is currently being rented out. A residuary fund, which is being invested in a number of places in order to provide income for life tenants, is another example. PRs will pay income tax on the income of that fund, but that is not the end of the matter: beneficiaries may also have to pay some income tax, as we will see below. Income tax is payable at the basic rate on all income, but there is no income tax personal allowance on deceased estates: all of the income is liable to income tax unless it falls under the interest on savings exception above.

Beneficiaries

As we have seen in the preceding paragraph, PRs must pay income tax on any residuary fund during the administration of the estate, but they will then pay out the income to any beneficiaries of the residuary estate entitled to income. Those beneficiaries will also have a personal liability to pay income tax on that income. As a result, beneficiaries can generally claim a tax credit for income tax already paid by the PRs. The rules here are complex and you should refer to your wider reading.

■ KEY POINT CHECKLIST

This chapter has covered the following key knowledge points. You can structure your revision around these, making sure to recall the key details for each point, as covered in this chapter.
• When IHT is chargeable.
• How IHT is calculated.
• Exemptions and reliefs.
• How to calculate the cumulative total.
• When and how to recalculate IHT.
• The composition of the death estate for IHT.
• Anti-avoidance.

■ KEY TERMS AND CONCEPTS

• lifetime chargeable transfer (LCT) (**page 164**)
• potentially exempt transfer (PET) (**page 164**)

■ SQE1-STYLE QUESTIONS

QUESTION 1

A businesswoman made a payment of £5,000 to her son to pay part of his living expenses while at university. She also gifted her old car, worth £10,000, to her sister. On the same day, the businesswoman sold a painting to a business associate for the sum of £4,000, wrongly believing that this was its true value. In fact, the painting was only worth £500. The businesswoman also sold a designer watch to her aunt for £350. The businesswoman knew that the true value of the watch was £3,000.

Which of the following transactions are transfers for value for IHT purposes?

A. The payment of £5,000 to the businesswoman's son only.

B. The payment of £5,000 to the businesswoman's son, the gift of the car to her sister and the sale of the painting.

C. The gift of the car to the businesswoman's sister and the sale of the watch to her aunt.

D. The payment of £5,000 to the businesswoman's son, the gift of the car to her sister and the sale of the watch to her aunt.

E. The gift of the car to the businesswoman's sister and the sale of the painting.

QUESTION 2

A man makes three transfers of value to his brother in three tax years. In the first tax year, the man transfers £1,500. In the second tax year, the man transfers £2,000. In the third tax year, the man transfers £500. The man makes no other transfers during this period.

What is the total amount of annual exemptions available to the man in the third tax year?

A. £3,500.

B. £2,500.

C. £6,000.

D. £5,000.

E. The man has no annual exemptions available.

QUESTION 3

A young man is going to be married shortly and he and his fiancée are planning to buy a house together. The deposit for the house is £25,000. The young man's father decides to give the young man the £25,000 as a cash gift. The young man has no annual exemptions available.

Which of the following statements best describes the IHT liability of this gift?

A. The full gift of £25,000 is exempt from IHT because it is a wedding present.

B. The full gift of £25,000 is a PET.

C. The first £5,000 of the gift will not be liable for IHT because it is a wedding present, but the balance of £20,000 is an LCT.

D. The first £5,000 of the gift will not be liable for IHT because it is a wedding present, but the balance of £20,000 is a PET.

E. The full gift of £25,000 is exempt from IHT because it is not a transfer for value.

QUESTION 4

A businessman decided to divest himself of some assets. The businessman was a partner in a public relations consultancy firm and sold his partnership interest to another one of the partners. The businessman also sold a car which was a partnership asset. The businessman then loaned £35,000 to the partnership to assist with cash flow problems arising from his departure. The businessman also decided to sell two shareholdings: 5,000 shares in a business he had bought 18 months ago, and of which he was the sole proprietor, and 10,000 preference shares of a public limited company of which he was the majority shareholder.

Which of the following transfers attracts business property relief at 100%?

A. The sale of the businessman's partnership interest.

B. The sale of the businessman's car.

C. The loan of £35,000 made by the businessman to the partnership.

D. The sale of 5,000 shares in the private company.

E. The sale of 10,000 shares in the public limited company.

QUESTION 5

A man owned a house worth £450,000 as a joint tenant with his cohabitee (he was not married or in a civil partnership). During his lifetime, the man set up a trust by which the proceeds of his life insurance policy would be paid to his cohabitee when he died. The man fell ill, and while he was in hospital, he told his brother that if he did not recover from his illness, he wanted his brother to have his motorcycle. The man also made a gift of £20,000 to his cousin while he was in hospital. Five days after he made the gift to his cousin, the man died.

Which of the man's assets are included in the death estate for IHT purposes?

A. Only the joint tenancy and the £20,000 gift are included in the death estate for IHT purposes.

B. Only the joint tenancy and the life insurance policy are included in the death estate for IHT purposes.

C. Only the £20,000 gift, the life insurance policy and the motorcycle are included in the death estate for IHT purposes.

D. Only the joint tenancy and the motorcycle are included in the death estate for IHT purposes.

E. Only the £20,000 gift and the life insurance policy are included in the death estate for IHT purposes.

■ ANSWERS TO QUESTIONS

Answers to 'What do you know already?' questions at the start of the chapter

1) False. IHT is payable on gifts made during a person's lifetime as well as on a deceased person's estate.

2) Every time there is a lifetime chargable transfer or potentially exempt transfer.

3) Yes. Even though the survivorship principle operates and the deceased person's share passes automatically to their fellow joint tenant(s) without becoming part of the estate for probate purposes (see **Chapter 6**), this undivided share *does* form part of the estate for *tax* purposes and is taxed at a modified market value.

4) False. Although the beneficiaries may sometimes have to pay tax on a specific gift that is made to them out of the estate, the responsibility for paying IHT on the estate itself is always on the PRs.

Answers to end-of-chapter SQE1-style questions

Question 1:

The correct answer was C. The gift of the car was a straightforward transfer of a £10,000 value. The sale to the aunt was a sale at an undervalue and represented a transfer for value of £2,650. However, the payment to her son was maintenance, and was therefore not a transfer for value, so A, B and D must be incorrect. The businesswoman did not know that she was selling the painting at below market value, which falls within the 'bad bargain' exception, and means that B and E are also incorrect on this ground.

Question 2:

The correct answer was A. A taxpayer is permitted an annual exemption of £3,000 in each tax year and can carry forward what remains of the allowance from the previous tax year, but from no earlier tax years. The man had £1,000 remaining from his allowance for the second tax year and a further £2,500 remaining from the third tax year: a total of £3,500. All other options are therefore incorrect.

Question 3:

The correct answer was D. Wedding presents are exempt transfers only up to an upper limit of £5,000, so A is incorrect. The first £5,000 of this gift will be exempt, but the balance of £20,000 will be chargeable, so B is incorrect. The transfer is to an individual, so it is not an LCT, and so C is incorrect. This is certainly a transfer for value as it has decreased the value of the father's estate by £25,000, so E is incorrect.

Question 4:

The correct answer was A. All of the other options either do not attract business property relief (BPR) at all or attract it at only 50%. The car belonged to the partnership; BPR is limited to 50% (therefore B is incorrect). C is not a transfer for value: it is a loan, which will be repaid by the partnership on the terms agreed. It therefore does not fall within the BPR rules. BPR is not available at all to the businessman in D, as it can only apply to sales where the individual concerned has owned the business for at least two years. The businessman in E has control of the plc and can claim only 50% BPR on the sale as the company is quoted.

Question 5:

The correct answer was D. The two items beneficially owned by the man at his death were his interest under the joint tenancy and the motorcycle, which passed to his brother immediately after his death as a *donatio mortis causa* but which was still owned by him at the time of death. Although usually an interest under a joint tenancy would not fall into the death inheritable estate, it does fall into the death estate for IHT purposes. The man did not own the proceeds of the life insurance policy at the time of his death: his cohabitee was the beneficiary of the trust set up for these. The man also did not own the £20,000, which was fully gifted to the cousin during the man's lifetime before he died (note the difference between this gift and the gift to his brother). Therefore, all other options are incorrect.

■ KEY CASES, RULES, STATUTES AND INSTRUMENTS

The SQE1 Assessment Specification does not require you to know any specific statutes, rules or cases for this topic. On this particular topic, it is probably much more important to understand how the taxation rules are applied than to be able to identify their source.

Will trusts: trustees and beneficiaries

■ MAKE SURE YOU KNOW

This chapter provides an overview of will trusts, including trustees and beneficiaries. It is essential, for this topic, that you know and thoroughly understand the key concepts from your trusts studies, because you are now asked to apply them in the context of wills.

■ SQE ASSESSMENT ADVICE

As you work through this chapter, remember to pay particular attention in your revision to:
- how the basic principles of trusts law apply to will trusts
- *how* and *why* a will trust may be created
- the differences between the executors' role as executors and as will trustees
- how to deal with a will trust containing land
- the basic principles of maintenance and advancement.

■ WHAT DO YOU KNOW ALREADY?

Have a go at these questions before reading this chapter. If you find some difficult or cannot remember the answers, make a note to look more closely at that area during your revision.

1) What are the three certainties required for every trust?
   [How a will trust is constructed, page 187]
2) How is a will trust created, and when does it take effect?
   [How a will trust is constructed, page 187]
3) Can a will trust also be a trust of land?
   [The Trusts of Land and Appointment of Trustees Act (TLATA) 1996, page 191]
4) True or false? Will trustees do not have the statutory powers of investment set out at s 3 of the Trustee Act 2000.
   [Introduction to will trusts, page 186]

INTRODUCTION TO WILL TRUSTS

Cast your mind back to the imaginative exercise we undertook at the start of **Chapter 3** when we imagined all of the testator's belongings spread out in one space. We examined what is in the testator's mind at the point of making decisions about who will benefit from the will. At that point, we were thinking primarily about the gifts that will be made from the will almost straight away: for example, a pecuniary legacy of £10,000 to a specified cousin or a gift of the testator's car to a son or daughter.

However, there are times when the testator will not want to make immediate, straightforward gifts. The testator may have a large amount of money in an investment portfolio, or may have one or more houses, and may not wish to give these items away directly or to just one person or two people. The testator might wish to allow the property to be used more flexibly by allowing some discretion to named controllers of the property to make payments to those who most need them. Nobody can foresee what will happen after they die, or which family member may be in most need of financial assistance or a roof over their head. In addition, it may either be impossible to transfer property to beneficiaries directly – because they are minors, for example, who cannot own property – or problematic to do so, perhaps because of their personal circumstances.

The solution is to create a **will trust**.

> ### Key term: will trust
>
> Any trust contained in a will is called a 'will trust'. These are express trusts written into the will itself, which will in most cases outlive the administration of the rest of the estate (see **Chapter 8** for more on general administration). By the time the will trusts have fulfilled their purpose, the testator may have been dead for many years and the estate long since wound up; but the creation of the will trusts has meant that their wishes can be carried out even long after death.

We are going to look in more detail in the rest of this chapter at some specific points relating to will trusts, but you should bear in mind as we do so that the basic rules on trusts (see *Revise SQE: Trusts Law*) also apply to will trusts.

In particular, the statutory powers given to trustees, including the powers of investment, apply just as much to will trusts as elsewhere. You should also bear in mind that all of the rights and remedies that beneficiaries have under trusts generally (including, for example, the right to bring a trust to an end under the rule in *Saunders v Vautier*, proprietary remedies such as tracing and third-party remedies in dishonest assistance and unconscionable receipt) apply just as much to will trusts as to other trusts. A detailed examination of these issues is outside the scope of this book, but you should ensure that you are aware of the relevant rules.

All of the statutory and common law duties of care, including the duty at s 1 of the Trustee Act 2000, apply to will trustees, and will trustees also owe a fiduciary duty to the beneficiaries of the will trust: see **Fiduciary duties and duties of care of trustees** below.

We will be referring to some of these more general points as we consider some of the specific issues that can arise in relation to will trusts.

> ## Revision tip
>
> As you go through this chapter, make sure that you understand all of the trusts concepts that are being discussed, and review your knowledge if you are unsure. Note in particular that for the SQE1 wills assessment, you should know about trusts for minors, life interest trusts and discretionary trusts.

HOW A WILL TRUST IS CONSTRUCTED

Where the testator's instructions make it necessary for a trust to be created, the trust will be expressly set out in the will. The will trust clause will state clearly that the testator is giving the specified property 'upon trust', which will satisfy the certainty of intention requirements (see also *Revise SQE: Trusts Law*).

The will then sets out the property which will be covered by the trust (certainty of subject matter) and expressly appoint the trustees of the trust. The trustees are usually, but not always, the persons named as executors of the will. However, it is possible to name non-executors as trustees of the trust.

The clause will also set out in clear terms who are the beneficiaries of the trust: in other words, that there is certainty of objects.

It is very common for a will first to make specific bequests and legacies (see **Chapter 3**) and then to create a trust of the residuary estate, or specific (usually large) items of property such as land/real estate or funds in a bank account or investment portfolio.

Even if the testator wishes the executors and testators to be the same people, it is vital for those people to be expressly appointed as trustees. The role of the personal representatives (PRs), as we have seen in **Chapter 2**, is to perform their duties as efficiently as possible and to wind up the estate within a reasonable time; but the trust will usually outlast the estate, and executors will have no powers under the trust if these are not expressly given to them in the will. If a will contains a trust as well as specific legacies and devises (again, see **Chapter 3**), the executors will distribute the estate and then wind it up. However, if they are also trustees, they will continue to manage the trust until the trust has come to an end.

INTRODUCTION TO WILL TRUSTEES' POWERS

All trustees have a number of statutory powers (see *Revise SQE: Trusts Law*), unless those powers are expressly excluded from the trust. In the case of will trusts, you can now see that the express exclusion of those powers would have to be in the wording of the will, as this is where the trust is set up.

As well as these statutory powers, the settlor (who in this case is also the testator) can give the trustees additional express powers: for example, the settlor/testator will often give the trustees an express power to insure the trust property. The settlor can also expressly limit or extend the statutory powers if they believe that that is appropriate.

Exam warning

Remember that any express wording in the will trust takes precedence over the implied statutory power: what is expressly set out in the will trust is always stronger. If a multiple-choice question (MCQ) sets out a valid will clause which apparently refines or contradicts a statutory power, it is the express will clause which will decide the issue.

Trustees' powers are often divided into two classes: administrative powers, which assist in managing the trust, and distributive powers, which are powers that allow them to give the beneficiaries trust money or property (often subject to certain conditions, particularly in discretionary trusts).

In the following sections, we are going to focus on two particular statutory powers which have particular relevance for will trusts: trustees' powers of investment and the powers of maintenance and advancement. Powers of investment are administrative (management) powers; powers of maintenance and advancement are distributive powers.

TRUSTEES' POWERS OF INVESTMENT

The general statutory investment power is contained in s 3 of the Trustee Act 2000. When exercising this power, the trustees must invest using the standard investment criteria (SIC) set out in s 4 of that Act. Remember that all trustees have this power unless the will expressly limits it in some way.

Investments (including stocks and bonds) do not have to be situated in the UK for the purposes of s 3/4, so if, for example, the testator had investments in the USA which were held in a US bank, they would nonetheless form part of the trust property.

Land as an investment

S 3(3) prohibits trustees from investing in land. However, Section 8 of the Trustee Act 2000 gives trustees the power to invest in any kind of land, freehold or leasehold, but only if that land is within the UK. Even if at the time of making the will, the testator does not own any land outside the UK, this could be a significant problem in the future (see **Practice example 11.1**). For that reason, the trusts clause in the will may grant the trustees an express power to acquire land outside the UK for investment purposes. Remember that it is the express wording of the will which takes precedence.

Practice example 11.1

Bjorn makes a will in 2010. At the time that Bjorn makes his will, he has a property portfolio consisting of a number of flats in and around central Manchester which he rents out to tenants. He owns no land outside the UK at that time.

Bjorn's will leaves the residue of his estate, which includes all of the Manchester properties, on trust for his three nieces. If Bjorn died in 2010, the trustees would be able, using the statutory power at s 8 of the Trustee Act 2000, to take ownership of the Manchester properties, because they are land within the UK.

However, Bjorn does not die in 2010. In 2015 he buys a flat in Stockholm, Sweden, intending to return there when he retires. He then sells all of the Manchester properties in early 2020 in preparation for going back to Sweden, but sadly dies of Covid-19 in May 2020. At the time of his death, the only land he owns is the Stockholm property. He has not made any amendments to his will.

What happens in this situation?

When Bjorn died in 2020, under s 8 the trustees only had the statutory power to invest in land in the UK and not land in Sweden. As you will see, this creates a major problem, because the trustees are not able to call for the Stockholm property to be vested in them as trustees. Although other items of Bjorn's property, including the proceeds of sale of the Manchester flats, may well fall into the residue, the Stockholm flat cannot become trust property because (if we use the terms we learned in basic trusts) constitution of the trust has failed. Title to the property cannot be transferred to the trustees.

In **Practice example 11.1**, if the original will trust had contained an express provision lifting the restriction in s 8 and allowing the trustees to invest in and acquire land outside of the UK, the flat in Stockholm would not have been an issue.

Land retained for occupation by a beneficiary

A testator may want land owned by them not to be immediately sold on their death but retained so that someone (perhaps a spouse or an adult child) can live in it. Their interest is called a **life tenancy**.

Key term: life tenancy

The word 'tenancy' does not mean that this is a leasehold interest: the phrase 'life tenancy' in a trusts context means that the beneficiary has an interest under the trust only for as long as the beneficiary lives. After their death, the property must pass on to someone else: this 'backstop' interest is called the 'remainder', as you may recall from your trusts studies.

If the testator wishes to have this arrangement, a trust *must* be set up to carry out those wishes. Executors cannot hold on to real property indefinitely; their primary job, as we have seen in **Chapters 2** and **8**, is to get in the assets of the estate, pay the liabilities, distribute the estate and then wind it up, using the 'executor's year' as their rough guide. These duties are incompatible with holding the title to real property for what may be many years and subject to a life interest and a remainder.

As we have seen, s 8 of the Trustee Act allows trustees to acquire land in the UK as an investment: but what happens if the land is being retained in order to allow someone to live there? That is not, strictly speaking, an 'investment', particularly if the occupant is living there without paying any costs.

This situation is dealt with by s 8(1)(b), which also allows trustees to acquire land for occupation by a beneficiary. As discussed above, this power, if left unamended, relates only to land in the UK, but will extend to land outside the UK if amended (see **Practice example 11.2**).

Practice example 11.2

Donal's will contained a will trust which permitted his partner Neve to live rent-free, for as long as she wished, in any property owned by Donal at the time of his death. The will clause expressly set out that the trustees were able to acquire and/or invest in property situated anywhere in the world. When Donal died, the only land he owned was a cottage in County Clare in the Republic of Ireland.

Is Neve able to live in this property?

Because the s 8 restriction had been lifted, this property could be transferred to the will trustees and Neve would be able to live there for as long as she wished.

The Trusts of Land and Appointment of Trustees Act (TLATA) 1996

Section 1(1)(a) of TLATA makes it clear that any trust which consists of or includes any land is a 'trust of land' (see **Chapter 8**). There are two main reasons why this is important in the context of will trusts.

The first reason is that if a trust is a trust of land, the trustees are given extra powers on top of the powers that they will have under the Trustee Act 2000. They also have extra duties. Not all of these are convenient or suitable for a particular will trust.

The second reason is that even if the testator did not intend to create a trust of land, and only intended to create a straightforward trust, there may be an unintentional trust of land at the testator's death – and that can have unintended consequences.

Let's look at the 'unintentional trust of land' point now (see **Practice example 11.3**), and after that we can consider the extra powers under TLATA.

Practice example 11.3

Fela makes a will which includes a trust of his residuary estate for the benefit of his two nephews, Adam and Brandon. At the time that he makes the will, Fela does not own any land.

However, four years after making the will, Fela inherits a house from his aunt Rosa. He makes no alteration to his will and dies two years later.

In this situation, is there a trust of land?

If Fela had died immediately after making the will, the trust of the residuary estate would not be a trust of land. However, as Fela goes on to inherit his aunt Rosa's house, he now owns land. The house falls into his residuary estate, and the trust of that estate is now a trust of land because it includes land.

It was not Fela's original intention to create a trust of land, but because of s 1 TLATA, that is in fact what has happened.

This situation is important because the beneficiaries under a trust of land (in **Practice example 11.3**, Fela's nephews) are given specific and quite powerful rights under TLATA. These rights can be modified or excluded in the will, but if they have not been, then the beneficiaries can use the rights to their full extent.

TLATA s 12: the beneficiary's right to occupy
Section 12 gives the beneficiaries rights, but those rights are subject to specific powers given to the trustees. Let's deal with the rights first. Section 12 of the 1996 Act gives a beneficiary the *right* to occupy trust property. However, the right only exists if either (i) the purpose of the trust includes making the land available for the beneficiary's occupation or (ii) the land is being held by the trustees so that it is available for the beneficiary's occupation (s 12(1)). It must also not be expressly excluded by the trust instrument itself. If the will trust contains

an express provision that s 12 is not to apply to the trust, then no beneficiary will have a right to occupy.

Where the trust of land has been created unintentionally, it is unlikely that the trust's purpose was to make land available for a beneficiary; in fact, the trust was not created on purpose, full stop. But if the trustees are holding on to a vacant property waiting for the right moment to put it on the market, that may well be land that is suitable for the beneficiary's occupation. Under s 12(2) however the right is restricted if the land is not available for the beneficiary or is not suitable for occupation by that beneficiary.

This can lead to conflicts between the trustees and all of the beneficiaries on the grounds that the trustees take the view that it is not in the best interests of the trusts for one of the beneficiaries to occupy. It can also lead to conflicts between the beneficiaries because one or more of them claim a right to occupy the property to the exclusion of the others.

Trustees' powers under s 13 to control the right to occupy

Fortunately for the trustees, under s 13(1) of the 1996 Act they are given the power to exclude or restrict any beneficiary's rights of occupation as long as they are not being unreasonable and as long as the restrictions are not unreasonable: ss 13(2) and (3).

Where the purpose of an express trust certainly was to allow occupation of the land by a beneficiary, the trustees can use s 13(3) to impose conditions on that occupation if they believe that this will benefit the trust overall. If, for example, the testator makes a will trust allowing their adult child to live in their former home for life after the testator dies, but says nothing about any payments for occupation, the trustees may require that adult child to pay for any repairs or improvements to the property out of their own pocket. The trustees cannot do this if the testator has expressly provided in the will that the beneficiary should be allowed to live in the property free of any costs or expenses: in that case, the express terms of the will would take precedence.

The duty to consult beneficiaries under s 11(1) of TLATA

The trustees of land have another statutory duty under s 11(1) of TLATA, which is to consult, so far as is practicable, all beneficiaries of full age who are beneficially entitled to an interest in possession in the land, every time the trustees take a decision about that land. The trustees are not obliged to carry out the collective views of the beneficiaries – their only duty is to listen – but even this path can be fraught with dispute and dissent. As a result, where there is a possibility that there may be a trust of land on death, the will almost invariably includes an express exclusion of s 11 of TLATA, meaning that the trustees can take decisions without any obligation to hear the views of the beneficiaries.

POWERS OF MAINTENANCE AND ADVANCEMENT

We have seen that one of the main things a testator, particularly an elderly testator, may want to do is to put aside a sum of money, often quite a large sum of money, for the benefit of future generations. The testator does not and cannot know how that money may be needed in the future. All the testator can do is to put the money in the hands of responsible trustees and give them sufficient powers to be able to use the money wisely for the benefit of the beneficiaries when the time comes. The testator therefore includes a will trust in the will. Two of the most important powers in this context are the **powers of maintenance** and the **powers of advancement**.

Key term: power of maintenance
This power gives the trustees the ability to give income to beneficiaries, particularly infant beneficiaries, in circumstances where they would otherwise not be entitled to income. Maintenance powers are set out at s 31 of the Trustee Act 1925.

Key term: power of advancement
This power gives trustees the ability to give beneficiaries of any age a capital lump sum before the beneficiary would be entitled to any money under the will. Advancement powers are set out under s 32 of the Trustee Act 1925.

These powers are statutory, and trustees therefore have these powers automatically unless the will excludes them or limits them in some way.

Before we go on to consider how the powers of maintenance and advancement work, let's just remind ourselves that in every trust of a capital fund, the trust will be invested to earn income. The trust itself will provide whether the income must be paid out in a specified way to specified people, or whether the trustees have discretion to hold on to the income and add it to the capital in the fund. You may remember that this latter practice is known as *accumulation*.

Where the beneficiary is an infant (that is, under the age of 18), the trustees have a primary duty to accumulate the income and hold it, together with the capital value of the beneficiary's share, until the beneficiary reaches the age of 18 or marries/becomes a civil partner before that age (s 31(2) of the Trustee Act 1925). The trustee of an infant beneficiary is therefore clearly directed to prioritise accumulating the income as opposed to paying it out.

Revision tip
The powers of maintenance relate to the trustees' powers over income; the powers of advancement relate to the trustees' powers over capital.

Maintenance

Let's take a look at a fictional scenario to see why the powers of maintenance are so important, and how they would work in the context of a will trust.

Philomena set up a trust in her will for the benefit of her five grandchildren. None of the grandchildren were over the age of five years when the will was written in 2015.

Philomena specified that after she died, the sum of £500,000 was to be held on trust for her five grandchildren in equal shares. The trustees are not under any express duty to distribute the income to the beneficiaries and, as we know, have a primary duty to accumulate until the beneficiaries become absolutely entitled to their share of the fund. Philomena has stipulated that this will be when they reach the age of 25.

The basic position therefore is that no grandchild will receive any money from the fund until they reach the age of 25, at which point they will receive their share, which would include some accumulated income.

Philomena cannot know what the future will hold for each of her grandchildren, but she can anticipate that one or more of them might need to be paid some of the income before they are entitled to their capital share; for university fees, for example, or for emergencies such as medical treatment. What she wants to do is to give her trustees the power to accumulate the income for some beneficiaries some of the time, and to pay out income to other beneficiaries some of the time.

This is the statutory power that the trustees are given under s 31(1) of the Trustee Act 1925. Section 31(1) allows trustees at their sole discretion (so here we have a good example of a discretionary power) to pay all or part of the income from an infant beneficiary's share while that beneficiary is under the age of 18 and as long as the payment is for the maintenance or education of that beneficiary. As we know from **Chapter 5**, an infant cannot give good receipt for the money, so s 31 provides that the payment can be made to the parent or guardian of the infant beneficiary.

Let us now imagine that Philomena died in 2020 with a will to this effect in place. Nuala, one of her grandchildren, is 12 years old and has obtained a place at a prestigious music summer school in the USA. Nuala's parents want her to attend the summer school but they do not have the funds to afford Nuala's travel and accommodation expenses. Nuala will not receive any capital from the fund for another 13 years, so that is not a help at the moment. However, Nuala's parents can make an application to the will trustees under s 31 asking the trustees to exercise their power to pay some or all of the income from the trust to pay for Nuala's trip. As this trip clearly benefits Nuala's education and is of general benefit to her, the trustees will probably agree.

You can see that this power gives the trustees flexibility, which is really important. Without it, Nuala would still get her share, but not for another 13 years. She really needs the money now and the trustees have the power to effect this.

Revision tip

It is very important to note that the trustees can only exercise their power under s 31 for the 'maintenance, education or benefit' of the infant beneficiary; they must be able to justify the payment on those grounds.

The power under s 31 lasts until an infant beneficiary has reached the age of 18 or has married/become a civil partner before that age. At that point, under s 31(1)(ii), the beneficiary becomes absolutely entitled to have the income (and any accumulated income) paid to them, even if their interest in the trust has not **vested** but is only **contingent**.

Key term: vested/contingent interest

A vested interest is one which allows the beneficiary rights under the trust straight away; there are no conditions to a vested interest. All rights under a trust must be either vested or contingent. Contingent interests depend on a condition being satisfied: the intended beneficiary will reach the age of 25, for example.

Maintenance powers apply to contingent interests only where they 'carry the intermediate income' (that is, trusts where the beneficiary's share accrues income from the time the testator dies until the money is paid out): s 31(3). It is worth remembering that *all* testamentary gifts – apart from contingent pecuniary legacies – carry the intermediate income. Section 31 therefore applies, for example, to the trust created by Philomena above.

Advancement

This power is contained in s 32(1) of the Trustee Act 2000. It allows trustees to pay out shares of the capital in the trust to a beneficiary who is not yet entitled to be paid the capital; in fact, it allows trustees to pay out shares of the capital to a beneficiary who has only a contingent and not a vested interest. Again, this is a power with a particular significance for will trusts.

Revision tip

Candidates frequently misunderstand the meaning of 'advancement'. It is *not* used in the sense of 'advancing money'. It is a power to *advance the beneficiary in life*: to help them with their studies or to start a career, for example.

Let's look at a fictional scenario of a will trust where the power of advancement would make a significant difference to a contingent beneficiary.

In 2016, Howard's will created a trust for all or any of Howard's nieces and nephews who obtain a gold Duke of Edinburgh (DofE) award. The amount in the trust fund is £450,000. Howard had four nephews and nieces, none of whom had obtained a Duke of Edinburgh award when Howard died. All four nephews and nieces therefore had *contingent* interests in the trust property.

In 2018, Howard's niece Brianna obtained a gold DofE award. Her interest therefore vested at that stage and she was entitled to her £112,500 share of the capital fund.

This leaves three potential beneficiaries. One of these, Howard's niece Tia, has currently obtained a bronze DofE award but cannot continue because of illness. It is therefore uncertain whether her contingent interest will ever be vested.

Tia has been given the chance to buy the flat that she currently rents for the sum of £50,000, which is well below the market rate. She has asked the trustees to give her this sum of £50,000 under the trustees' power of advancement.

In this scenario, the trustees are able to use the s 32 power of advancement to assist Tia, even though her interest has not vested and may never vest. Note also that they can do this even though one beneficiary has already received her share of the capital fund and there are other beneficiaries who may be entitled to a share in the future.

The 'presumptive share' of the beneficiaries in this case is £112,500 (that is, one-quarter each of £450,000). If the trustees decide to use the power of advancement in Tia's favour, they can never give her more than the amount of her presumptive share: s 32(1)(a). However, Tia is seeking a payment of less than her presumptive share.

The trustees must be certain that the power is being used for the 'advancement' of Tia: that is, that it is being used to give Tia a good start in life. Obviously, being able to acquire a property at a reduced price is a very good start in life, so this standard is met.

If Tia's interest never becomes vested – that is, she does not ever obtain a gold DofE award – she does not have to repay any money to the trust. However, if it does become vested, the money given to Tia must be taken into account when her share is paid out: s 32(1)(b). If she does obtain a gold DofE award and her total share is worth £112,500, she will only get £62,500 because she has already received £50,000 of her share.

It is possible for a will trust to expressly exclude or limit the power of advancement. The testator/settlor may well have strong views that no potential beneficiary, even where all of the interests are vested from the outset, should be able to obtain money before the age specified either by law or in the trust. The difficulty, again, is the loss of flexibility for the beneficiaries as well as the trustees. If the beneficiary cannot get their share until they are 25, but has a life-changing opportunity at age 21, they will lose that opportunity if the power of advancement has been completely excluded.

One compromise is to limit the amount which can be given under the power. Under the unamended statutory power, the trustees are able to give up to 100% of the presumptive share in advance. However, settlors will often write in an express limitation that the trustees can only give up to a certain percentage of the share.

FIDUCIARY DUTIES AND DUTIES OF CARE OF TRUSTEES

One final point to note is the often concurrent nature of the fiduciary duties and duties of care of executors who are also will trustees. We dealt in **Chapter 8** with the fiduciary duties and duties of care of PRs. Those duties correspond with the fiduciary duties and duties of care of will trustees, including the statutory duty of care at s 1(1) of the Trustee Act 2000. When executors are also acting as will trustees, therefore, they are under two separate sets of fiduciary duties and duties of care: one set relating to their administration of the whole estate and one set relating to the management and administration of the will trust. Gradually, as we have seen, the estate will be wound up and executors' duties will fall away. However, as long as the trust is in existence and the trustees are in place, the trustees will continue to have both fiduciary duties and duties of care in relation to the will trusts.

◼ KEY POINT CHECKLIST

This chapter has covered the following key knowledge points. You can structure your revision around these, making sure to recall the key details for each point, as covered in this chapter.
- How the basic principles of trusts law apply to will trusts.
- *How* and *why* a will trust may be created.
- The differences between the executors' role as executors and as will trustees.
- How to deal with a will trust containing land.
- The basic principles of maintenance and advancement.

◼ KEY TERMS AND CONCEPTS

- will trust (**page 186**)
- life tenancy (**page 190**)

- power of maintenance (**page 193**)
- power of advancement (**page 193**)
- vested/contingent interest (**page 195**)

■ SQE1-STYLE QUESTIONS

QUESTION 1

A testator dies, leaving a will which contains three pecuniary legacies of £10,000 each ('the legacies') to his sisters and a specific gift of a car 'the gift') to his nephew. After these dispositions are made, the residuary estate is worth approximately £450,000. The will contains a trust directing that the residue should be held for the benefit of the testator's two infant grandchildren. The testator appoints his wife and his brother to be the executors of his will and his father-in-law as the trustee of the will trust.

Which of the following best describes the executors' powers under the will?

A. The executors can distribute the legacies and the gift but cannot distribute the £450,000 because it is trust property and does not fall into the estate.

B. The executors can distribute the legacies and the gift and can pay the £450,000 residue directly to the infant grandchildren.

C. The executors can distribute the legacies and the gift and can pay the £450,000 residue into the trust.

D. The executors can distribute the legacies and the gift and can distribute the £450,000 under the intestacy rules because the will creates a partial intestacy over the residue.

E. The executors can distribute the legacies and the gift, pay the £450,000 into the trust and then manage the trust fund for the grandchildren together with the father-in-law.

QUESTION 2

A testator appoints his only niece and nephew to be executors under their will. The will contains a trust of the residue of the testator's estate. The testator also appoints his nephew, who is an executor, and an old family friend, who is not an executor, as trustees. A solicitor is asked to advise the executors about the validity of the appointment of the trustees.

What advice should the solicitor give?

A. The appointment of the nephew and the old family friend as trustees is valid.

B. The appointment of the nephew and the old family friend as trustees is not valid unless the niece is also appointed as a trustee.

C. The appointment of the nephew and the old family friend as trustees is not valid unless the old family friend is removed as a trustee and replaced by the niece.

D. The appointment of the nephew and the old family friend as trustees is not valid unless the old family friend is removed as a trustee.

E. The appointment of the nephew and the old family friend as trustees is not valid unless the nephew is removed as a trustee.

QUESTION 3

A testator died last year. The will contains a trust of the residuary estate. The residuary estate includes a three-bedroom house ('the house') in a good neighbourhood. The will trust does not expressly exclude any rights of the beneficiaries to occupy the house. The house has been rented out to a tenant for the past 10 years. There are two beneficiaries of the will trust, a man and a woman. Both the man and the woman are claiming that they should be allowed to exercise their right to occupy the house to the exclusion of the other. The tenant is still in occupation of the property and is about to sign a new 10-year lease, which was negotiated with the testator before the testator died. The will trustees seek advice from their solicitor.

Which of the following most accurately describes the advice that should be given to the will trustees?

A. As the beneficiaries' right to occupy the house has not been excluded, the trustees must allow both the man and the woman to occupy the house.

B. As the beneficiaries' right to occupy the house has not been excluded, and both beneficiaries are in conflict, the property must be sold.

C. Although the beneficiaries' right to occupy the house has not been excluded, the trustees have absolute discretion to refuse to allow either beneficiary to occupy the house.

D. As the beneficiaries' right to occupy the house has not been excluded, the trustees must allow either the man or the woman to occupy the house.

E. Although the beneficiaries' right to occupy the house has not been excluded, the trustees can refuse to allow either beneficiary to occupy on the grounds that the house is not available.

QUESTION 4

A will trust contains an investment portfolio of stocks and shares, the sum of £10,000 in a bank account and shop premises with a flat above the shop. The will appoints the executors as the trustees of the will trust. There are three beneficiaries of the will trust. The first and second beneficiary do not live in the UK. The third beneficiary has, for the past 20 years, operated a business from the shop and has lived in the flat above the shop. Her lease of the property is about to expire. The third beneficiary has not yet decided whether she wishes to continue to occupy the flat. The will trust contains no clause which limits or excludes any express rights of the beneficiaries under any statute. The trustees have received an offer to buy the freehold of the shop and flat from a third-party purchaser. The price offered is slightly higher than the market value. The trustees have asked for advice from a solicitor.

What advice should the solicitor give to the trustees?

A. The trustees do not have to ask for the views of any of the beneficiaries in order to sell the freehold of the shop and flat, but they must first consider amongst themselves whether they should ask for the views of any of the beneficiaries.

B. The trustees must ask for the views of the third beneficiary in order to sell the freehold of the shop and flat.

C. The trustees must ask for the views of first and second beneficiaries in order to sell the freehold of the shop and flat.

D. The trustees must ask for the views of all of the beneficiaries in order to sell the freehold of the shop and flat.

E. The trustees do not have to ask for the views of any of the beneficiaries in order to sell the freehold of the shop and flat, nor are they required to consider amongst themselves whether they should ask for the views of any of the beneficiaries.

QUESTION 5

A girl aged 12, a talented dancer, has a contingent interest in a trust fund set up under her grandfather's will. The girl's interest in the trust, currently valued at £65,000, will vest when she is 21 years old. The gift carries the intermediate income and the current accumulated income is £6,000. The girl's mother has asked the trustees for the sum of £5,500 to pay for the girl and her mother to travel to, and stay in, Paris for the duration of a three-month ballet course. The trustees seek advice as to whether they can pay money from the trust to the girl's mother.

What is the most likely advice to be given to the trustees?

A. The trustees can use either their power of maintenance or advancement, but should prefer the use of their power of maintenance.

B. The trustees can use either their power of maintenance or advancement, but should prefer the use of their power of advancement.

C The trustees cannot use either their power of maintenance or advancement because the requested payment would also benefit the girl's mother and this is not permitted.

D The trustees can use their power of advancement, but cannot use the power of maintenance because the requested payment is not for the education or benefit of the girl.

E The trustees can use their power of maintenance, but cannot use the power of advancement because the requested payment will not help to set the girl up in life.

■ ANSWERS TO QUESTIONS

Answers to 'What do you know already?' questions at the start of the chapter

1) Certainty of intention, certainty of subject matter and certainty of objects.

2) A will trust is created by a clause or clauses within the will; it takes effect at the same time as the will – that is, when the testator dies.

3) Yes. All trusts which contain land as part of the trust property are trusts of land.

4) False. All trustees, whether of will trusts or any other kind of trust, have the powers of investment set out at s 3 of the Trustee Act 2000 unless the trust instrument expressly excludes or restricts those powers.

Answers to end-of-chapter SQE1-style questions

Question 1:
    The correct answer was C. This question demands careful reading, and in particular that you identify that the executors were not appointed as trustees. As executors, they have power to distribute the estate, including paying the £450,000 into the trust: in fact, it is their duty to do so, so B and D are incorrect. As to D in particular, there is no partial intestacy in this case as the three certainties are met in full. However, they have no power whatever as trustees, so E is incorrect. Once the money has been paid over, only the named trustee has power over it. A is also incorrect as the trust is not in existence until it is set up, so the residue is not 'trust property' at the time that it comes into the estate.

Question 2:
    The correct answer was A. Although it is commonplace for executors also to be appointed as will trustees, there is no requirement that they should be so appointed. In this case, the testator has chosen to appoint one of the executors (the nephew) as a trustee together with a non-

executor (the old family friend). There is no bar on the testator doing so. B, C and D assume, wrongly, that an executor must be appointed as a will trustee. E assumes, conversely, that an executor cannot be appointed as a will trustee, which is again incorrect.

Question 3:

The correct answer was E. This property has been occupied (by the same tenant, though this is not conclusive) for a considerable period and a new lease has been negotiated by the tenant. Such a property is not available for occupation by the beneficiaries and the trustees are not under any obligation to remove a lawful occupant of the property in order to make way for any beneficiary. All other options are therefore incorrect.

Question 4:

The correct answer was D. This is a trust of land, and in compliance with statute, the trustees have a duty to ask for the beneficiaries' views about any decision that they take in connection with the trust. Deciding whether or not the freehold of the property should be sold is clearly one such decision (therefore A and E are incorrect). There is no express exclusion of this duty in the will, therefore D remains the best answer. By being under such an obligation to take soundings from the beneficiaries, it must be all of them and not just some of them. Therefore, B and C are both incorrect.

Question 5:

The correct answer was A. Although the trustees could pay over capital using the power of advancement, this request can be met from the accumulated income and is for the education and benefit of the girl, so A is the best solution as opposed to B. Because the money will clearly assist the girl's education, D is incorrect, and it is likely that it will also advance her in life as she is already a talented dancer, so E is incorrect. As to C, a payment which will incidentally benefit a third party (here, the mother) is permissible as long as the primary purpose is to maintain the beneficiary, so this answer is also incorrect.

■ KEY CASES, RULES, STATUTES AND INSTRUMENTS

The SQE1 Assessment Specification does not require you to know the specific numbers of the sections of the Trustee Act that we discuss in this chapter. However, it is worth paying attention to the numbering and contents of:

• Trustee Act 2000, ss 1, 3, 4, 5 and 8.

Index